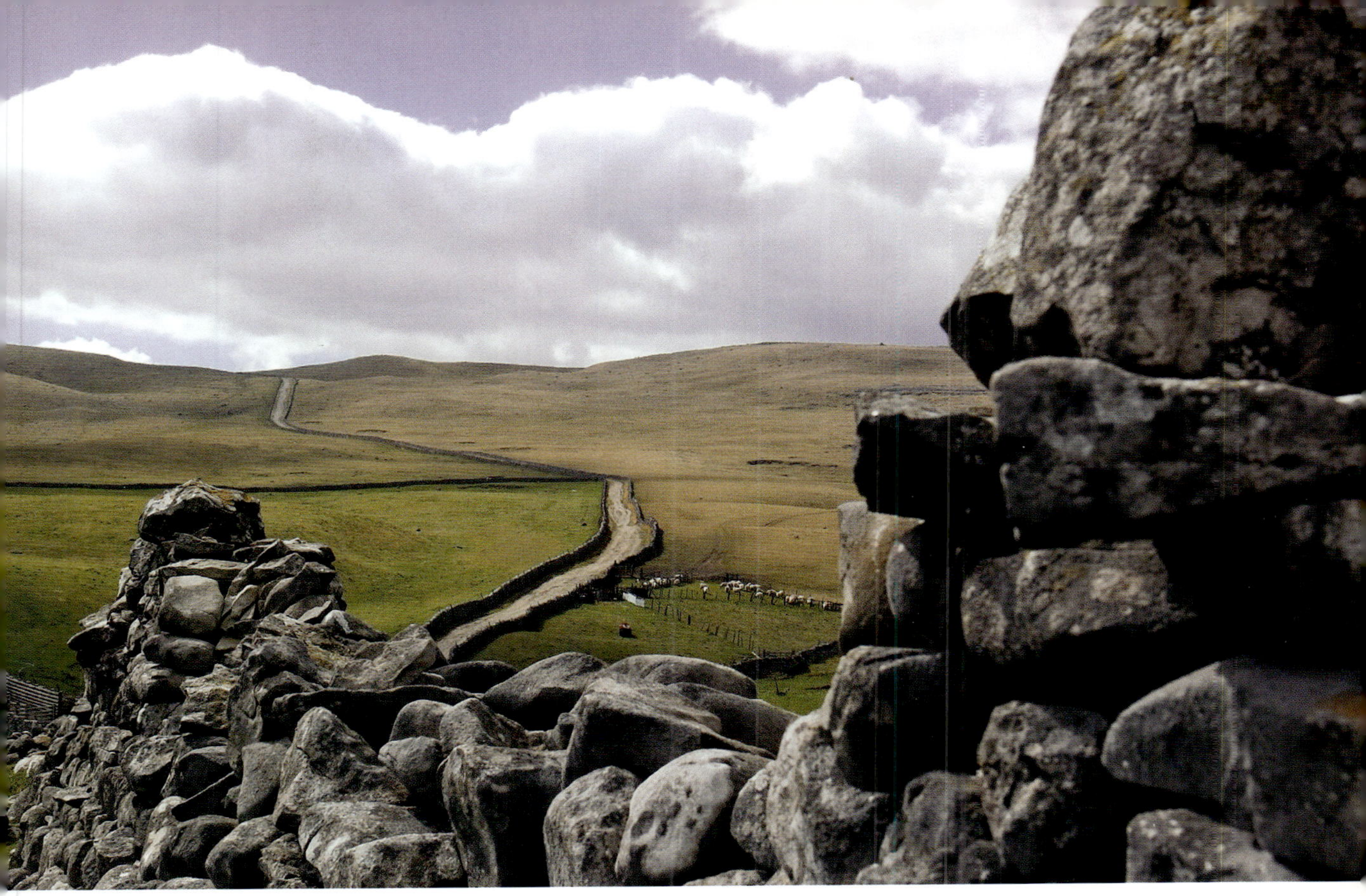

Yorkshire's
Picture Post 2

A special publication brought to you by

YORKSHIRE POST Yorkshire Evening Post

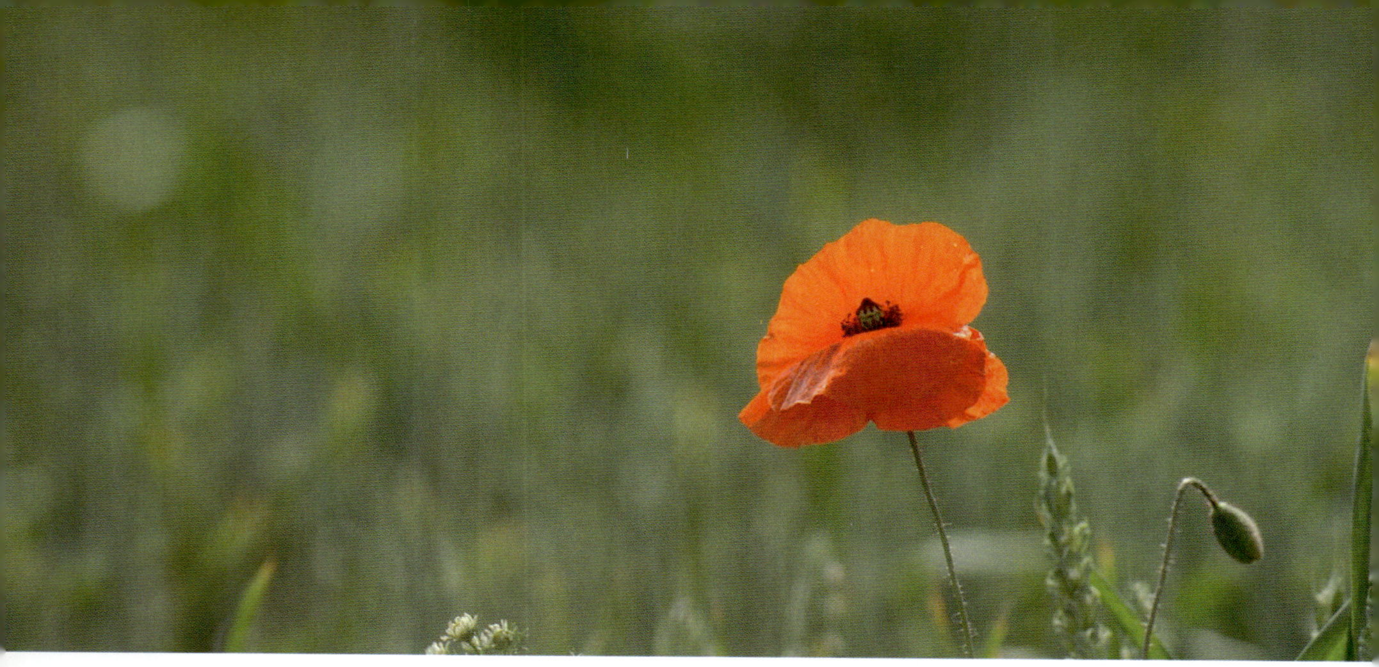

All pictures taken by the staff photographers of the
Yorkshire Post and the Yorkshire Evening Post,
YP Photographers are:

Mike Cowling
Bruce Rollinson
Jim Moran
Gary Longbottom
Simon Hulme
Gerard Binks
Terry Carrott
Chris Lawton.
EP Photographers are.
Mark Bickerdike
Mel Hulme
Steve Riding
Tony Johnson
Jonathan Gawthorpe
James Hardisty

First published in 2007 by: At Heart Ltd, 32 Stamford Street, Altrincham, Cheshire, WA14 1EY in conjunction with Yorkshire Post Newspapers Ltd PO Box 168, Wellington Street, Leeds, LS1 1RF

ISBN: 978-1-84547-114-9

Yorkshire's
Picture Post 2

Scenes that are striking for their beauty or novelty or quirky character abound in the Yorkshire countryside and around its coast, and while they register fleetingly in the eye of the beholder, the camera allows them to be captured and kept for posterity.

Here, then, the momentary glimpses which reward a day's outing for the observer are made permanent. That sun, low in the sky, painting a landscape high in the Dales with subtle colours here and glorious hues there; a footpath lost beneath snow, and night rushing in, and from cooling towers' gaping mouths, dramatic clouds of steam fringed with gold. There are abbeys here, and castles and mansions, and like an inquisitive alien, just landed, a sunflower peers into the camera.

Leaf through these pages, and enjoy what they offer.

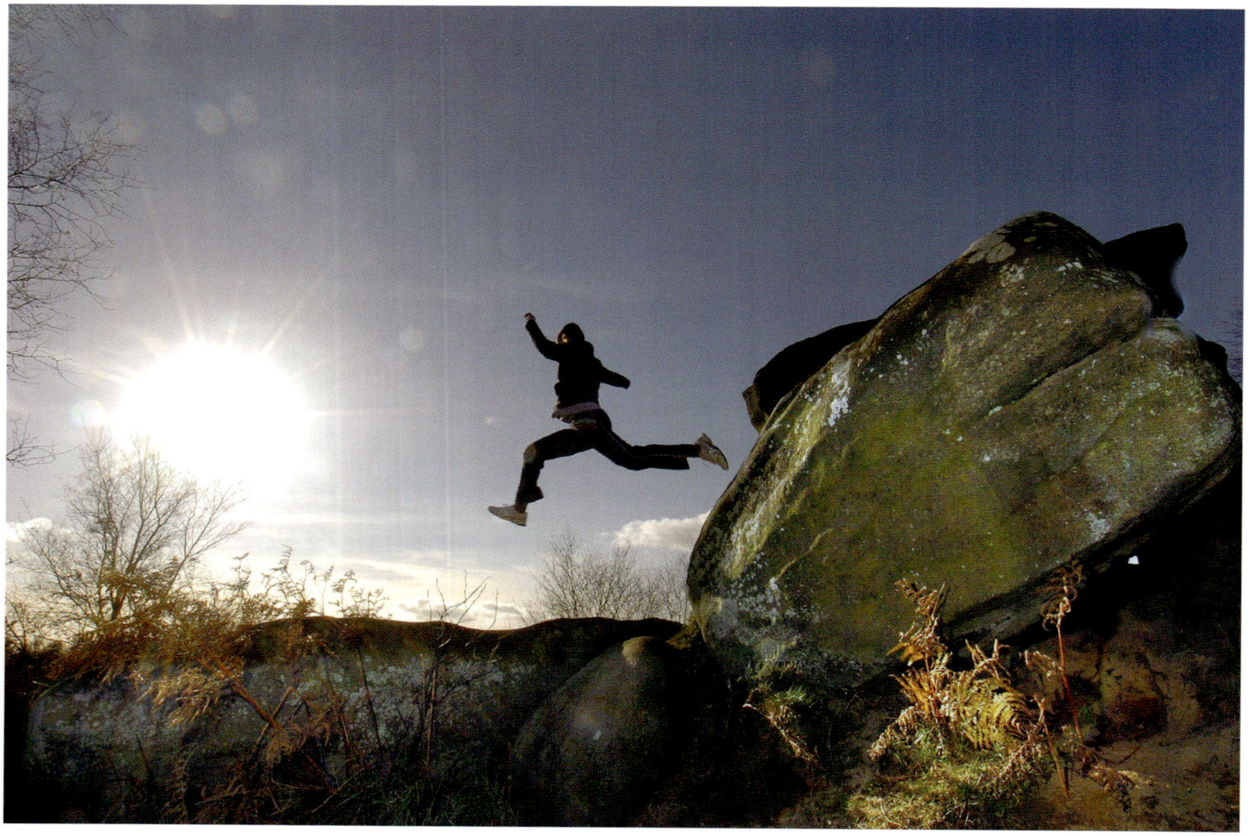

Brimham Rocks near Pateley Bridge are Nature's adventure playground. Here 15-year old Holly Workman from Swindon, on a work experience week with a local outdoor training centre, makes an exhilerating leap. (YPP2001)

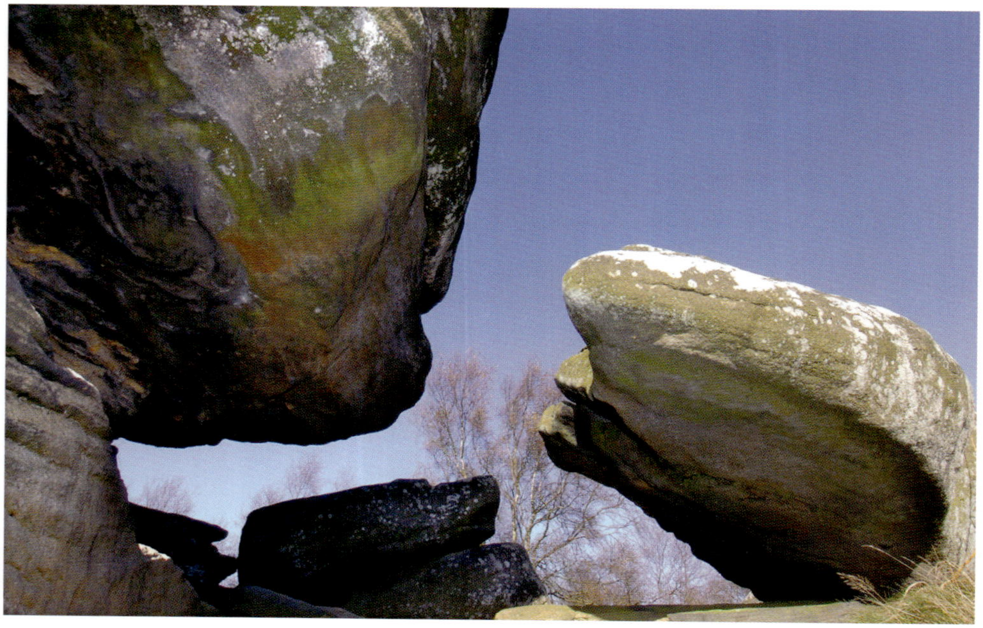

The extraordinary rock formations have been attracting visitors since time immemorial, whether to clamber among them or wonder at their amazing shapes. (YPP2002)

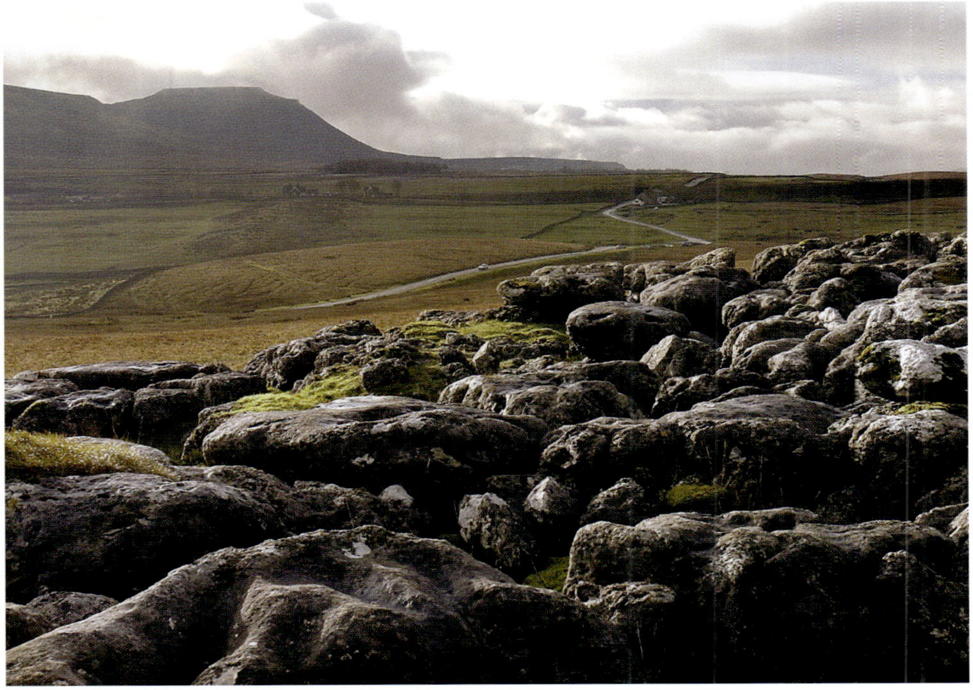

Limestone pavement and Ingleborough. (YPP2003)

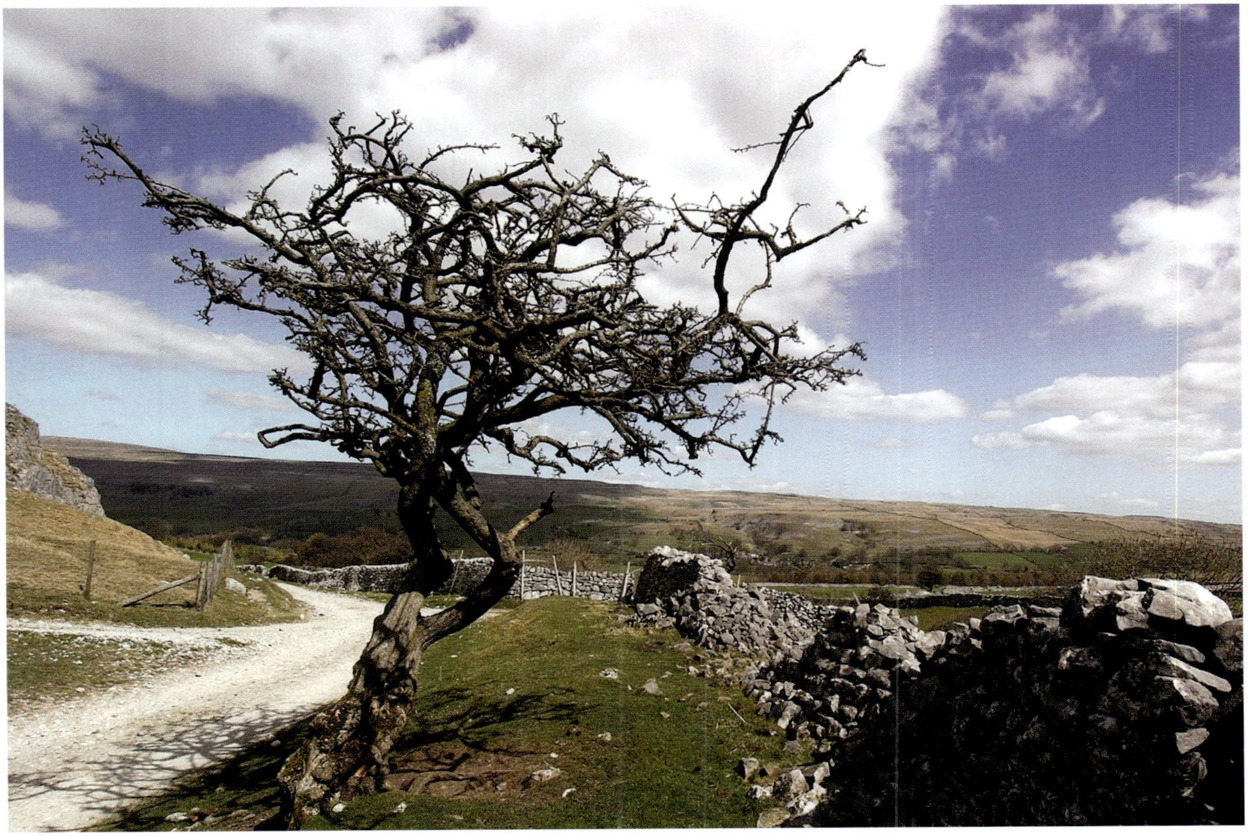

A tangled tree stands lonely sentinel beside Mastile Lane. which ascends steeply to Malham Moor from Kilnsey. (YPP2004)

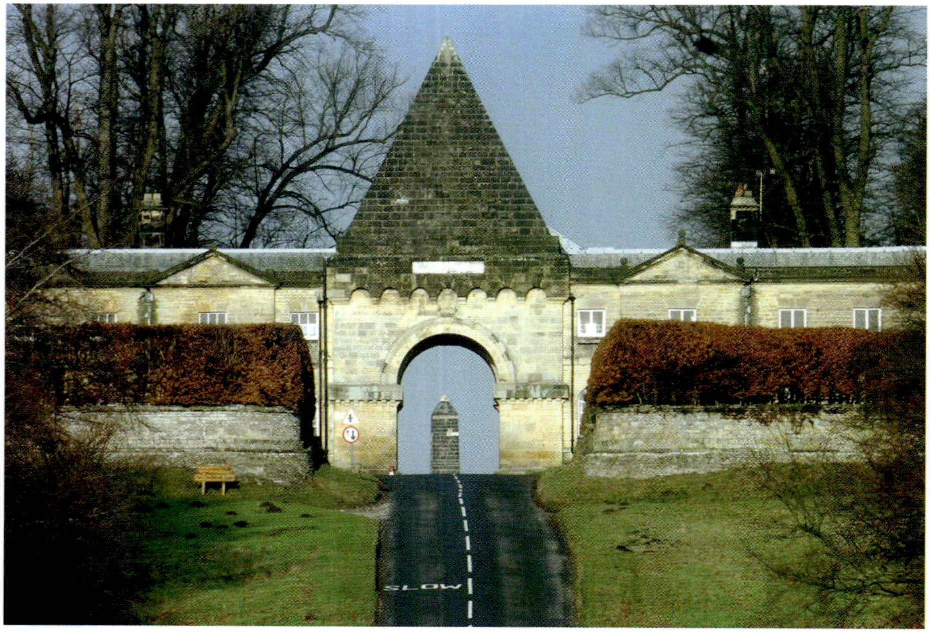

The Obelisk at Castle Howard as many visitors to Vanbrugh's stately pile first see it. (YPP2005)

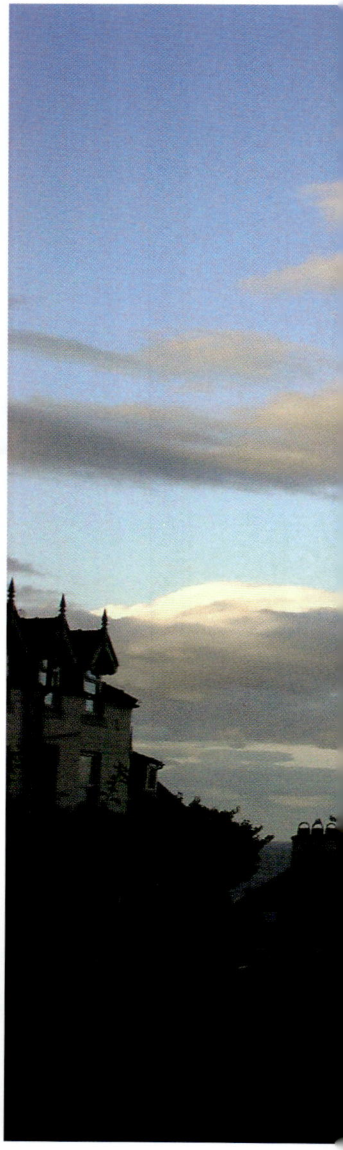

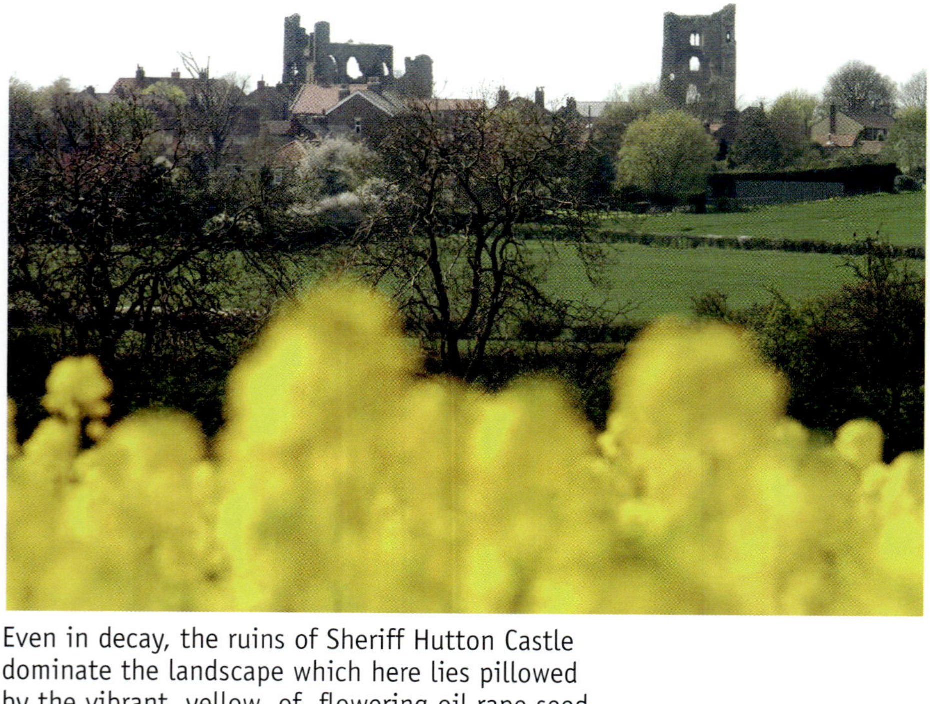

Even in decay, the ruins of Sheriff Hutton Castle dominate the landscape which here lies pillowed by the vibrant yellow of flowering oil rape seed. (YPP2006)

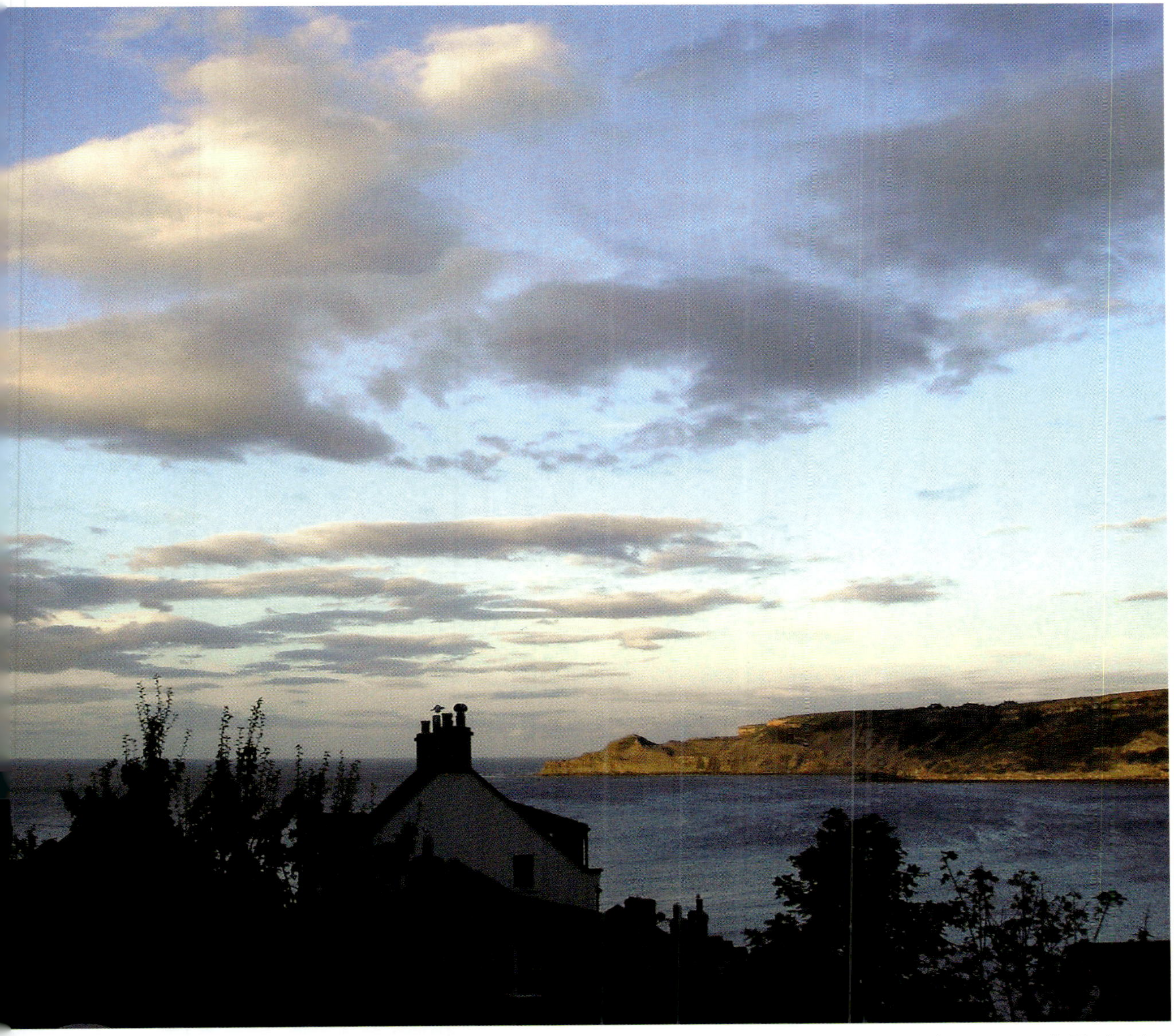

Sunset over Runswick Bay, North Yorkshire (YPP2007)

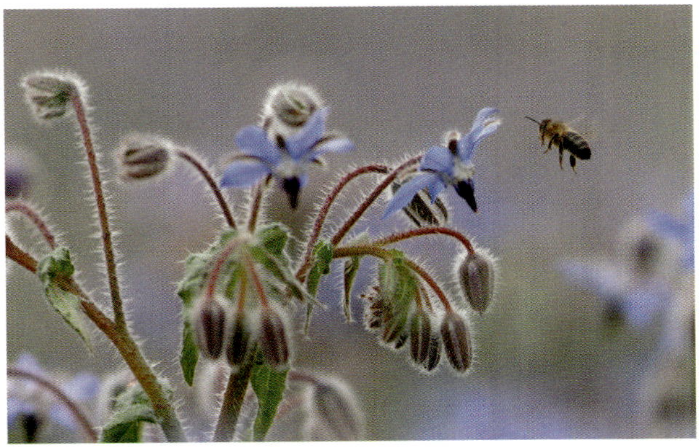

Bees visit borage flowers at Well Green Farm, Barnby, near Doncaster. (YPP2008)

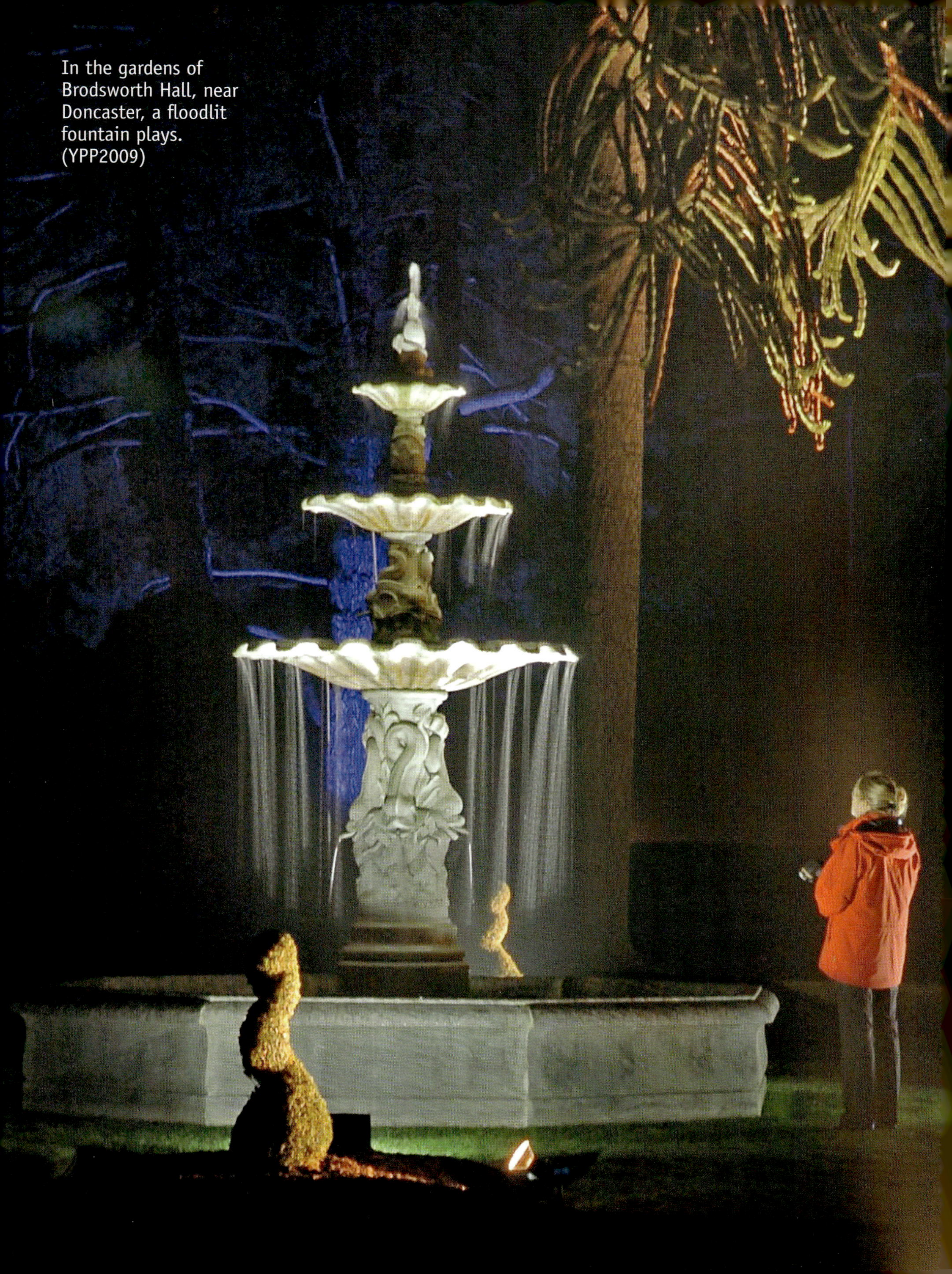

In the gardens of Brodsworth Hall, near Doncaster, a floodlit fountain plays. (YPP2009)

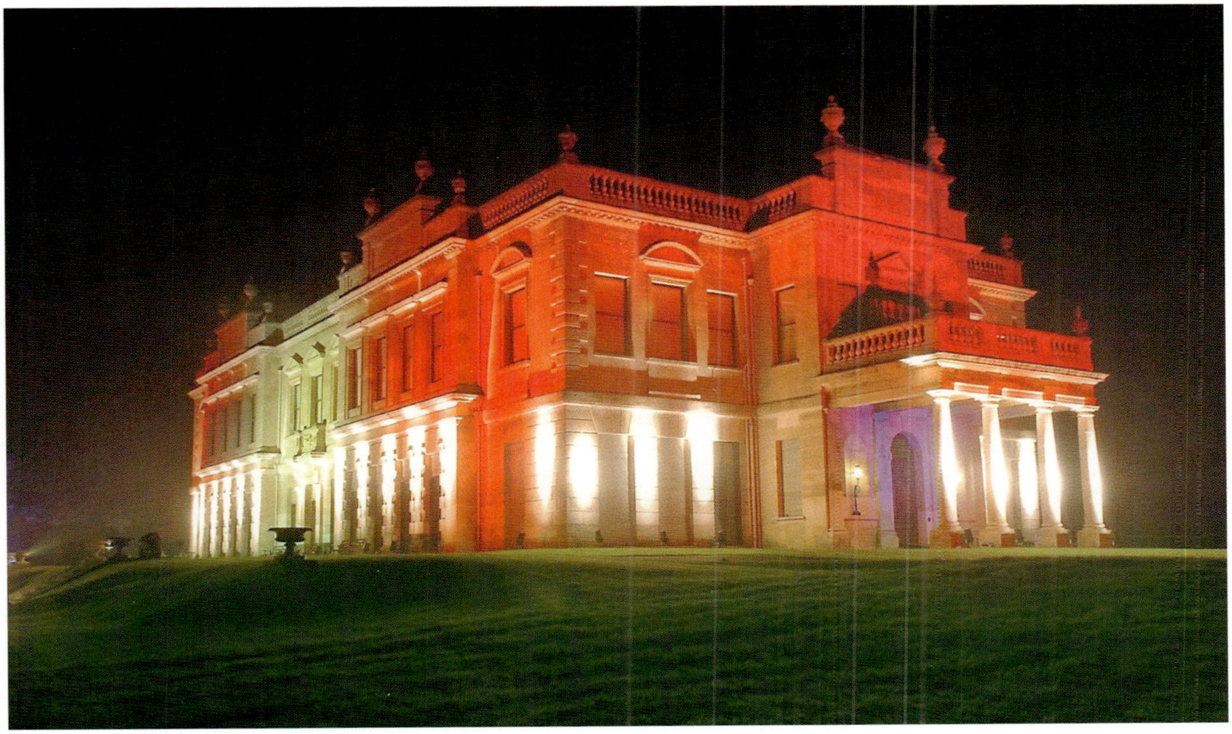

As darkness descends, the Hall glows as never seen before.
(YPP2010)

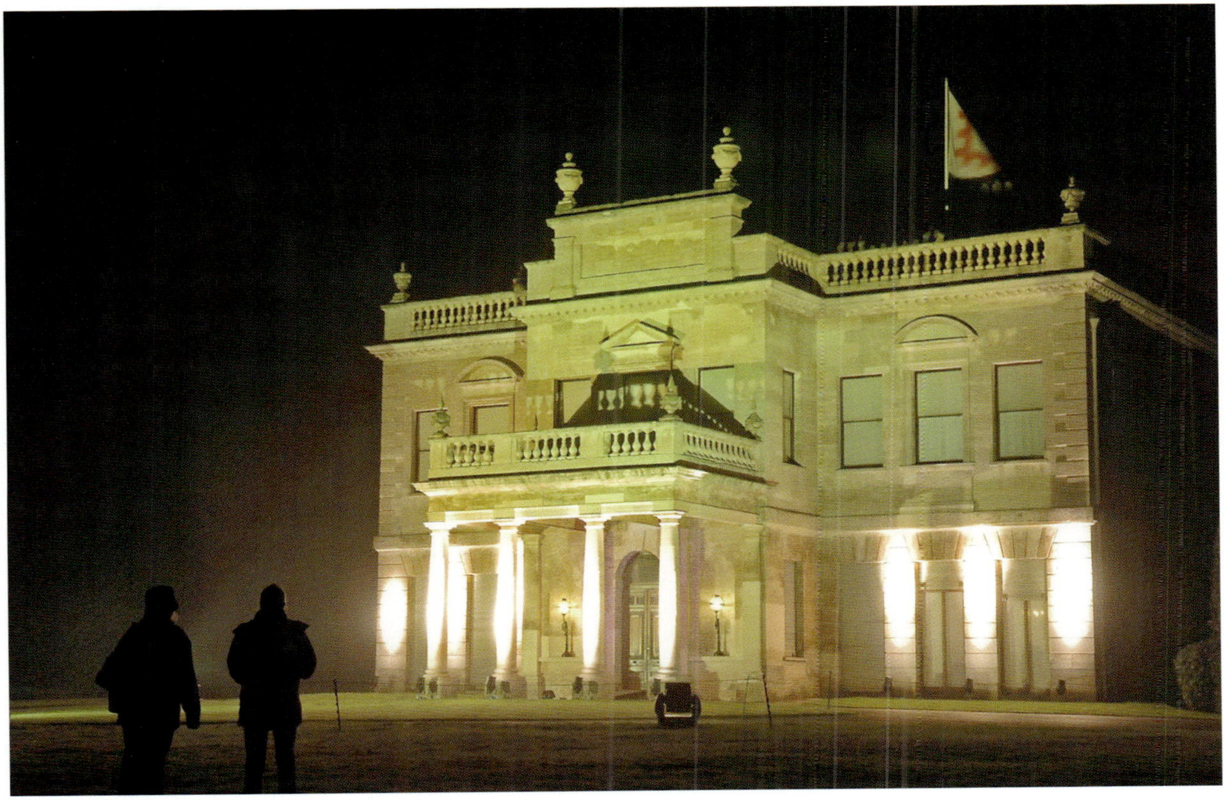

The lighting changes colour - and the Hall is transformed again.
(YPP2011)

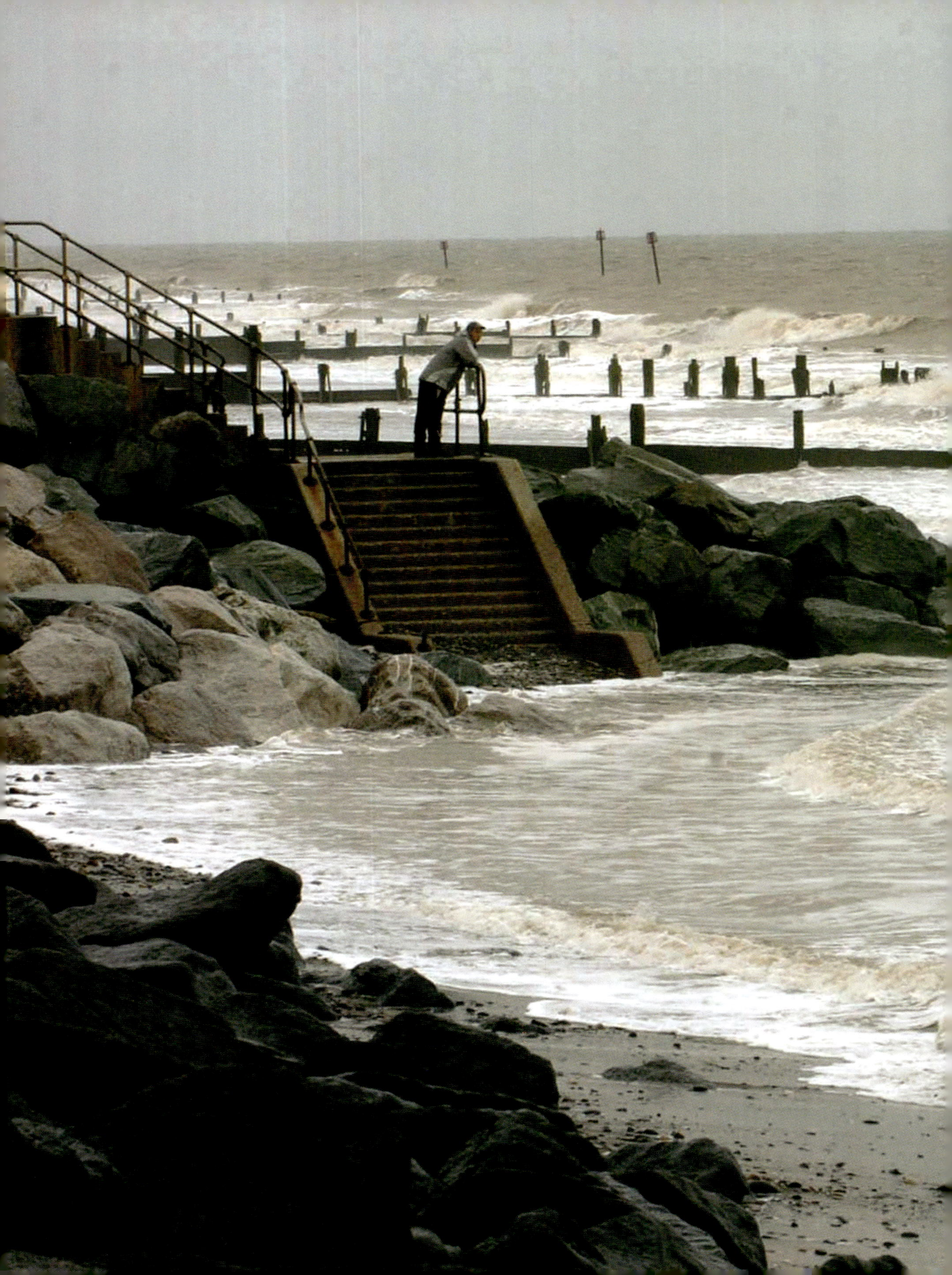

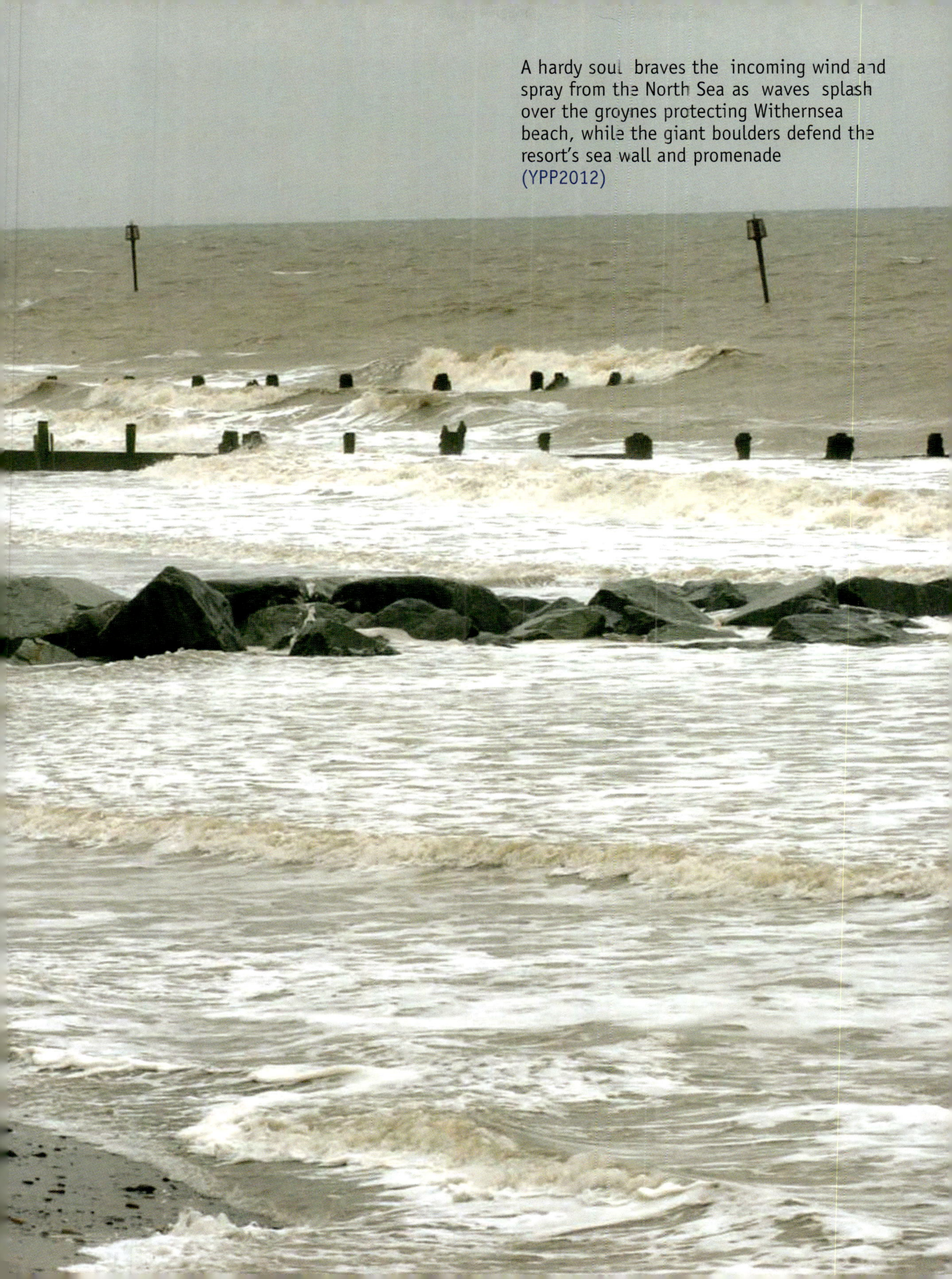

A hardy soul braves the incoming wind and spray from the North Sea as waves splash over the groynes protecting Withernsea beach, while the giant boulders defend the resort's sea wall and promenade (YPP2012)

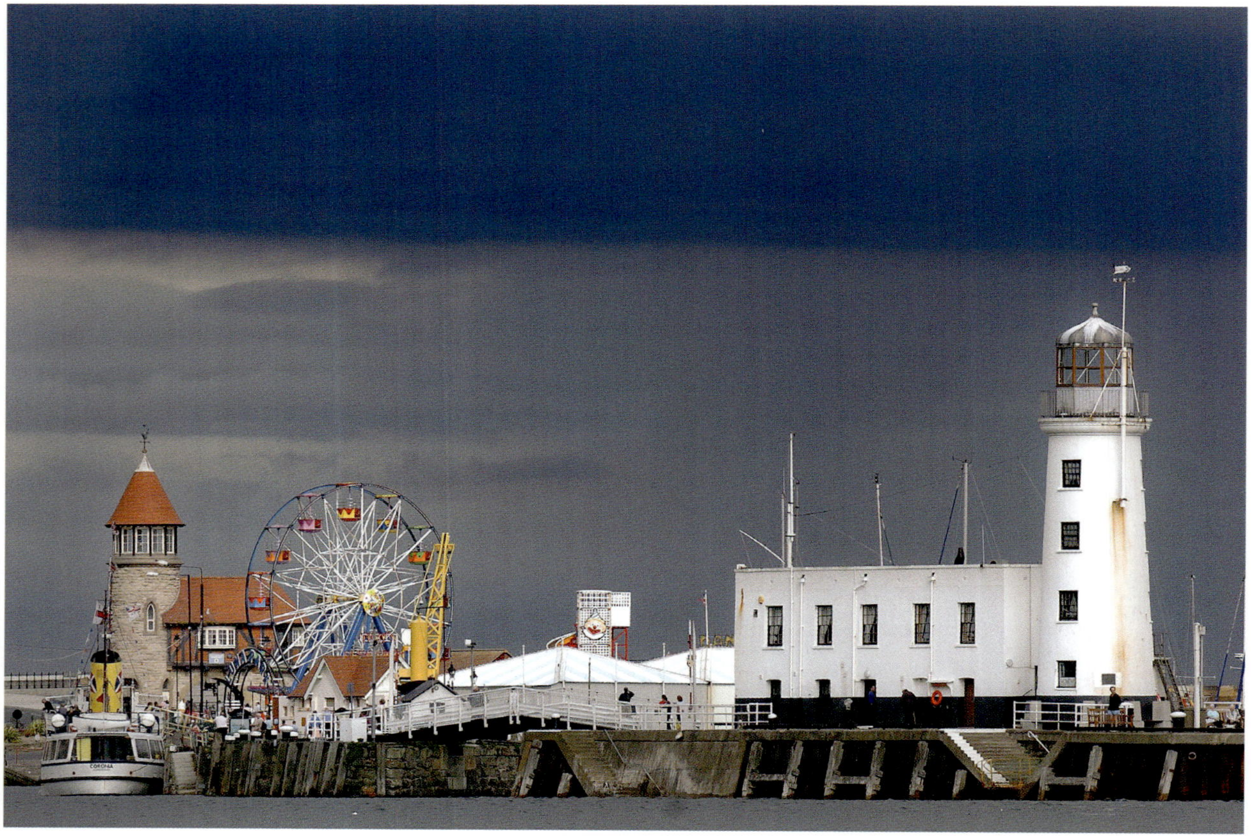

Taken from across Scarborough's South Bay, this picture shows the harbour wall, lighthouse and small funfair on the sea front. The rust smear stretching down the whitwashed lighthouse wall bears testament to the salty seaside winds. (YPP2013)

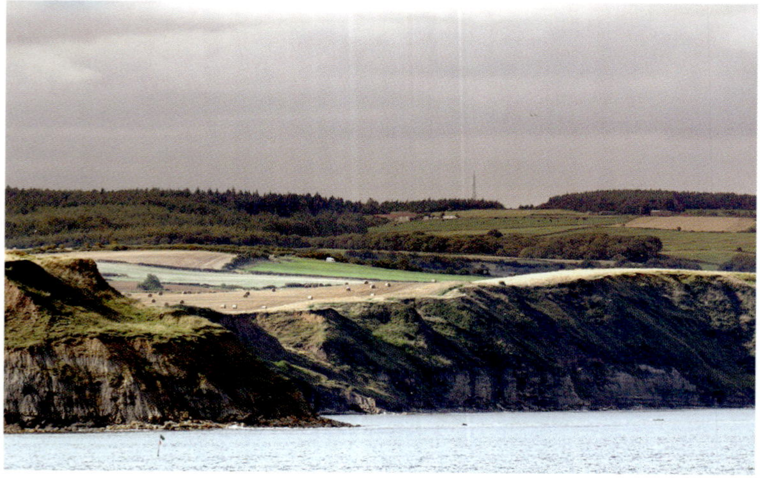

The North Bay on a late summer's day in Scarborough. (YPP2014)

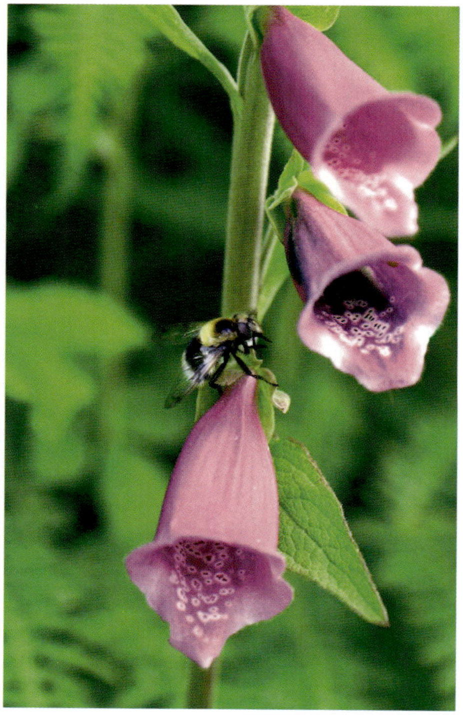

A bee visits a foxglove to gather its gifts of nectar and pollen. (YPP2015)

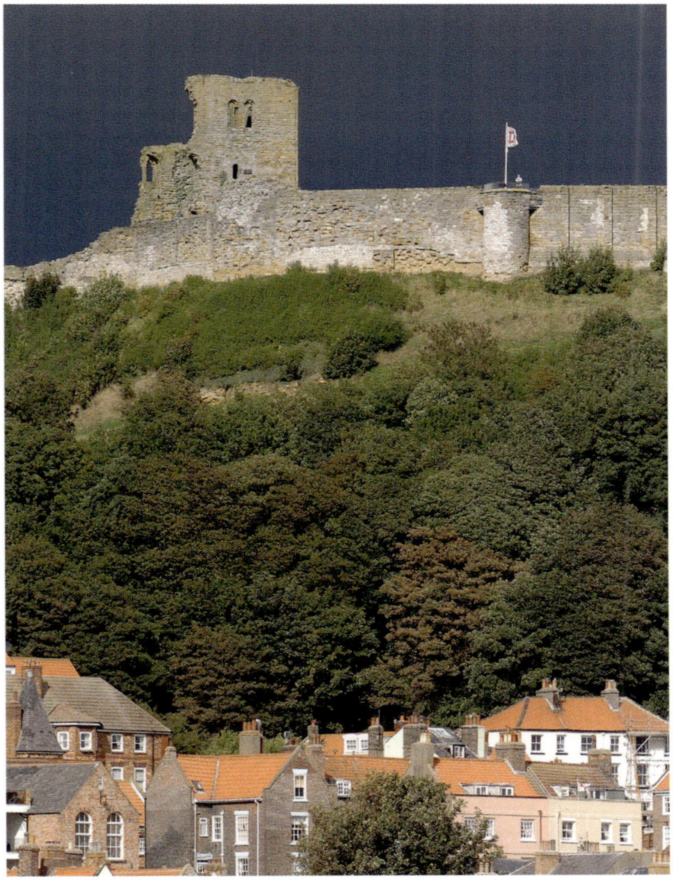

Scarborough Castle elevated high above the seaside resort that developed long after need for a castle's protection had past. (YPP2016)

Seagulls search for food as a farmer ploughs his field at East Knapton, between Malton and Scarborough. (YPP2017)

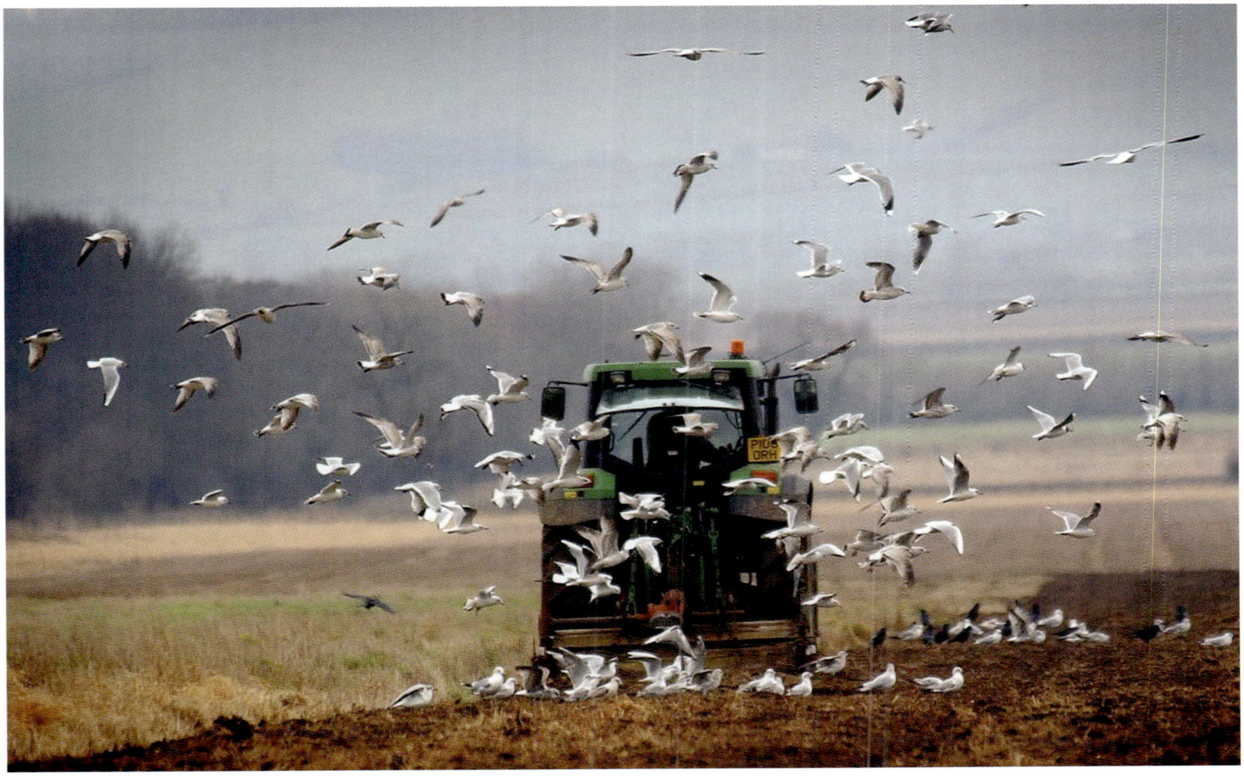

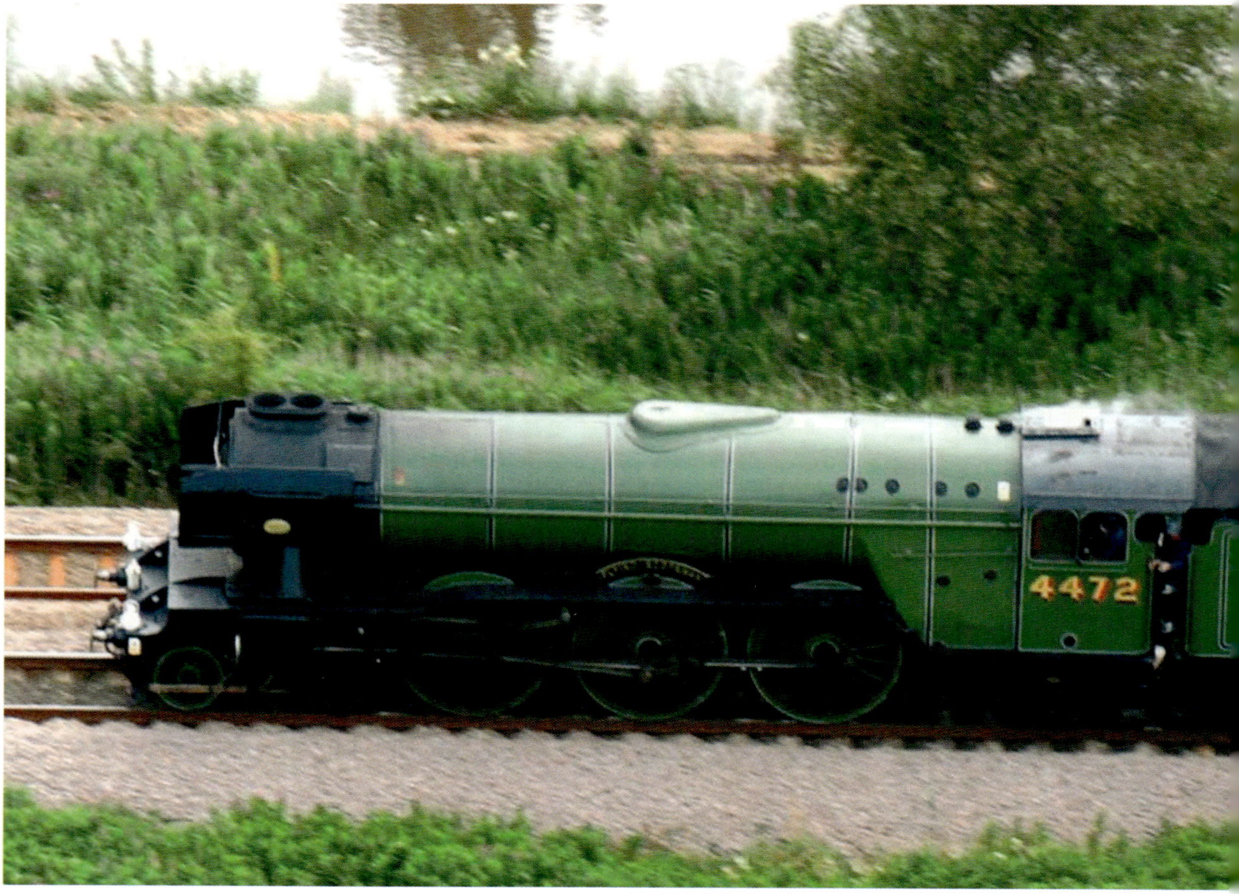

The Flying Scotsman steams its way to Scarborough from York. A passenger leans out of a carriage window to sense the grand old lady of rail transport thunder through the North Yorkshire countryside. (YPP2018)

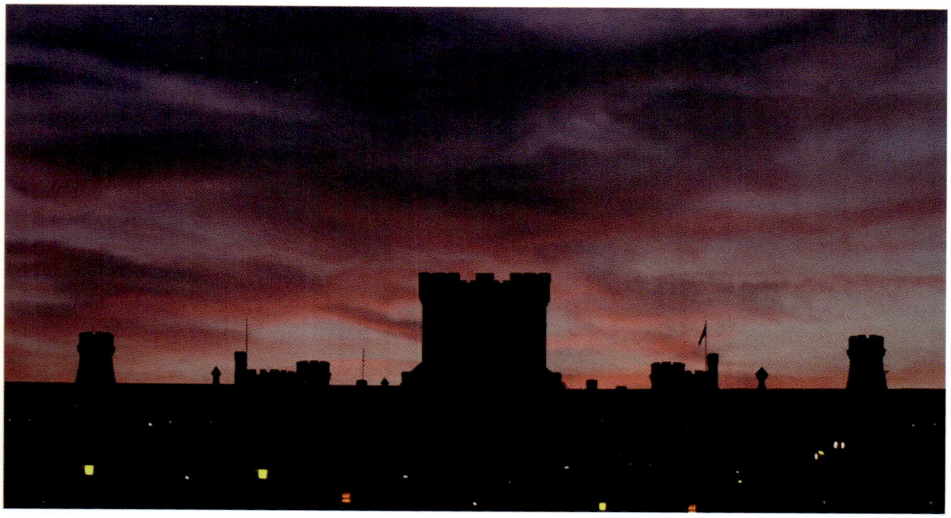

The sun sets over Armley Jail, Leeds. (YPP2019)

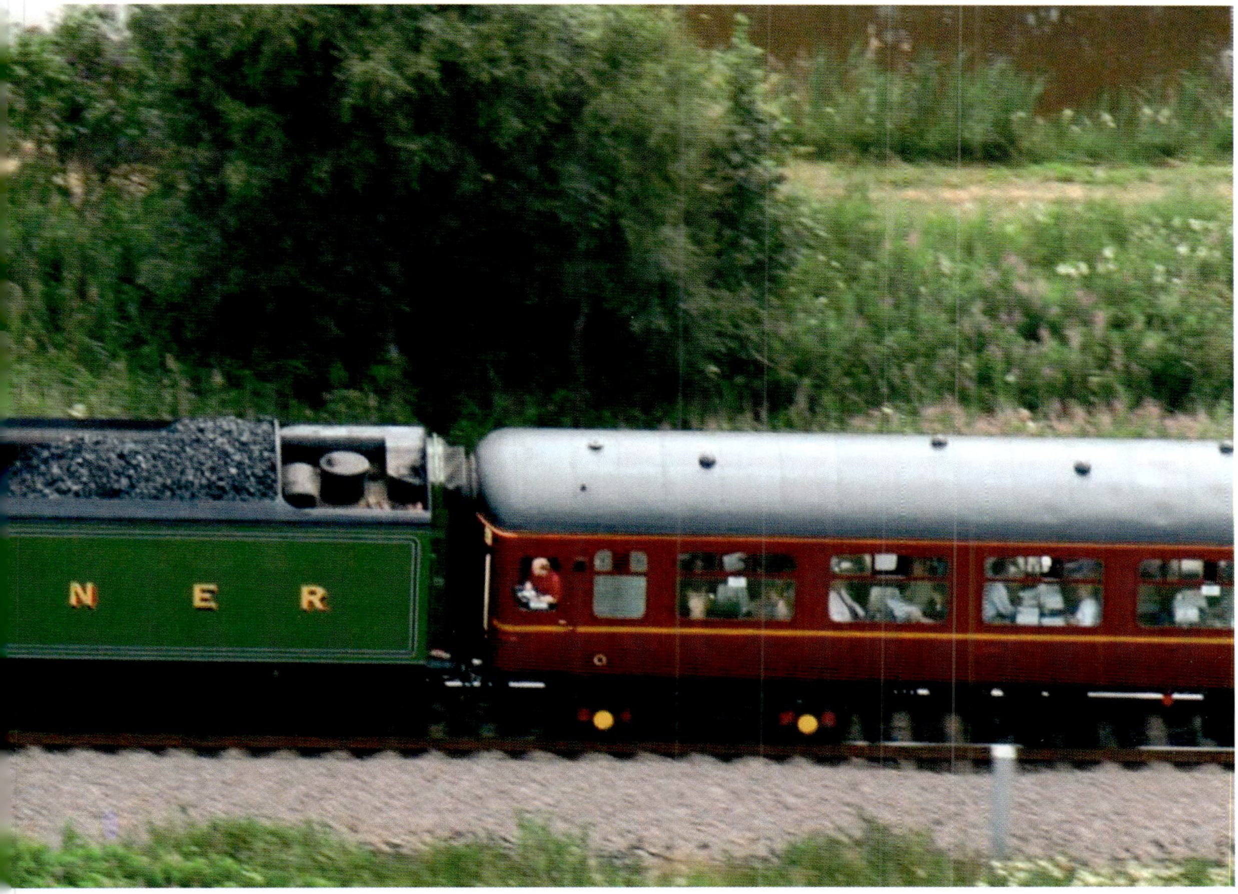

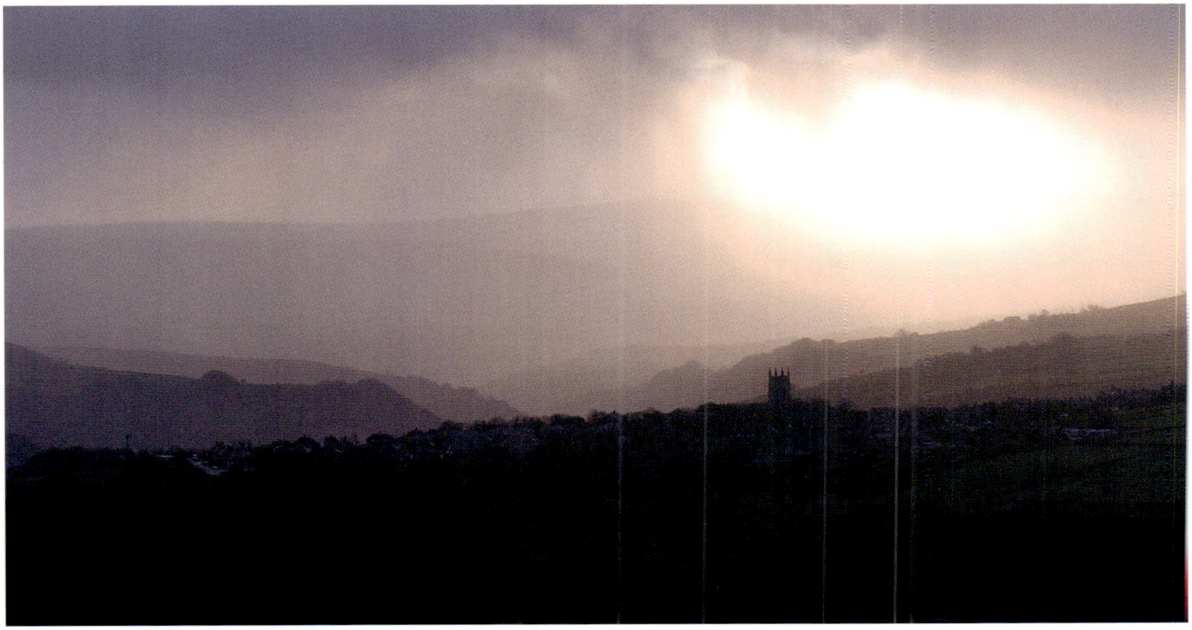

Late winter sunshine over the village of Heptenstall above Hebden Bridge taken fron Pecket Well. (YPP2020)

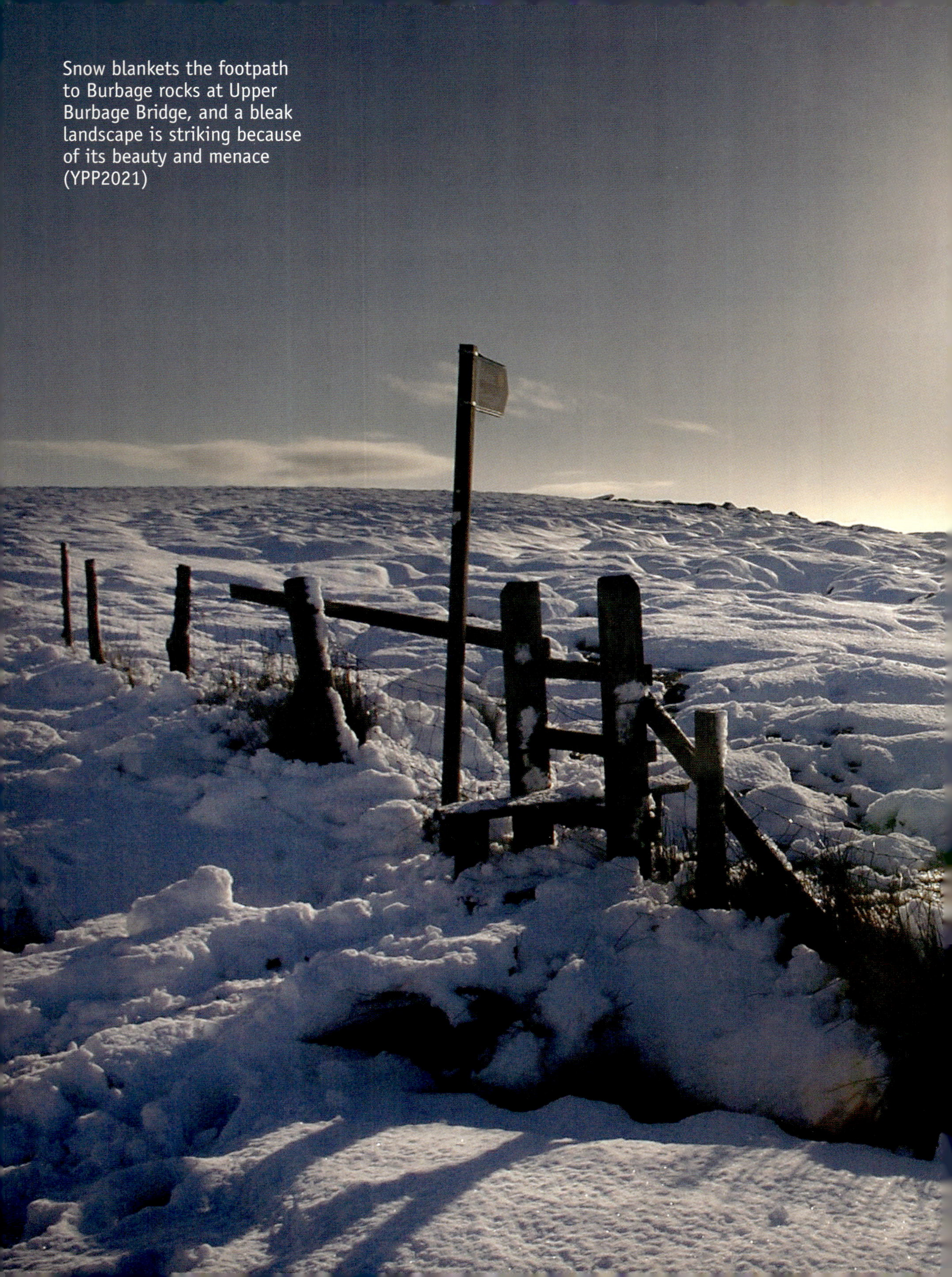

Snow blankets the footpath to Burbage rocks at Upper Burbage Bridge, and a bleak landscape is striking because of its beauty and menace (YPP2021)

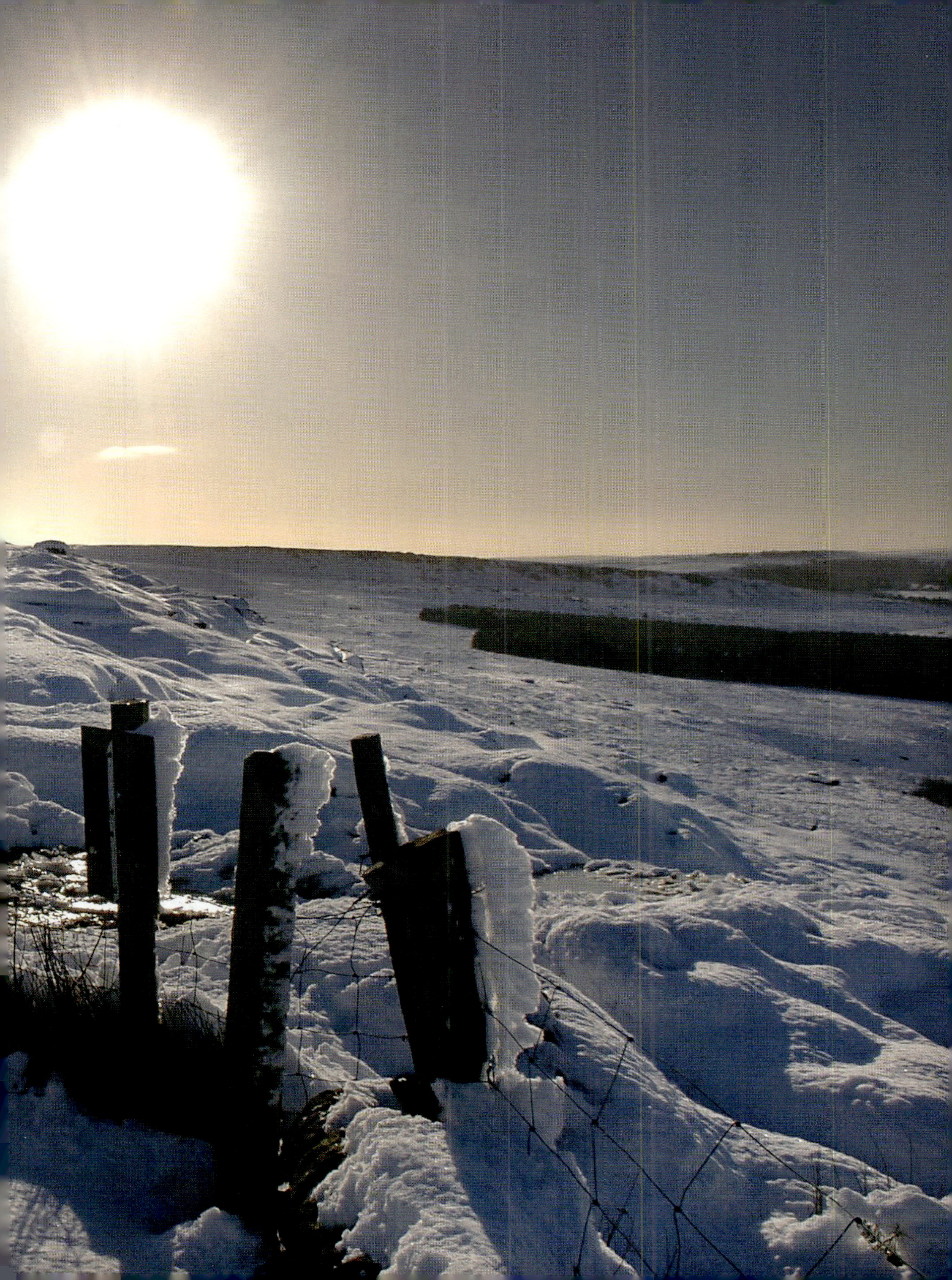

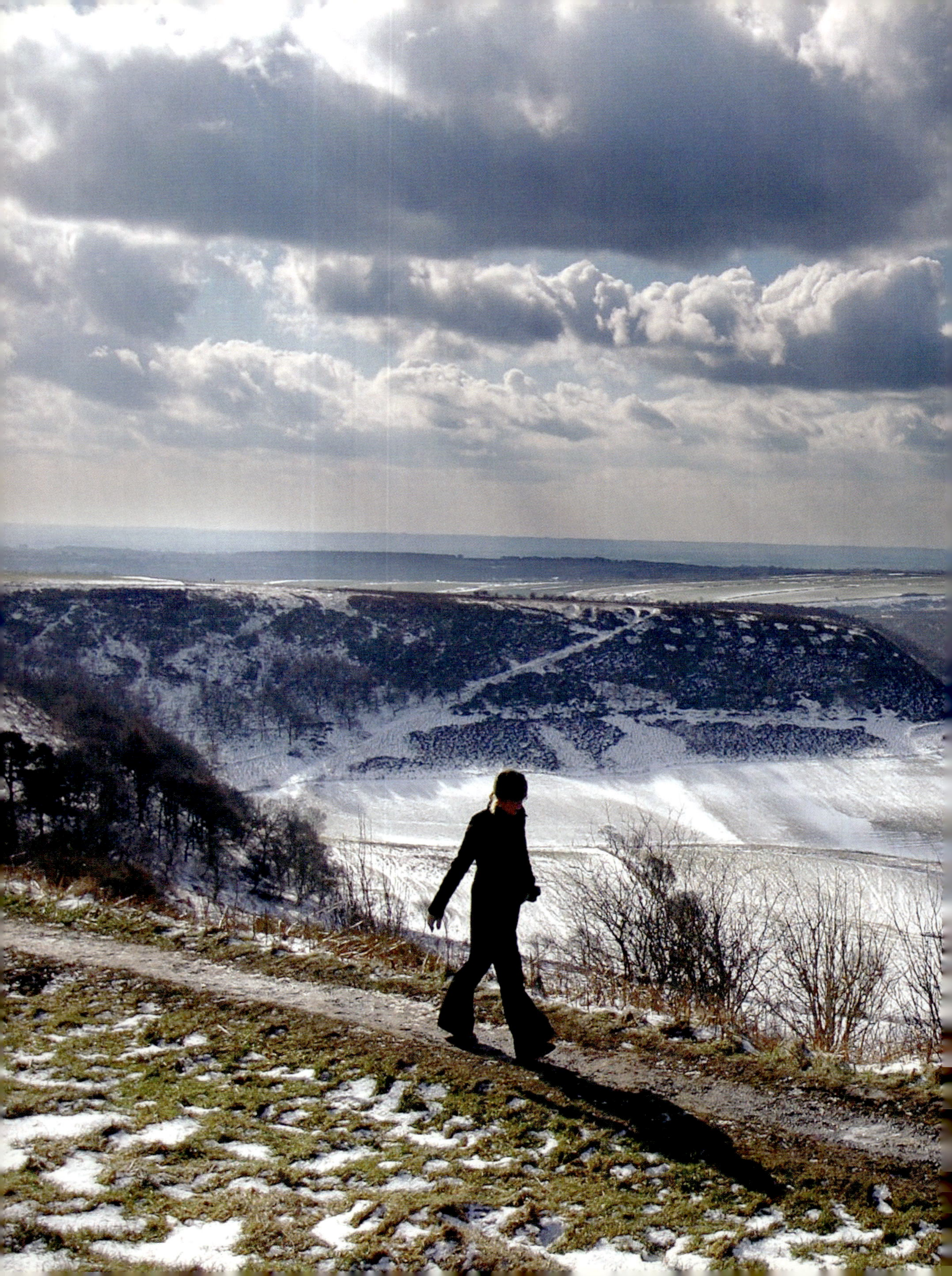

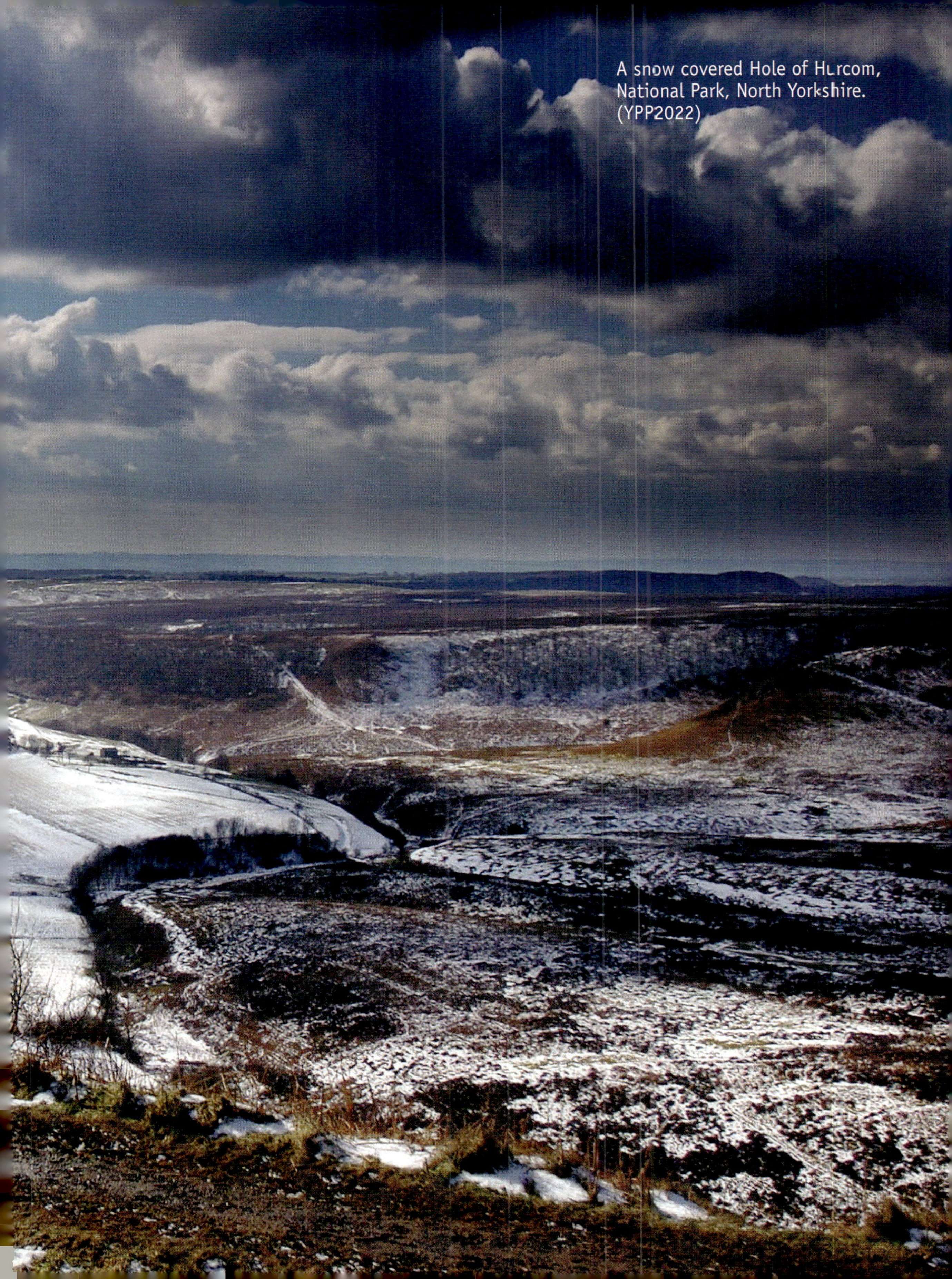

A snow covered Hole of Horcum, National Park, North Yorkshire. (YPP2022)

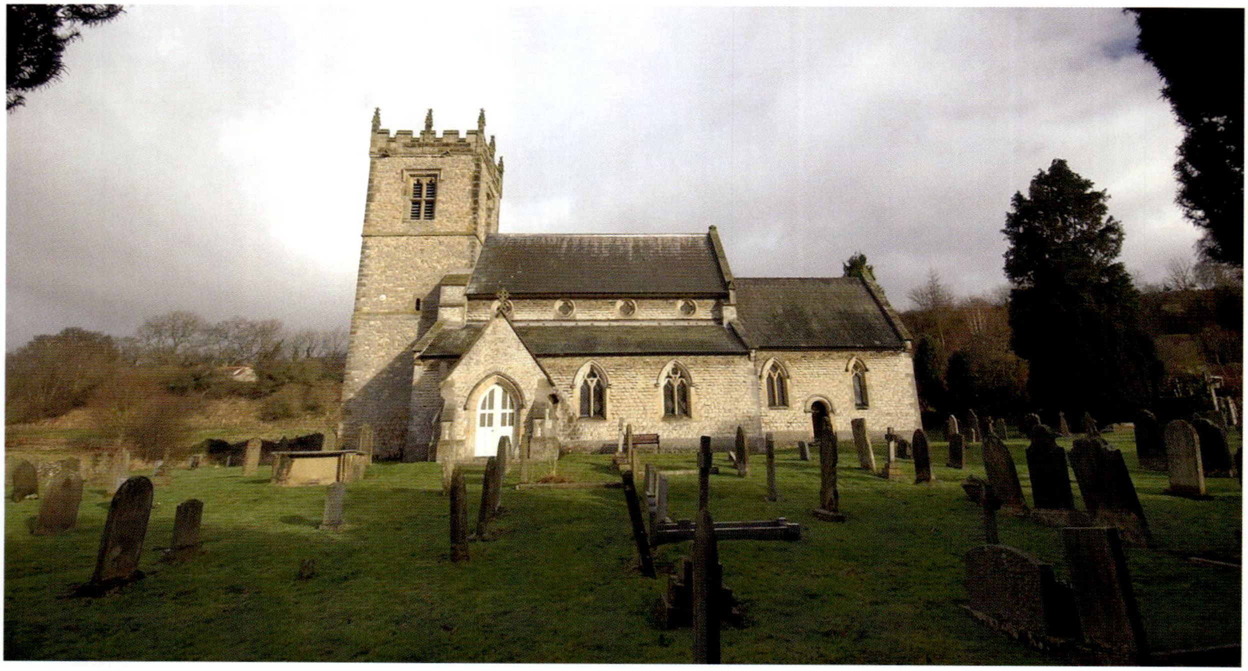

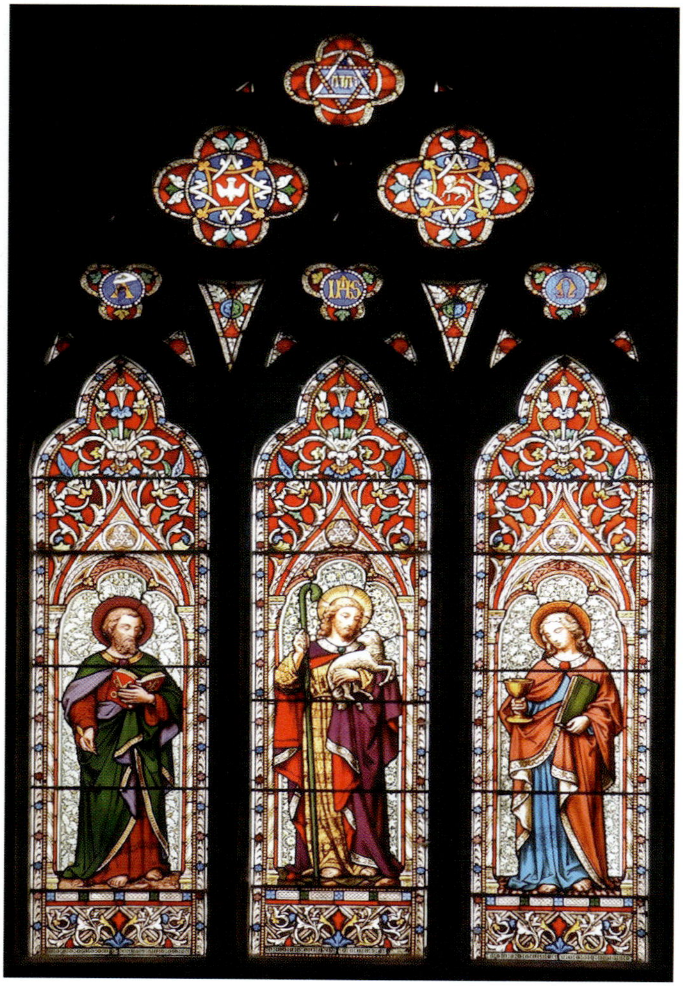

Stonegrove Minster near Helmsley, and rather more compact than certain other ministers in the county. (YPP2023)

Its charms include a brilliant stained-glass window. (YPP2024)

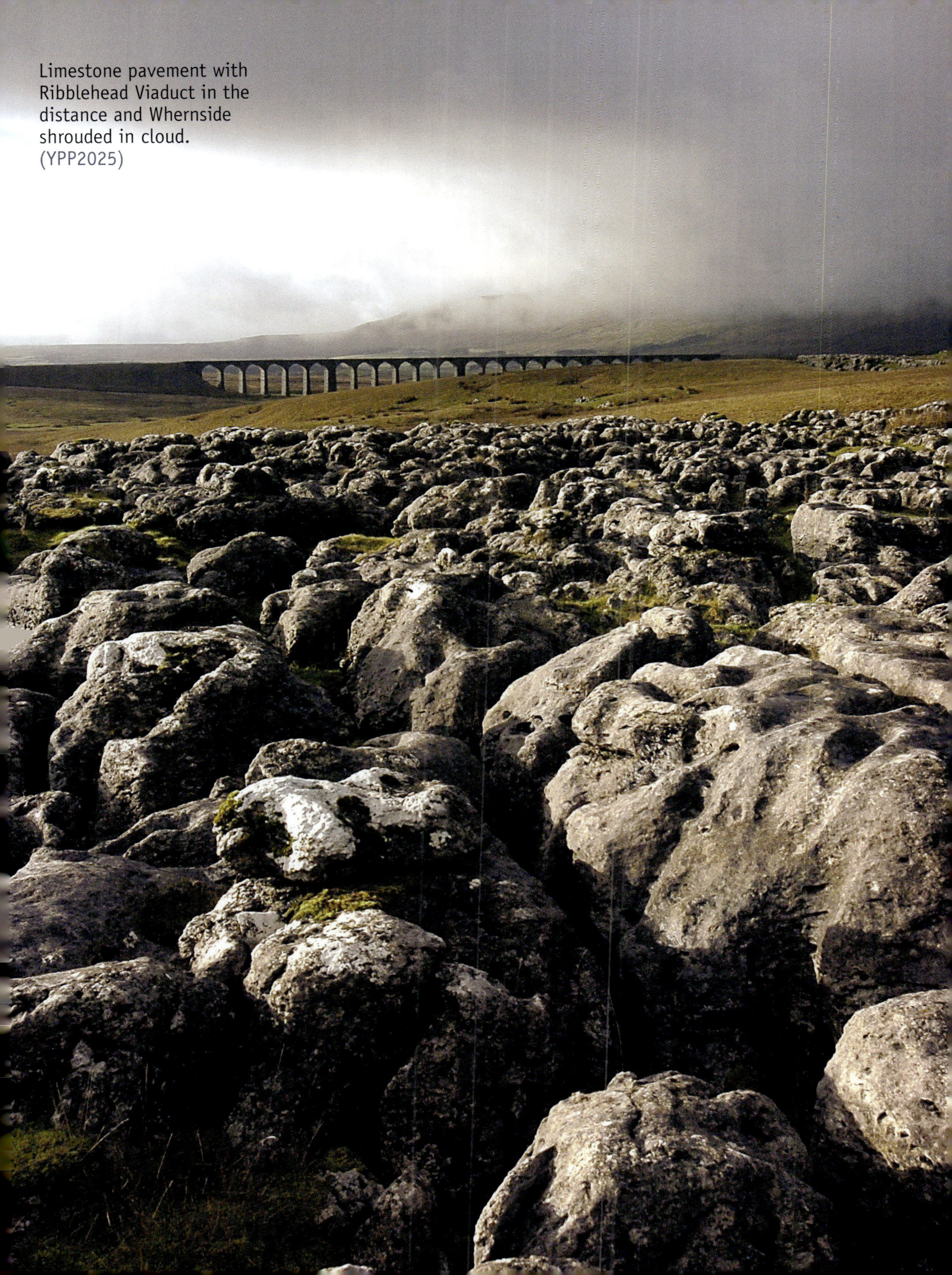

Limestone pavement with Ribblehead Viaduct in the distance and Whernside shrouded in cloud. (YPP2025)

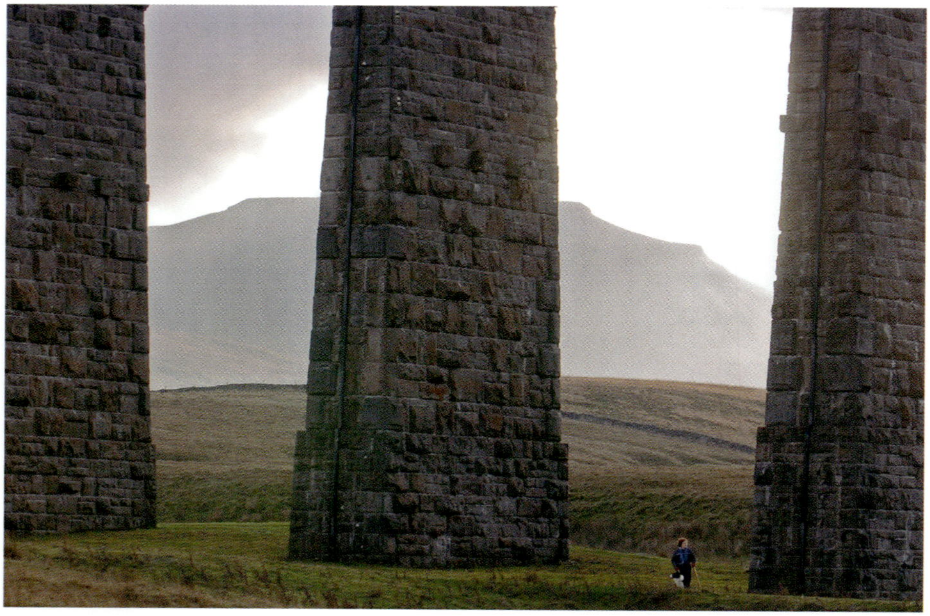

The arches of Ribblehead Viaduct dwarf a walker and her dog. While brooding in the background is a darkened Ingleborough. (YPP2026)

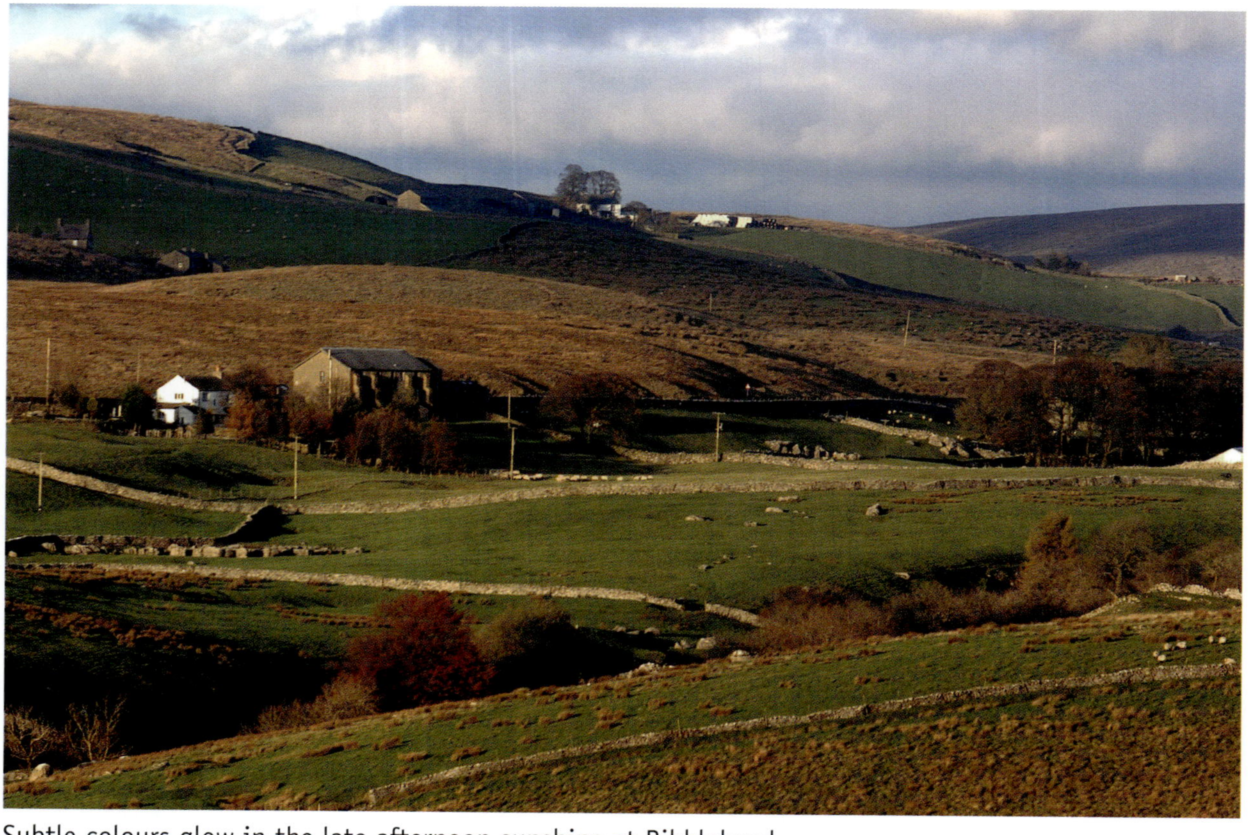

Subtle colours glow in the late afternoon sunshine at Ribblehead (YPP2027)

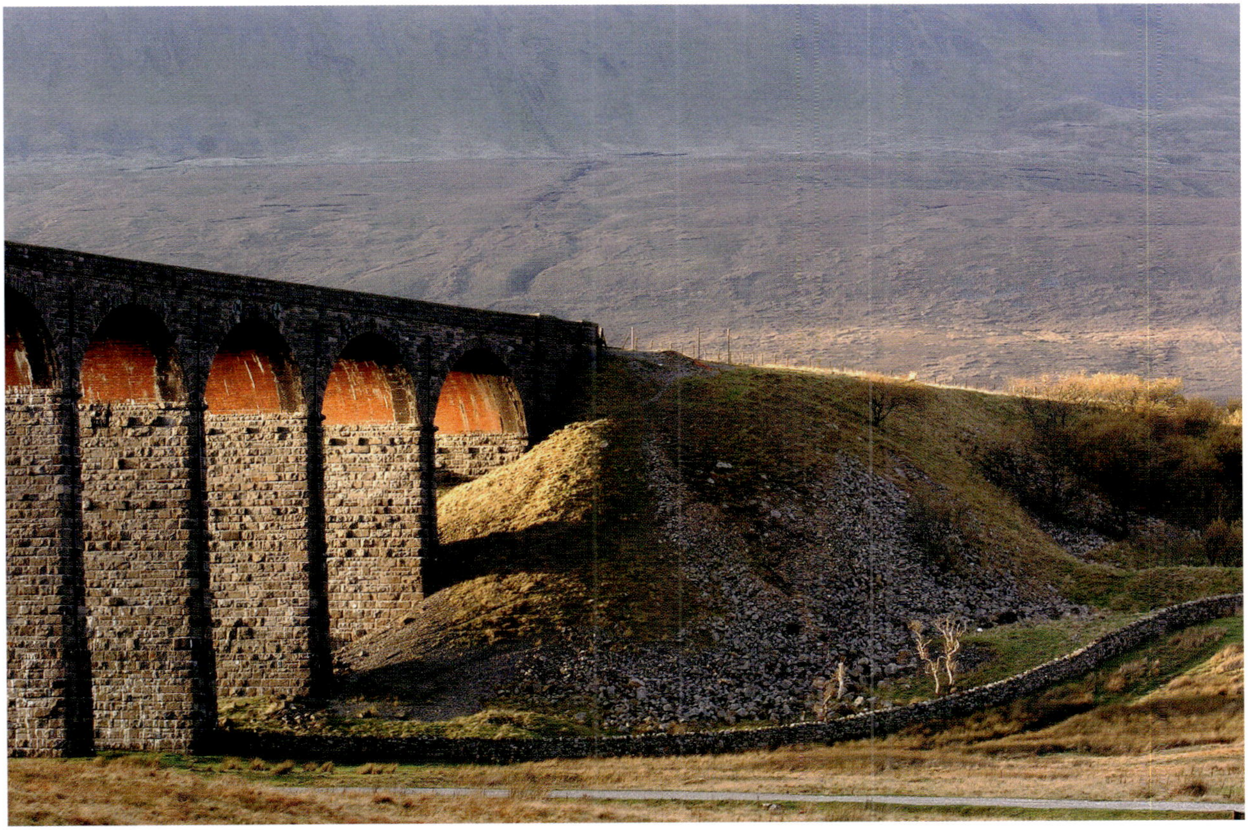

Stone stanchions cast long shadows as a sinking sun illuminates the the viaduct's vast arches.
(YPP2028)

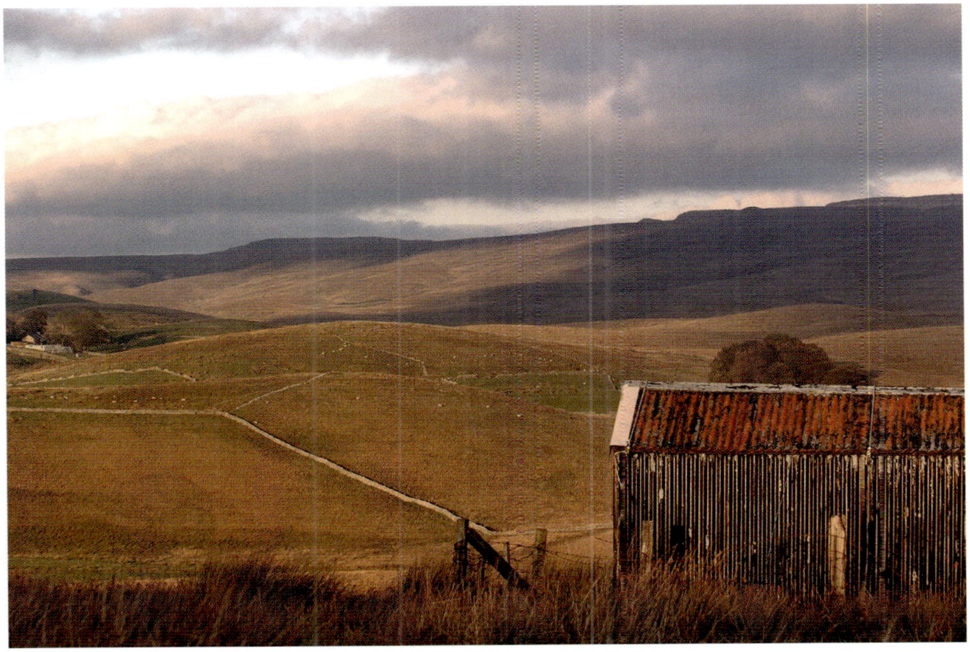

A poem for the eye in contours and colours.
(YPP2029)

Tom Benstead, a member of Bradford Waltonians Angling Club, casts his line on Chelker reservoir near Skipton while on the hillside beyond, twin-bladed turbines lazily turn, grinding out electritcity for Yorkshire Water. (YPP2030)

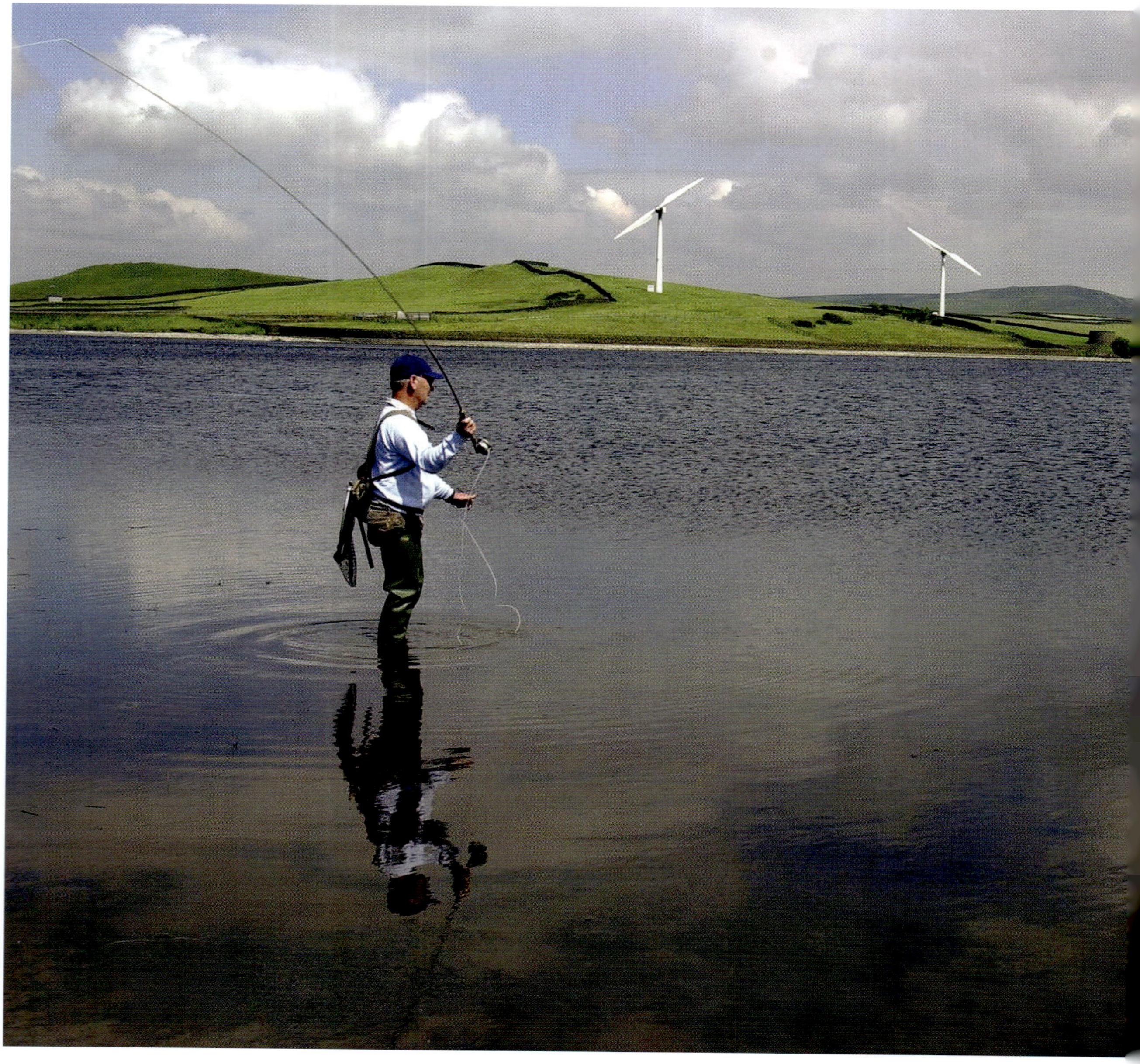

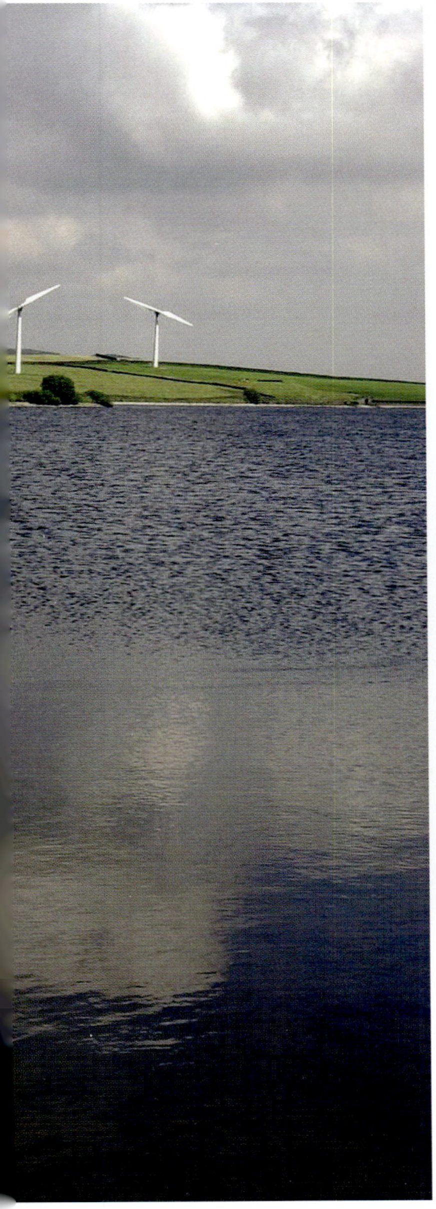

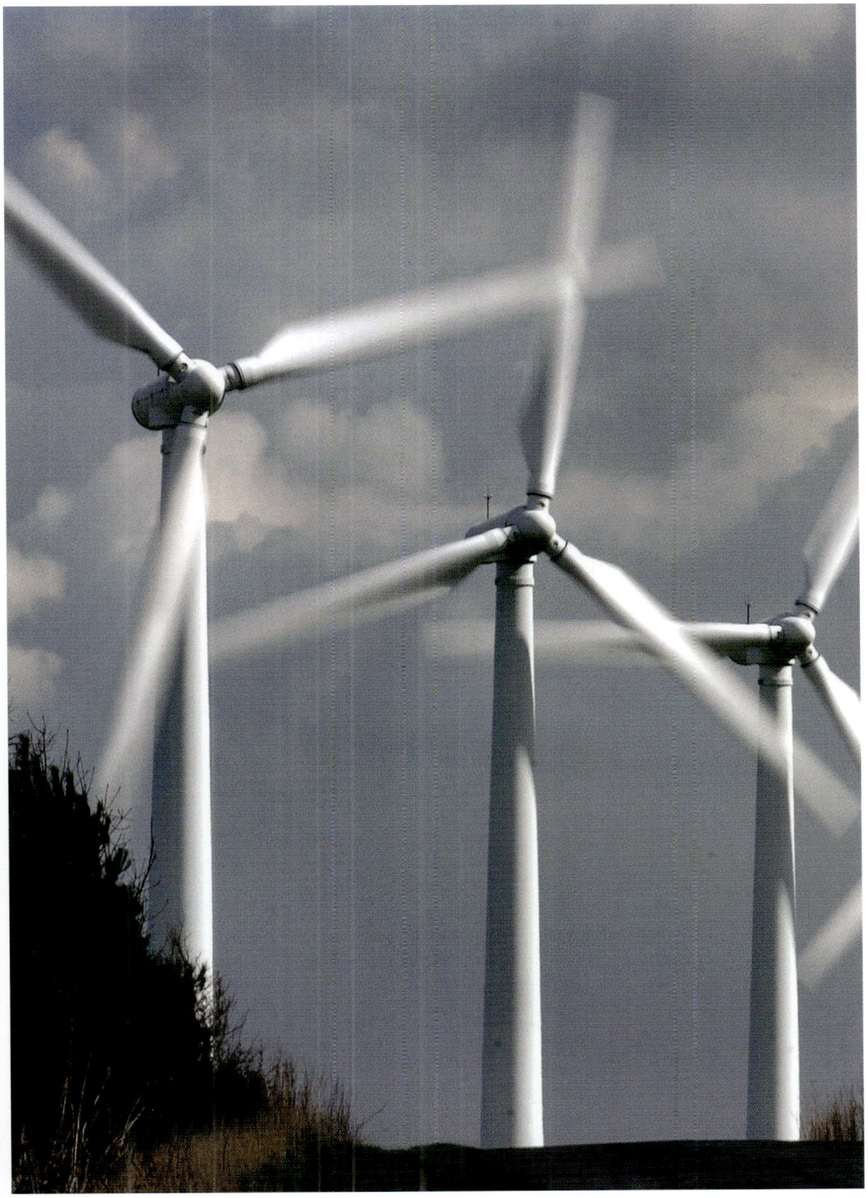

Wind turbines spinning a on a windy day at Royd Moor near Penistone. (YPP2031)

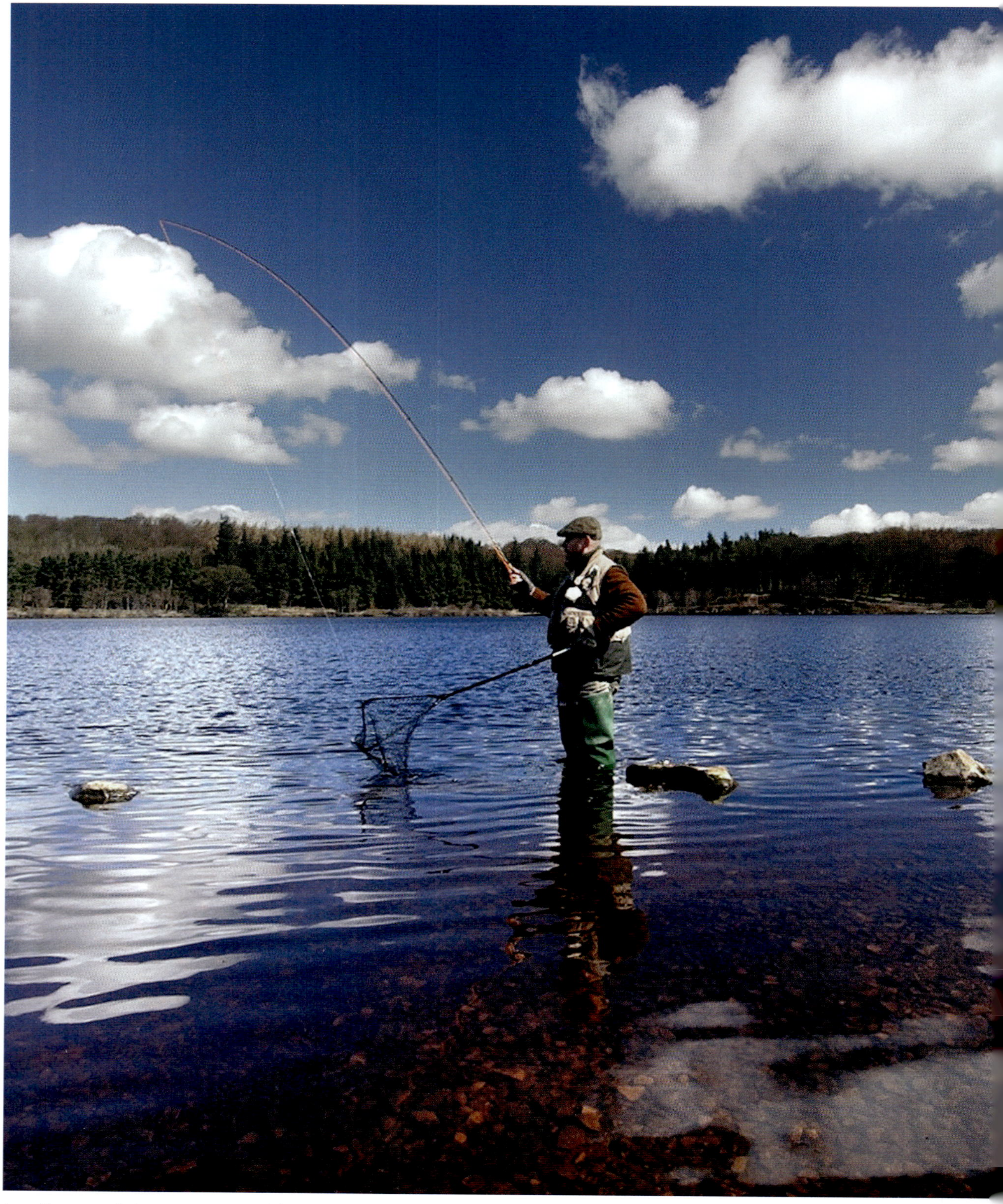

Landing a rainbow trout, David Lawrence fly fishing at Fewston Reservoir, in the Washburn Valley. (YPP2032)

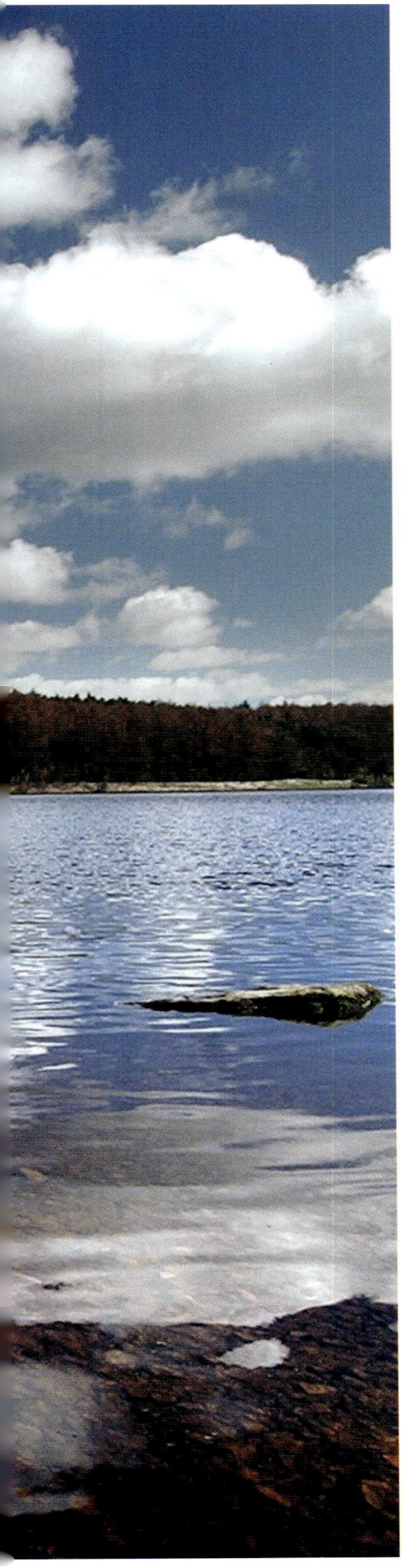

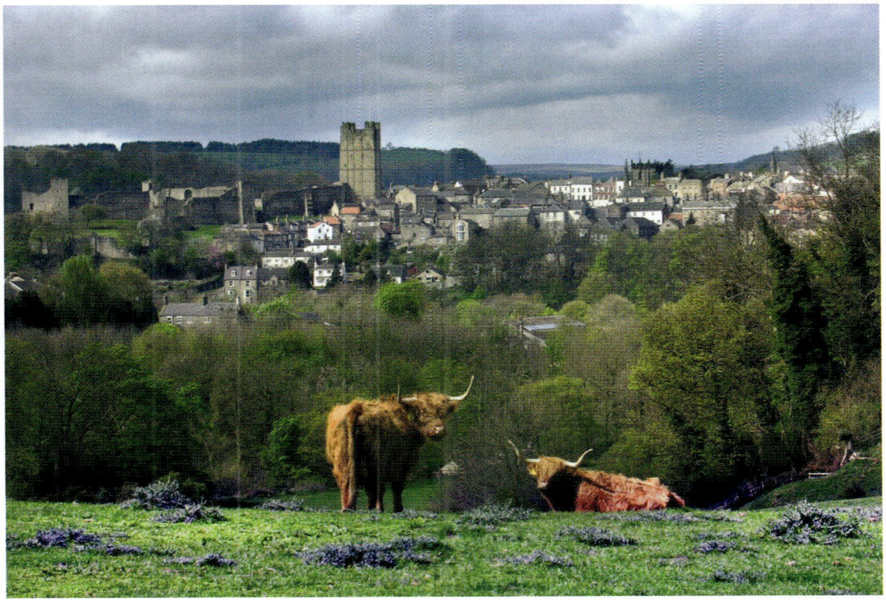

Highland Cattle graze in the fields above Richmond.
(YPP2033)

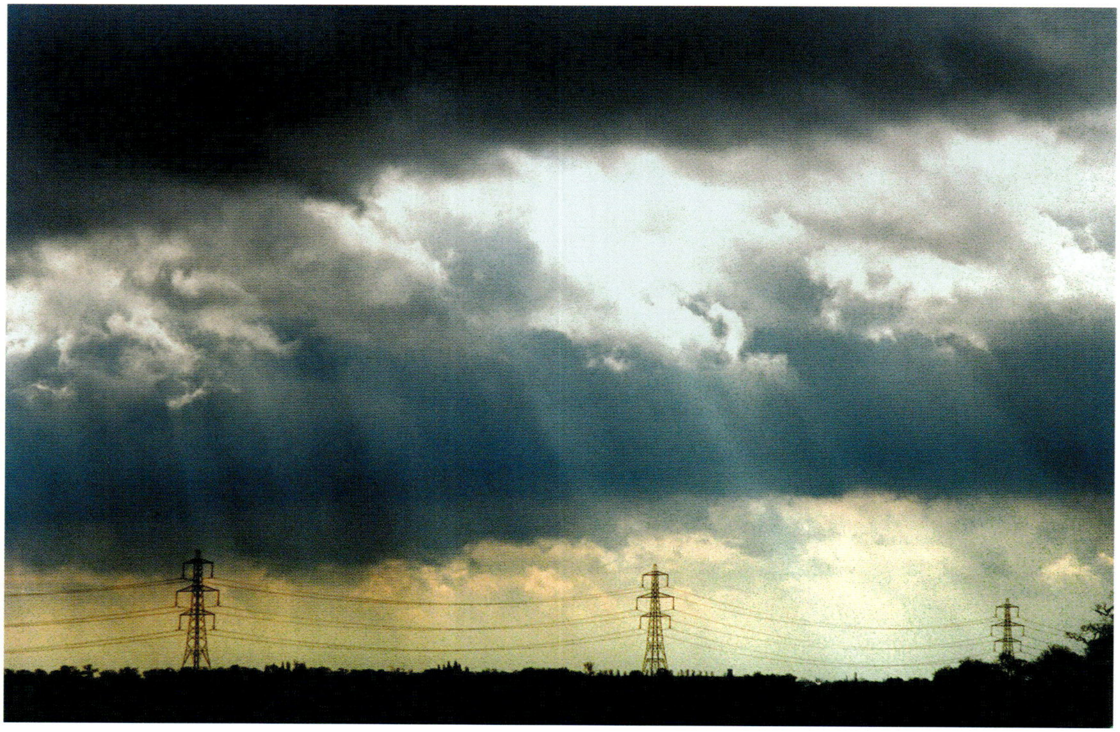

Sunlight filters through the clouds drifting over a landscape near Howden that's dominated by striding pylons. The power in the lines they carry from Ferrybridge, Eggborough and Drax slots into the national grid. (YPP2034)

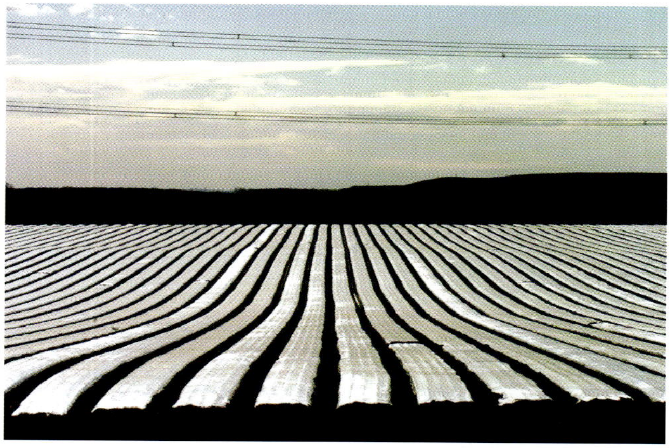

Plastic sheets, laid in sharp rows to protect young crops from winter frosts give a machined look to a field near Kellington. (YPP2035)

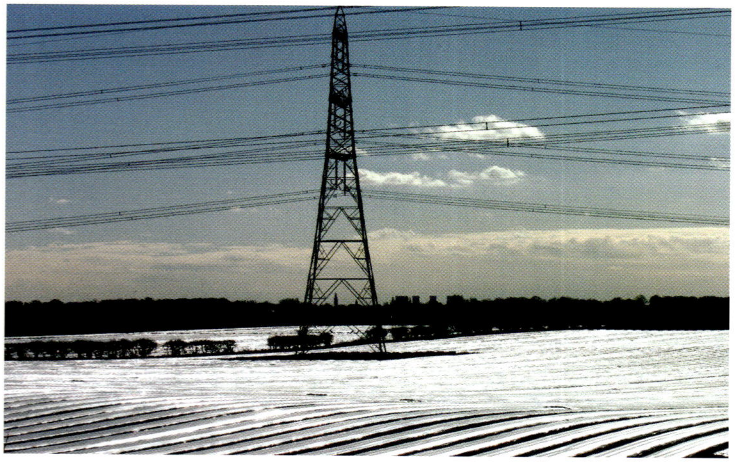

In this view, the sheets look like a thin covering of snow, and high above, the power lines sing to a skeletal pylon. (YPP2036)

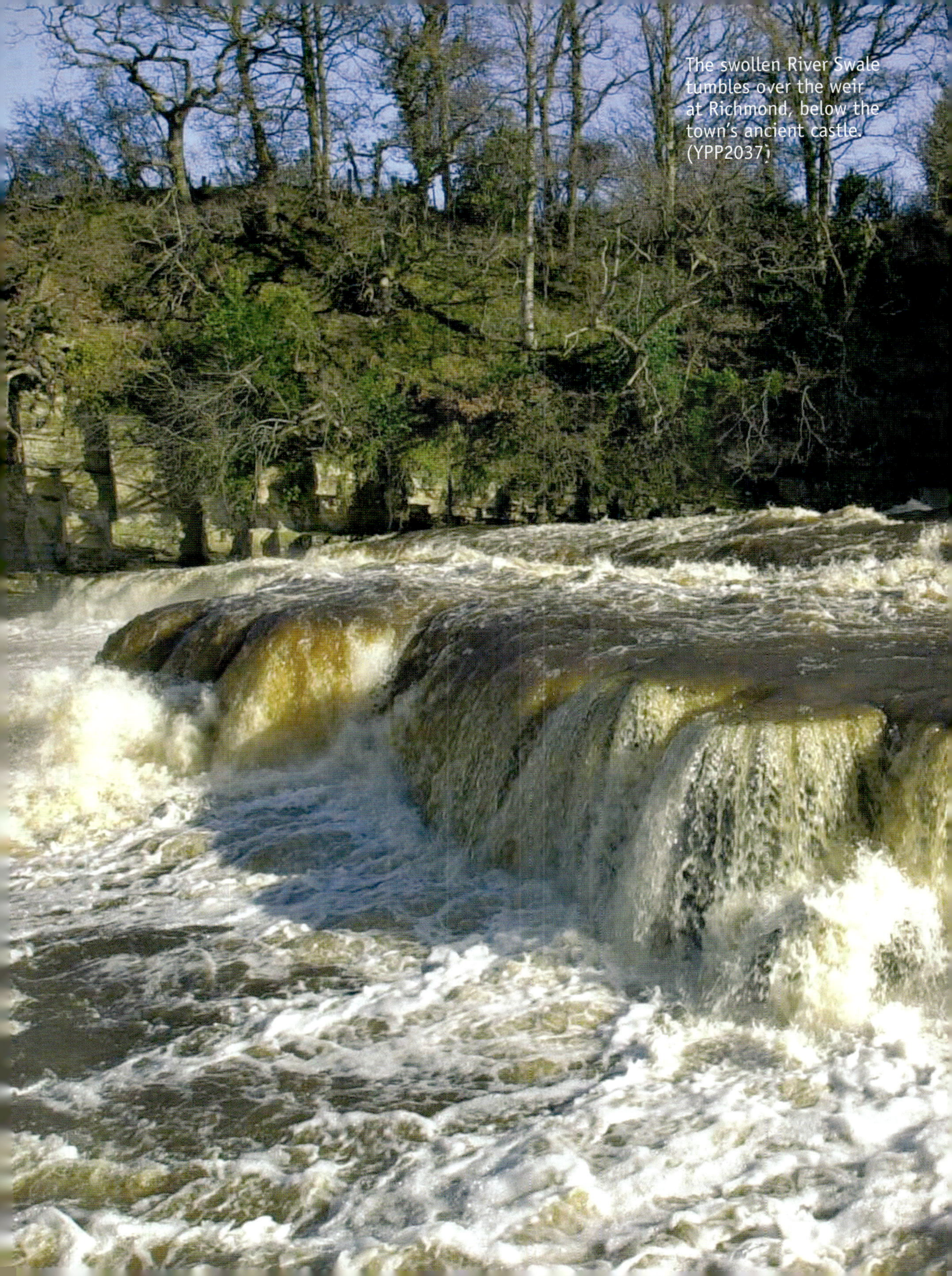

The swollen River Swale tumbles over the weir at Richmond, below the town's ancient castle. (YPP2037)

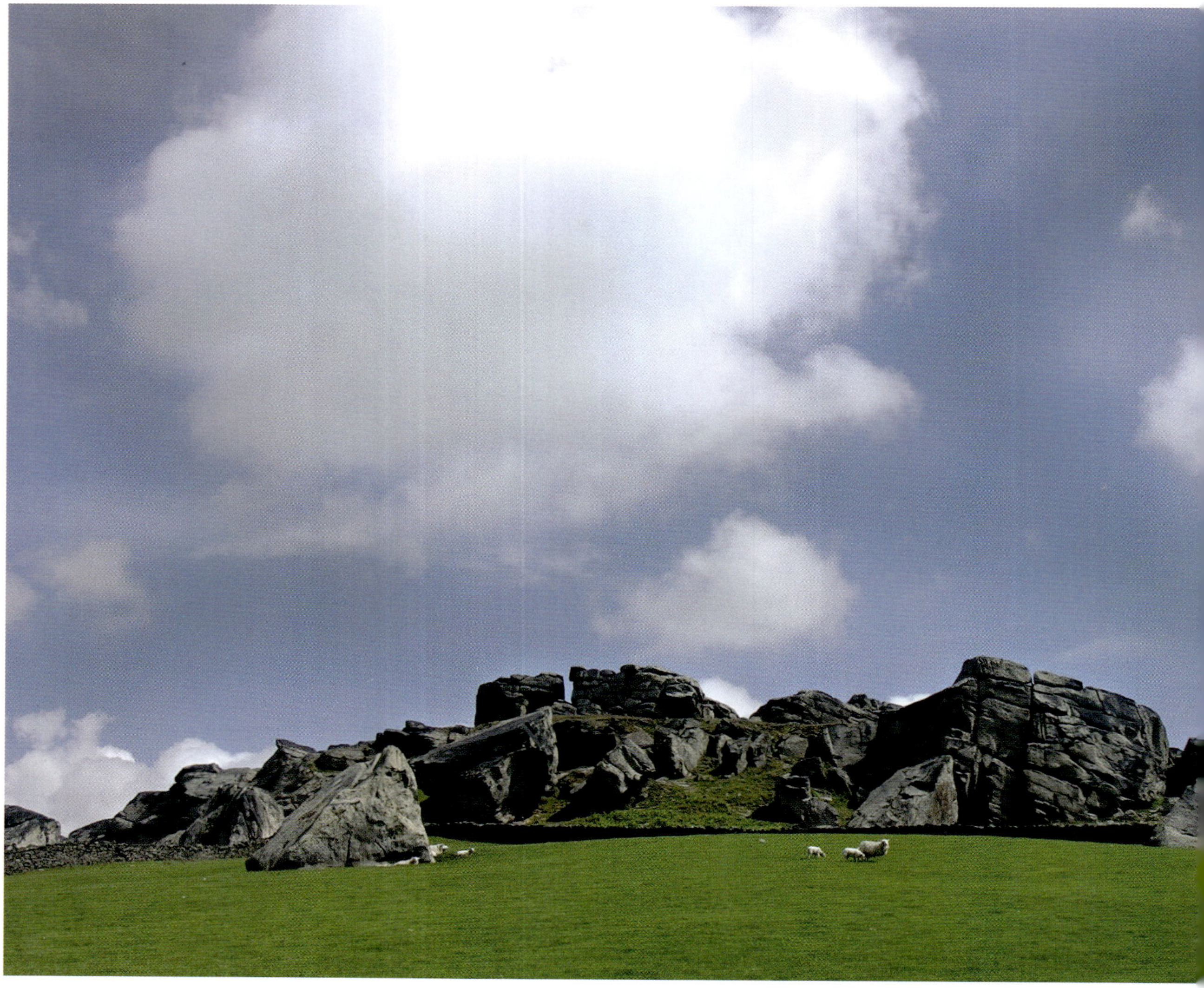

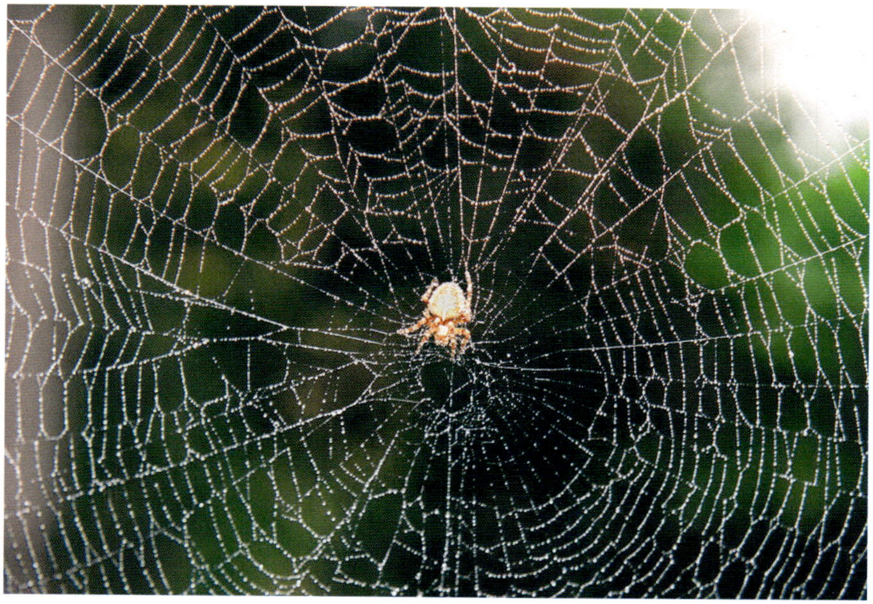

Early-morning dew defines the delicate structure of a spider's web with jewels while the architect, fat and deadly, awaits her breakfast. (YPP2039)

The gritstone mass of Almscliffe Orag appers to erupt from the fields between Harewood and Harrogate. (YPP2038)

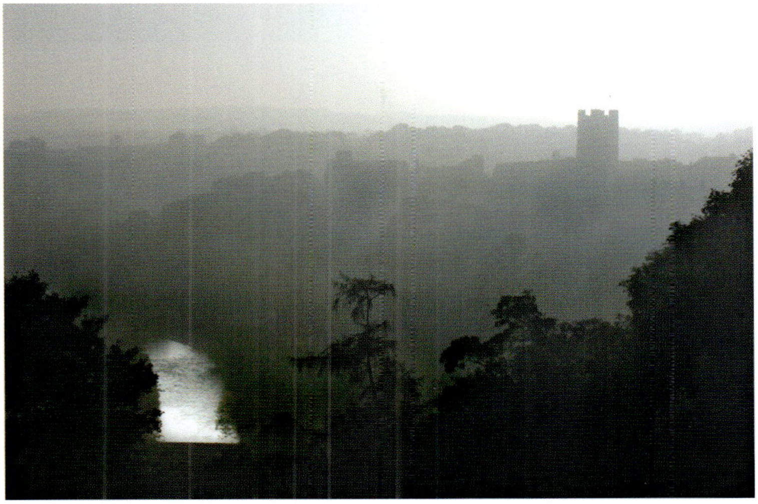

Season of mists and mellow fruitfulness. Richmond is swathed in an autumnal mist as a pale sun lights the sky (YPP2040)

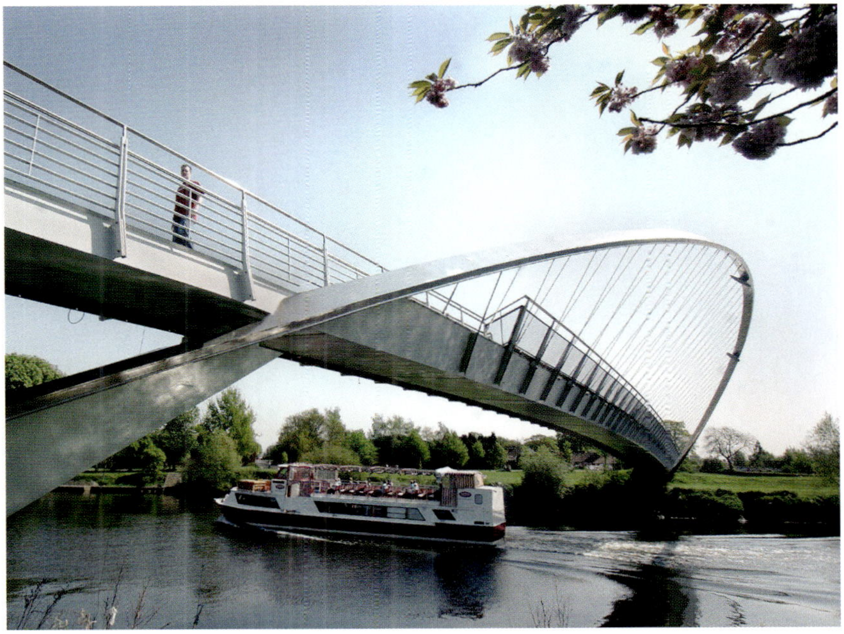

A York Boat pleasure cruiser moves down River Ouse in York under the the Millennium Bridge. The bridge is the first permanent bridge on the site. A temporary bailey bridge was erected in July 1955 during the York Tattoo.
(YPP2041)

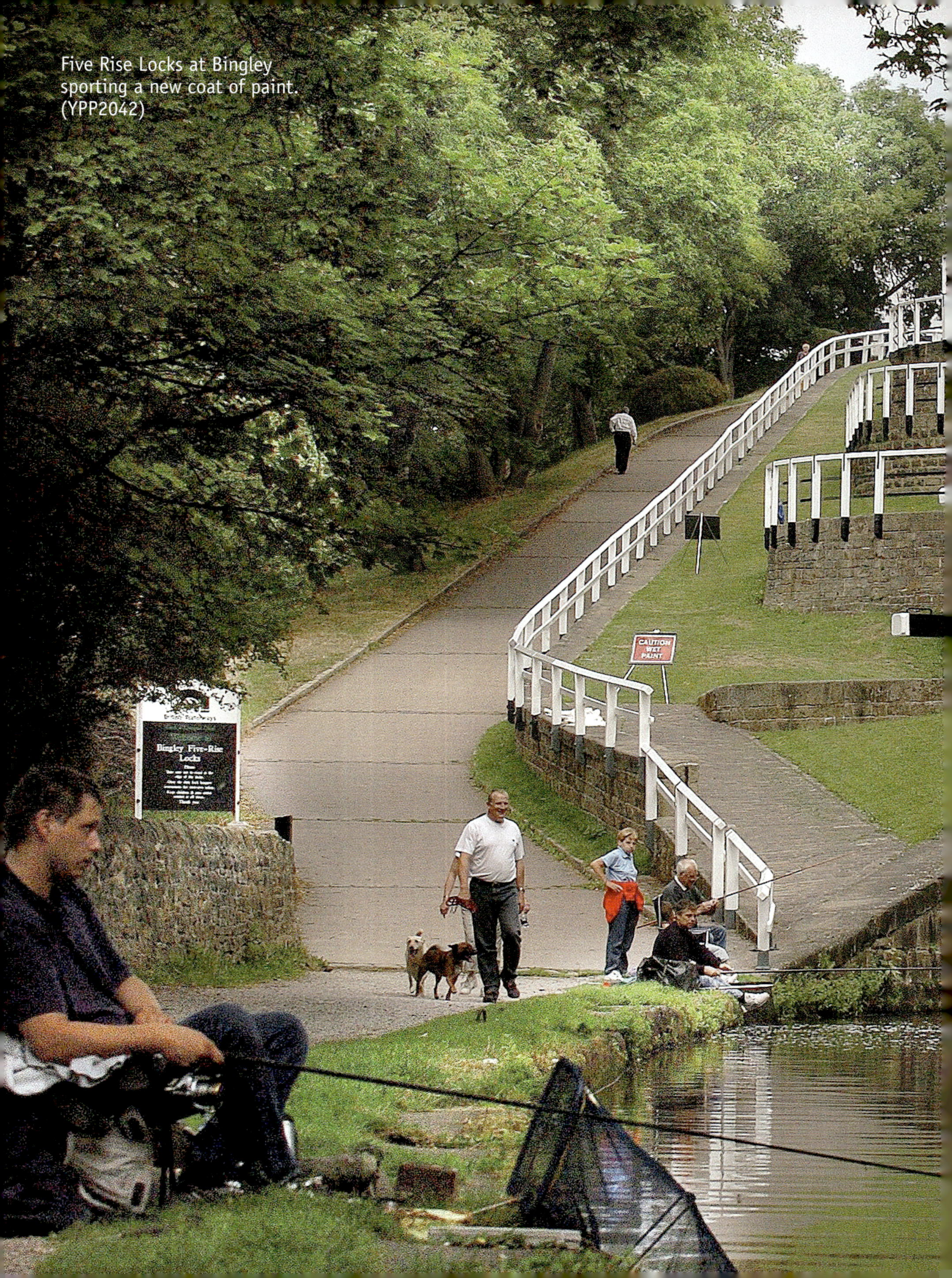

Five Rise Locks at Bingley sporting a new coat of paint. (YPP2042)

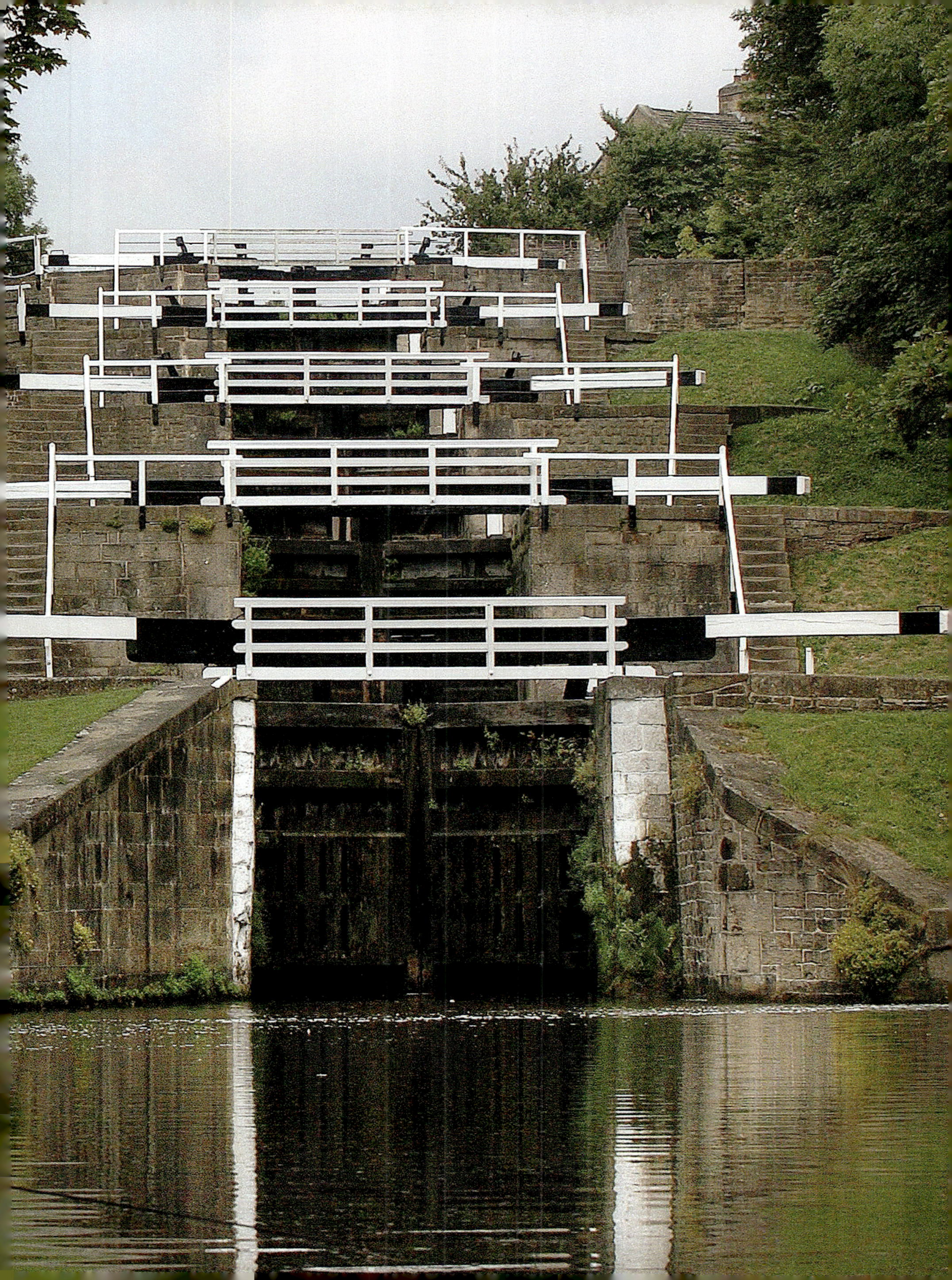

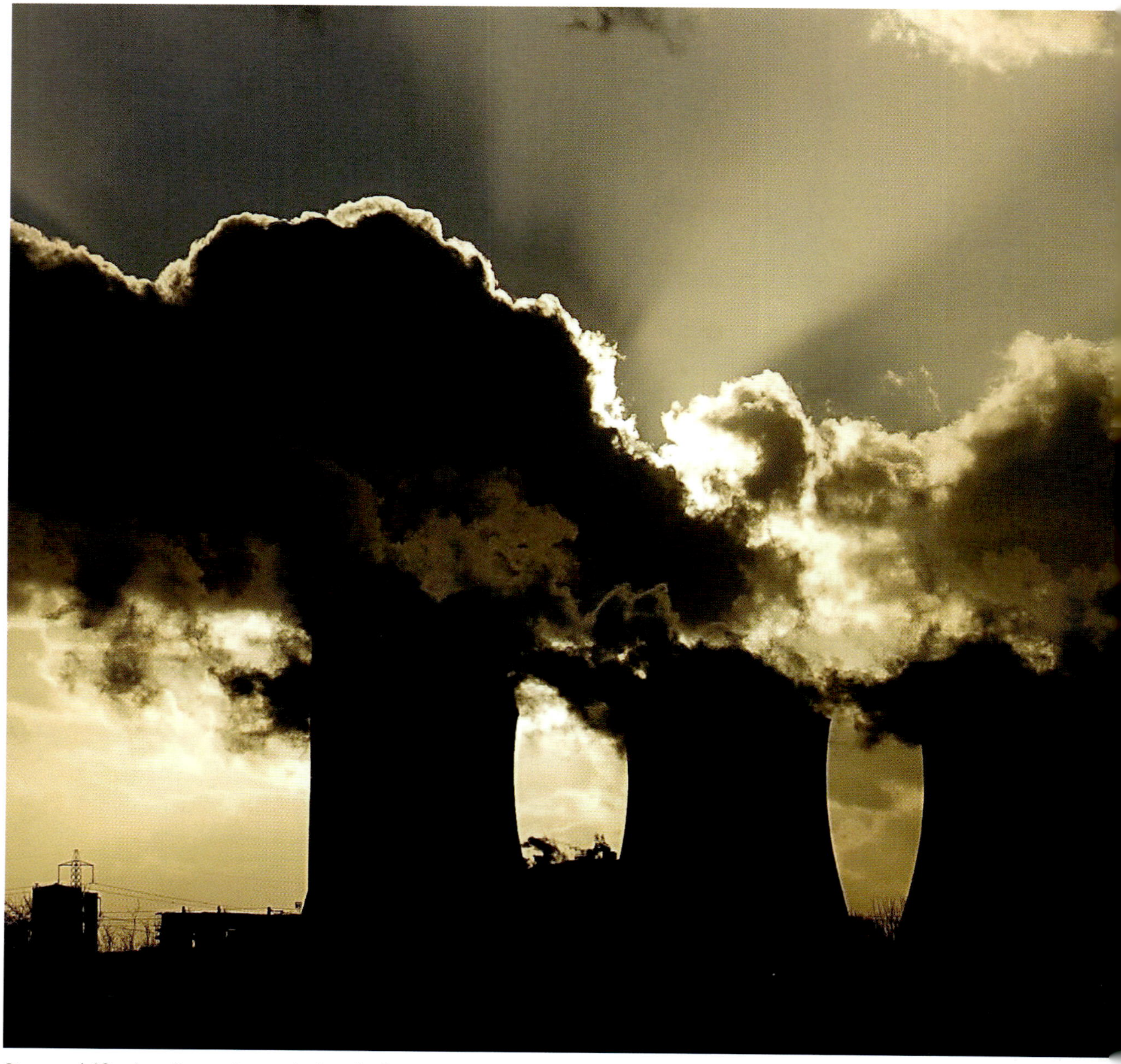

Steam drifts in silver-rimmed clouds from the wide gaping mouths of the cooling towers at Eggborough Power Station, near Selby.
(YPP2043)

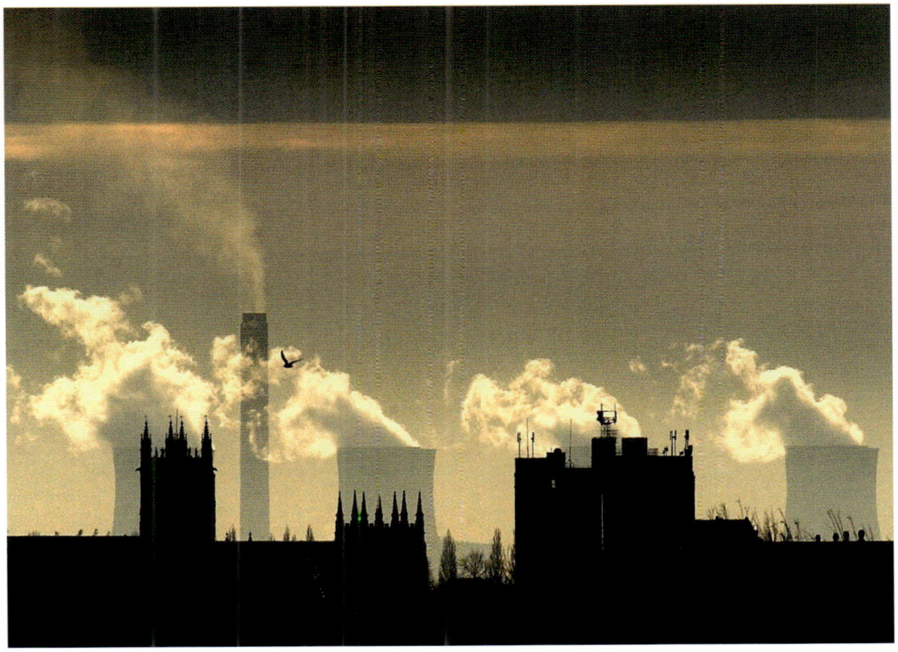

Selby Abbey in silhouette on a cold winter's day against the grey distant shapes made on the horizon by Eggborough. (YPP2044)

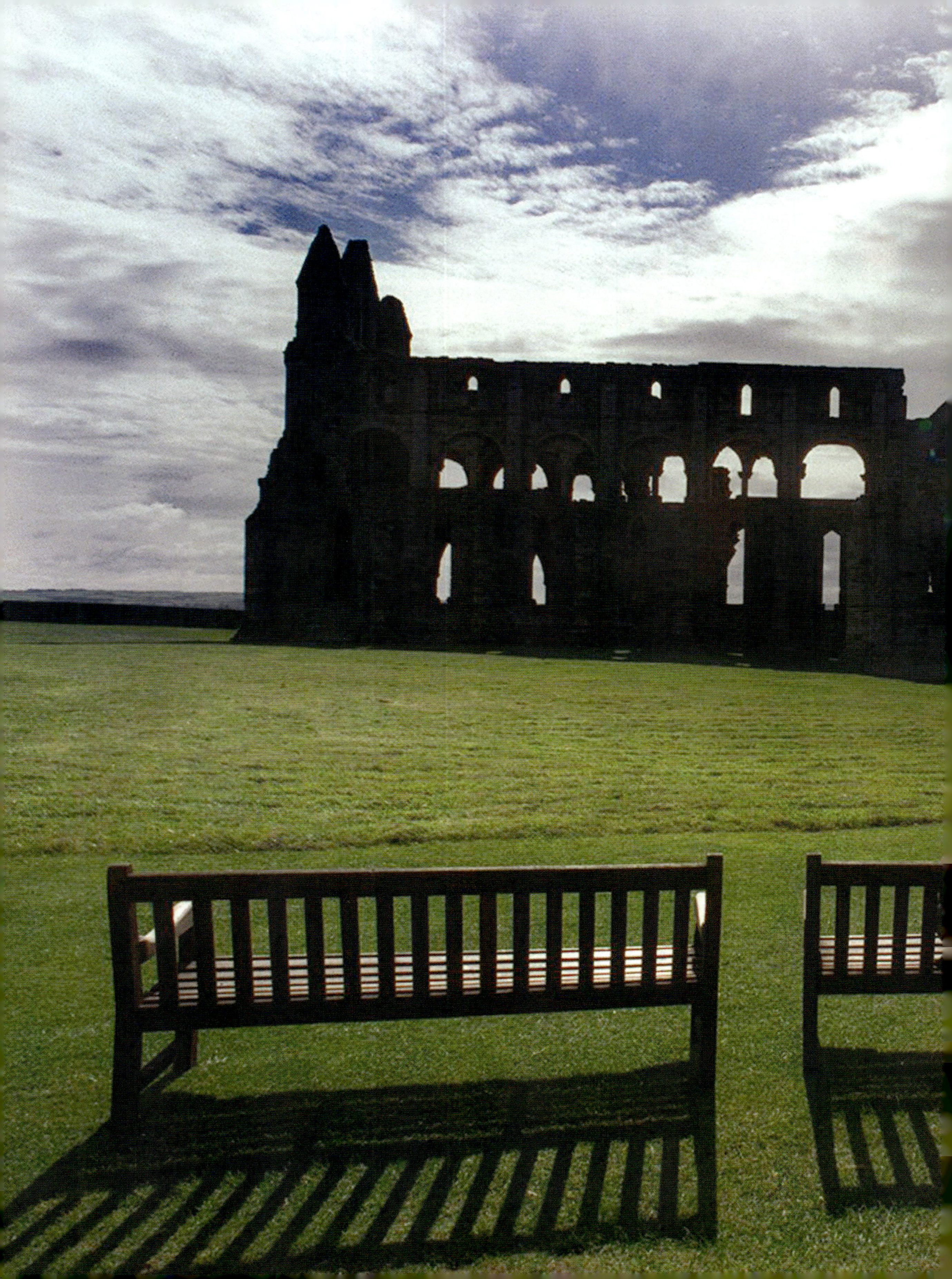

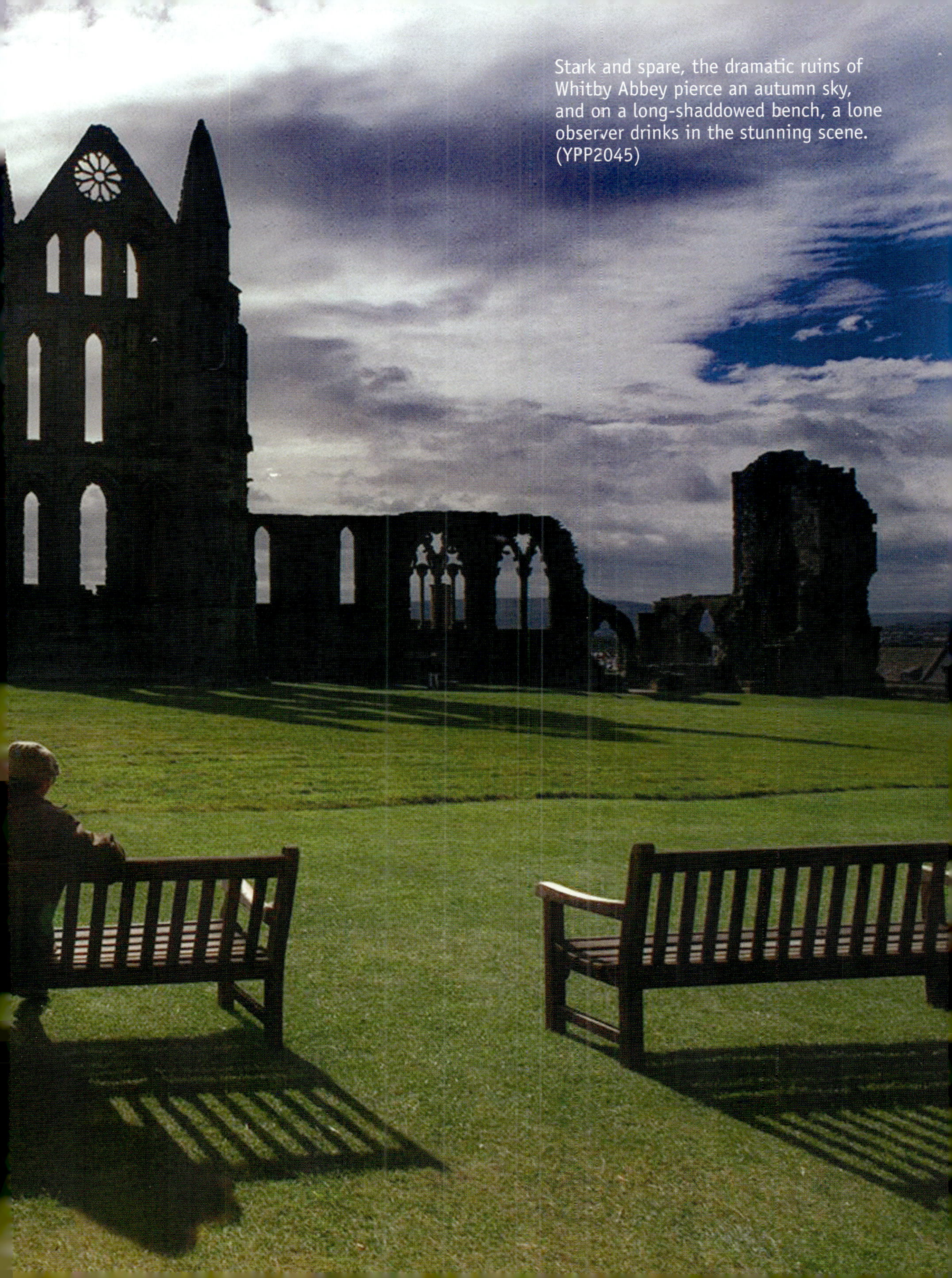

Stark and spare, the dramatic ruins of Whitby Abbey pierce an autumn sky, and on a long-shaddowed bench, a lone observer drinks in the stunning scene. (YPP2045)

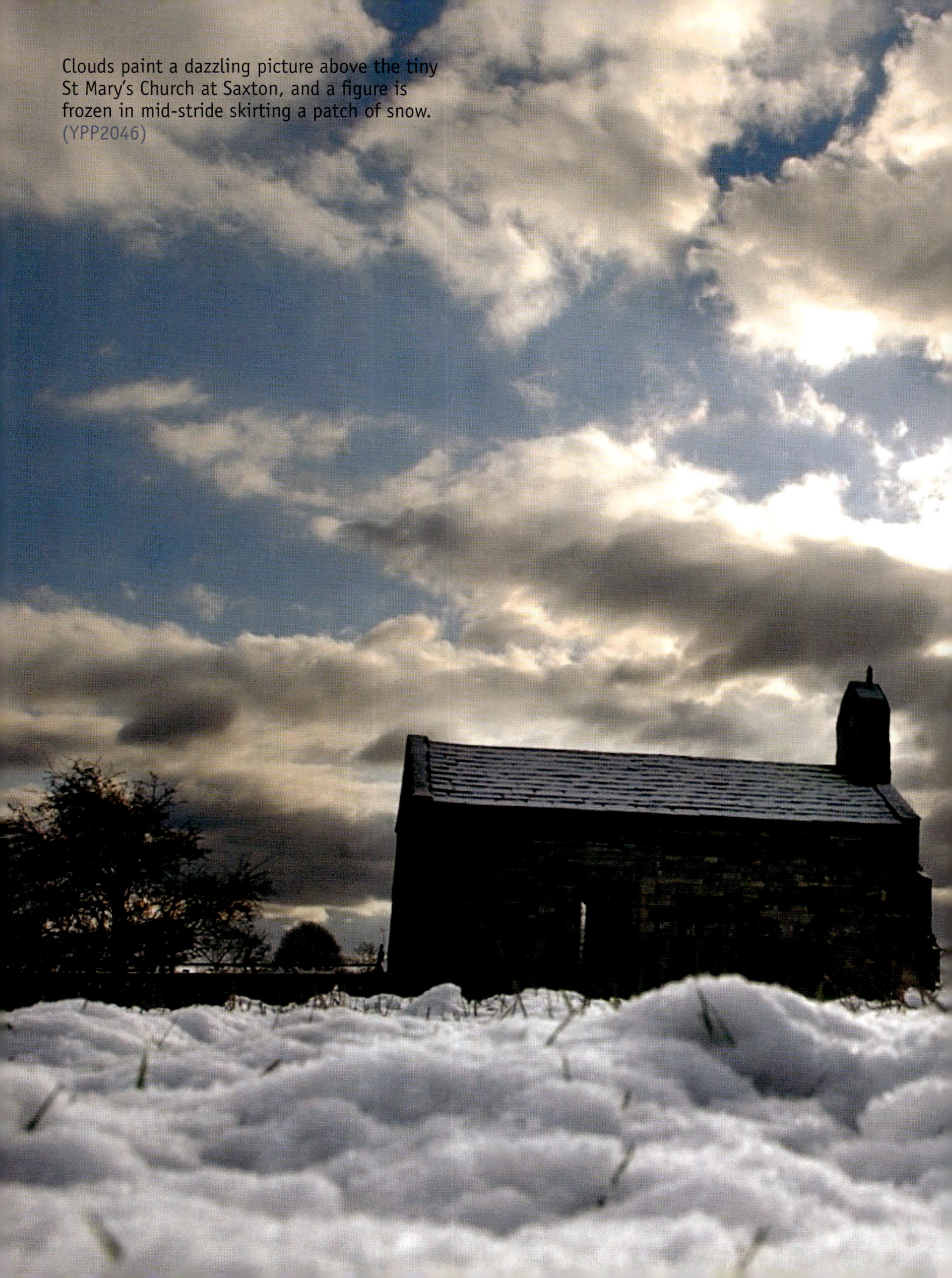

Clouds paint a dazzling picture above the tiny St Mary's Church at Saxton, and a figure is frozen in mid-stride skirting a patch of snow. (YPP2046)

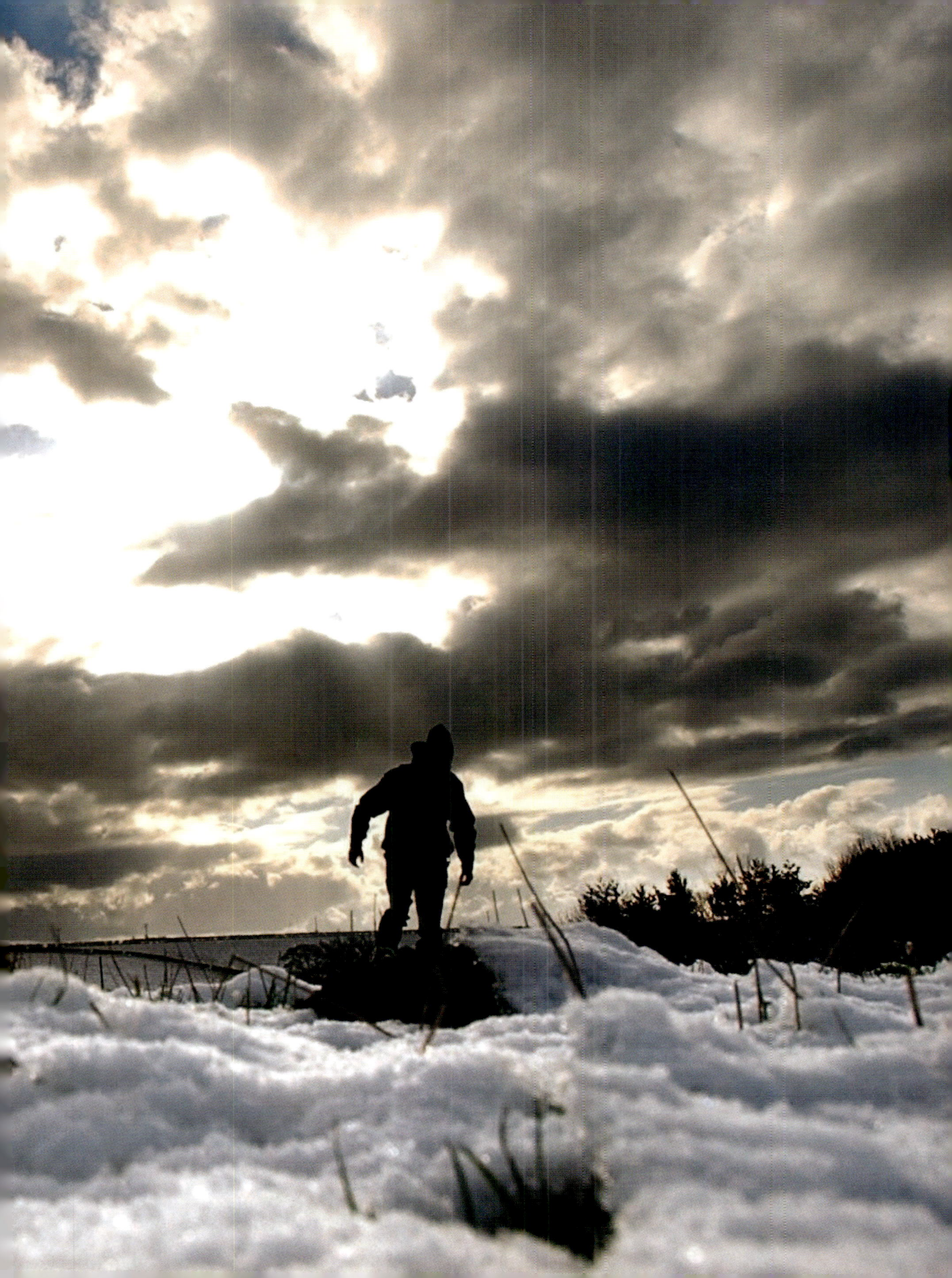

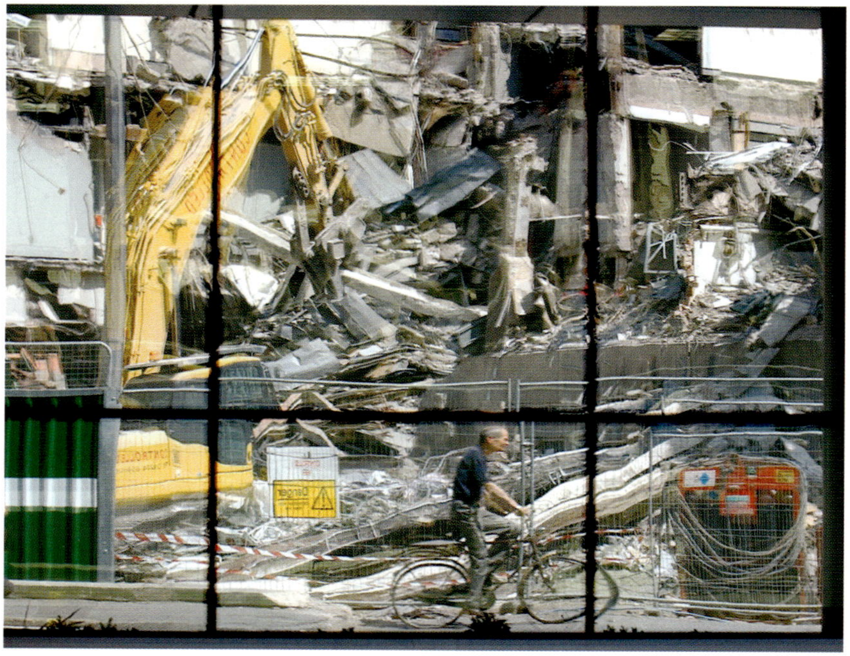

The mirror-glass wall of a brand new office block reflects a cyclist passing by, and, on the far side of the road, the demolition of the hideous Royal Mail building which had dominated Wellington Street, Leeds, for too many years. (YPP2047)

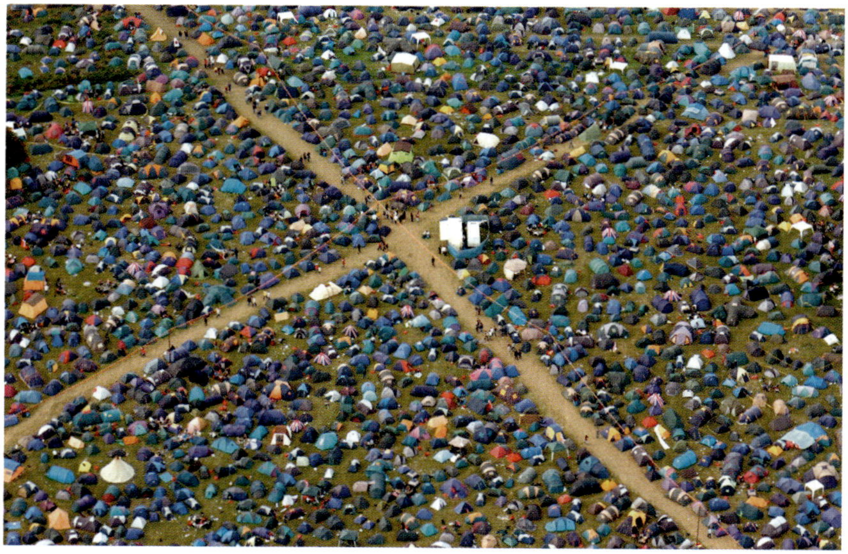

Tents put up by festival goers smother the ground in Bramaham Park for the Leeds Festival. (YPP2048)

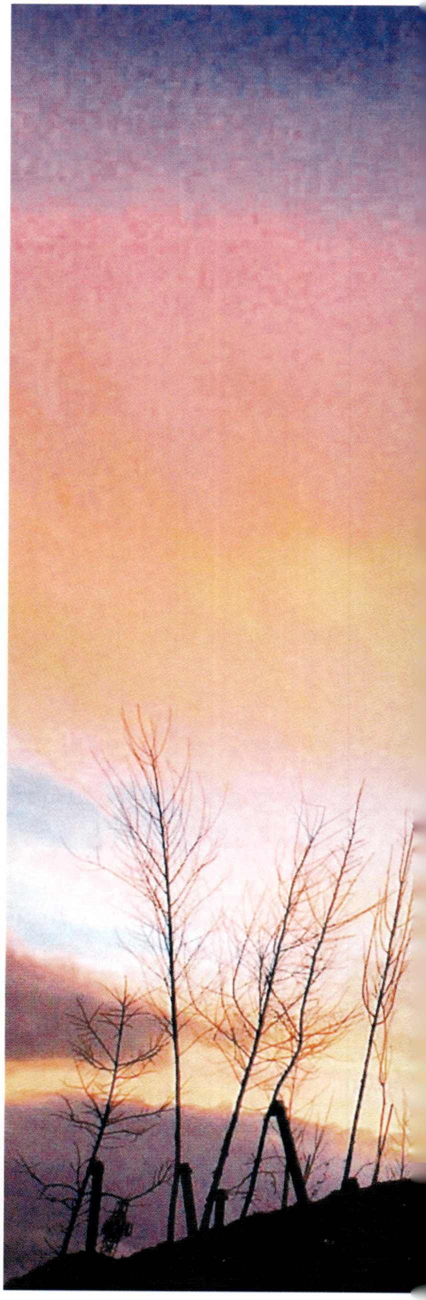

A 6 metre high Stainless Steel sculpture of a women named 'Triumphant' at Leeds Valley Park, Stourton, Leeds. (YPP2049)

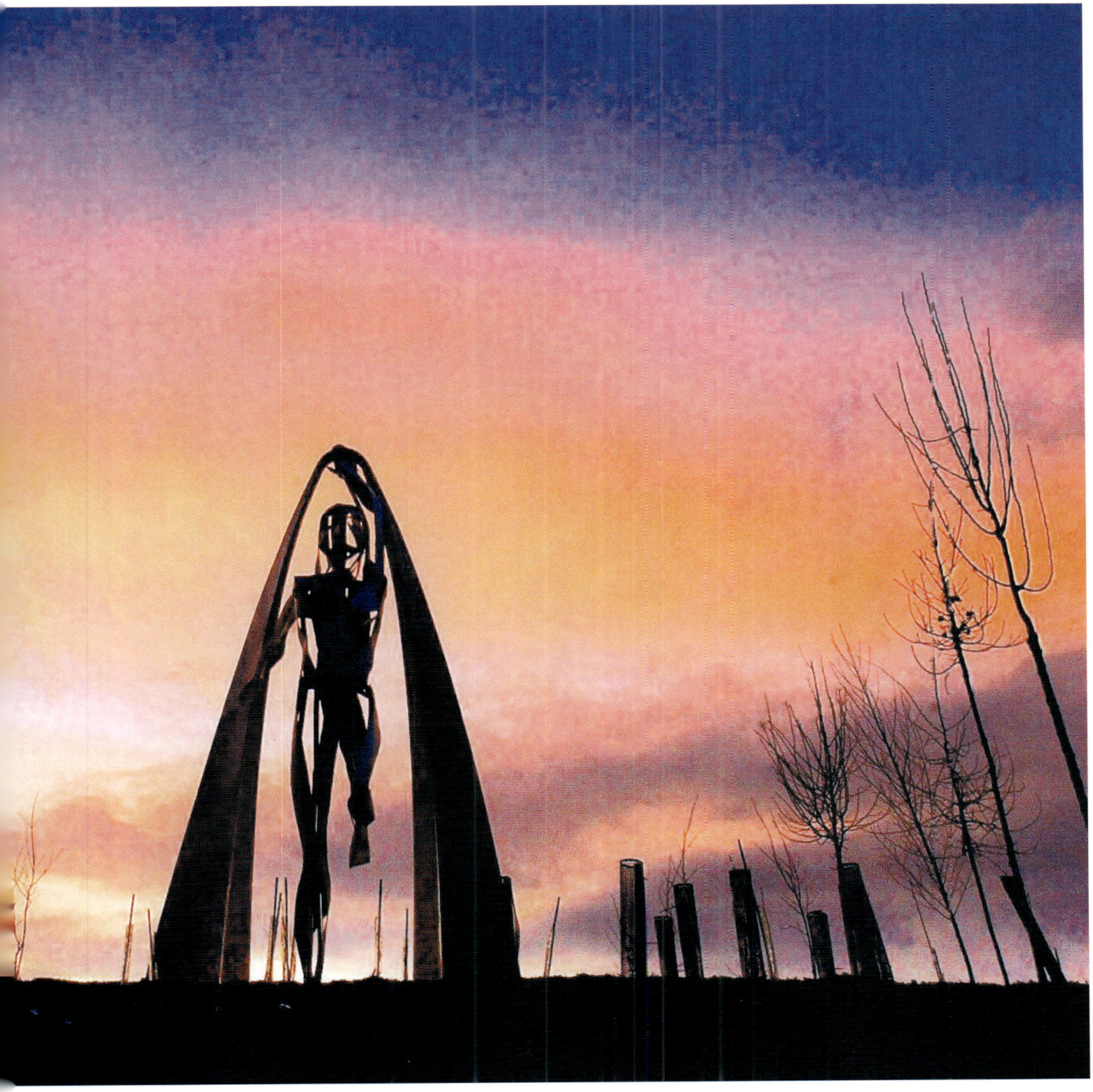

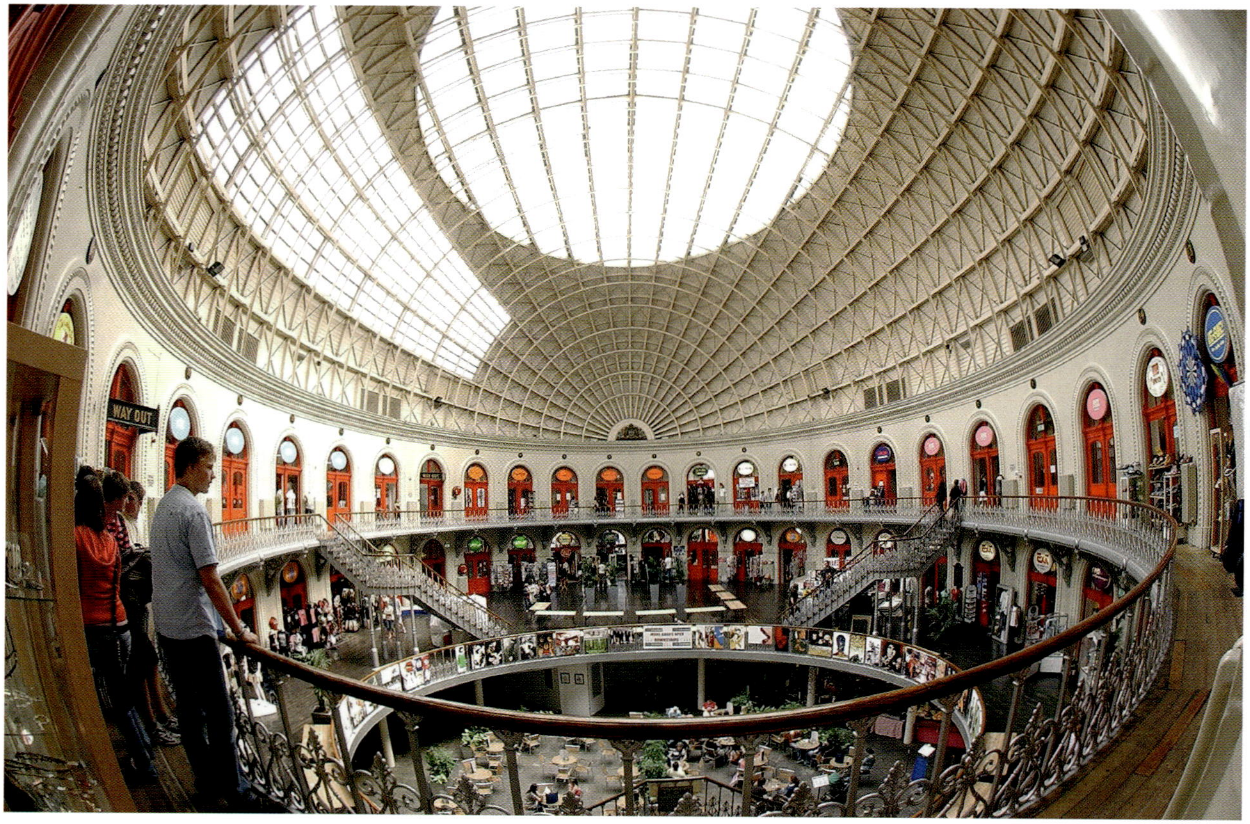

The oval shape of the Corn Exchange, Leeds, can be seen in its unique roof, looking like a gigantic up-turned boat. (YPP2050)

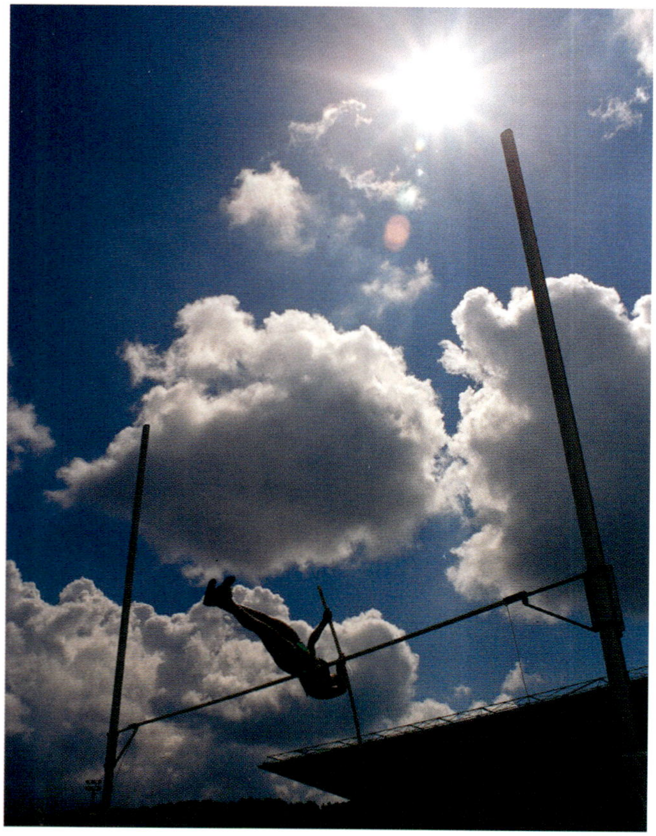

A pole vaulter in silhouette against a cloud-strewn sky as he flings himself over the bar at an international athletics event at South Leeds Stadium. (YPP2051)

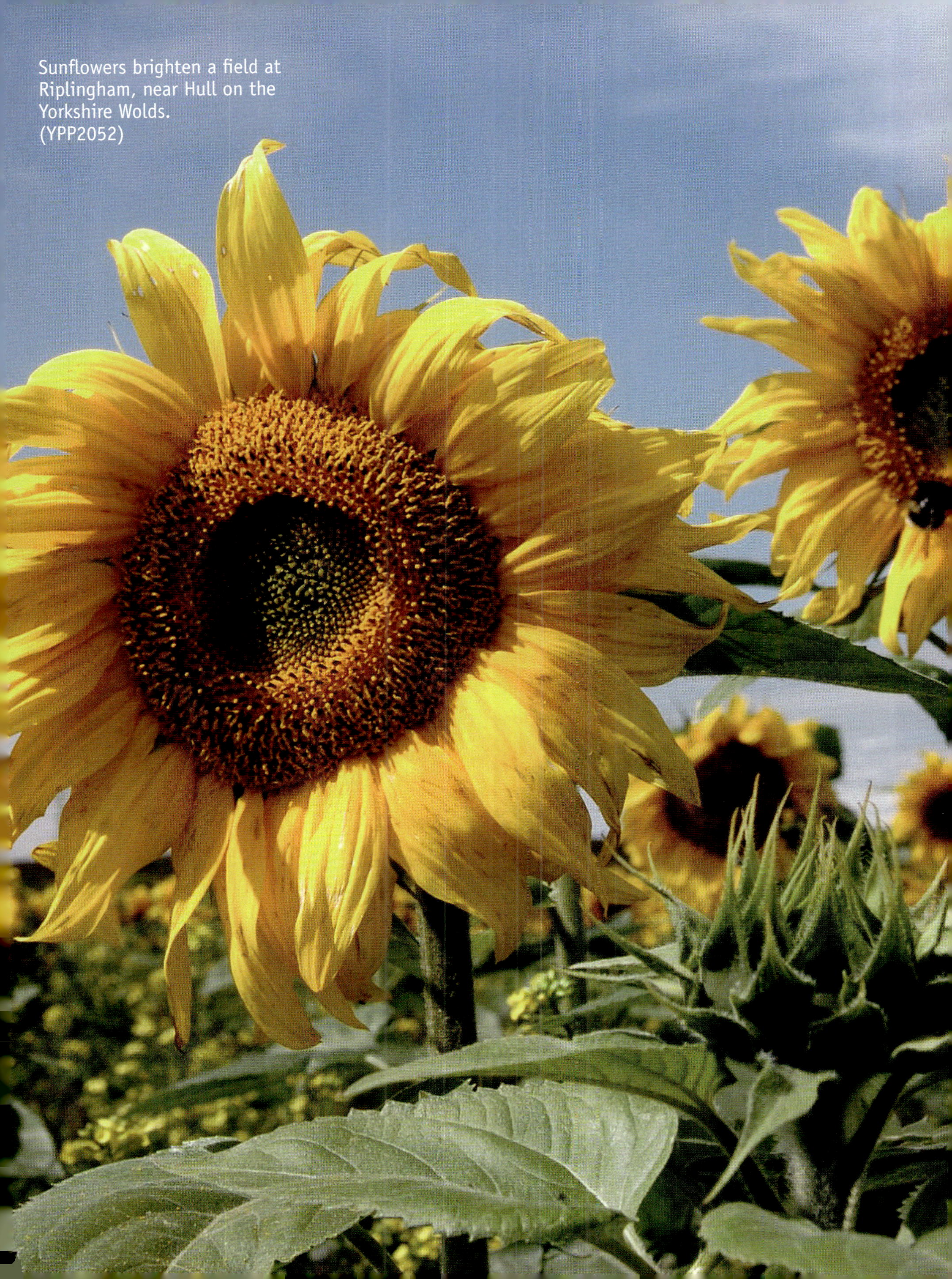

Sunflowers brighten a field at Riplingham, near Hull on the Yorkshire Wolds. (YPP2052)

Wakefield Cathedral.
(YPP2053)

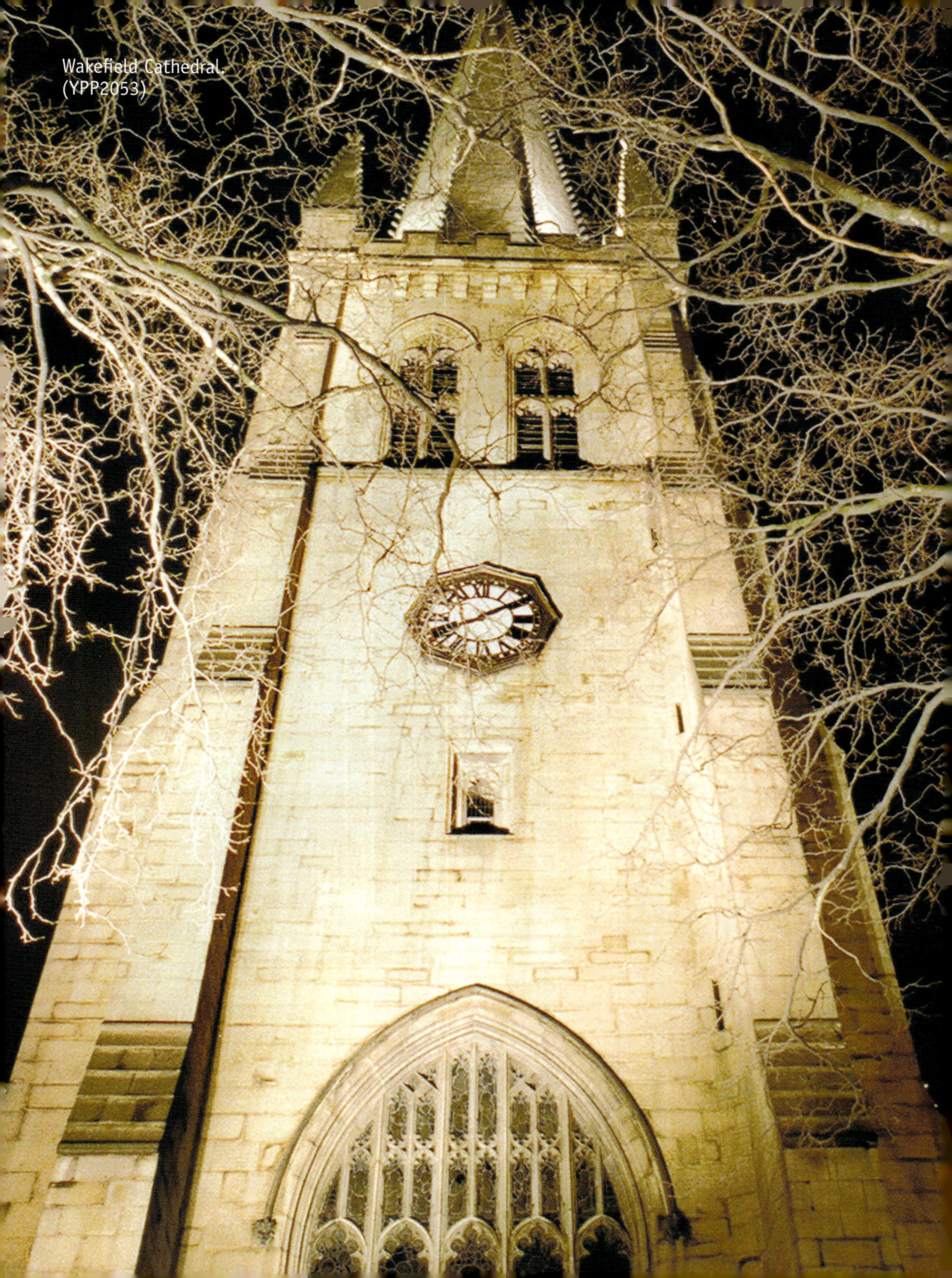

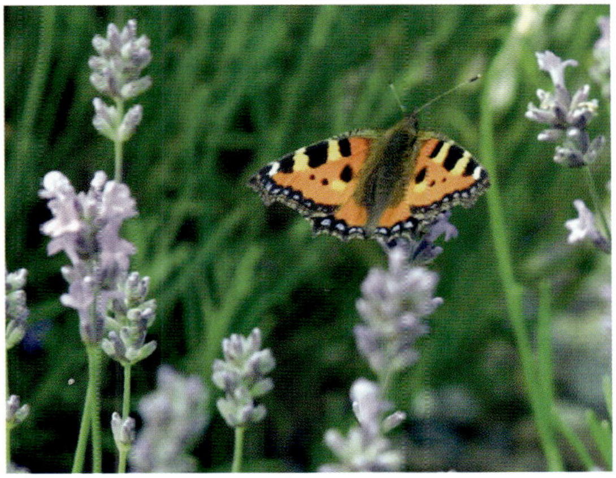

A butterfly is attracted to the lavender at 'Wolds Way Lavender', probably Yorkshire's largest lavender and herb farm.
(YPP2054)

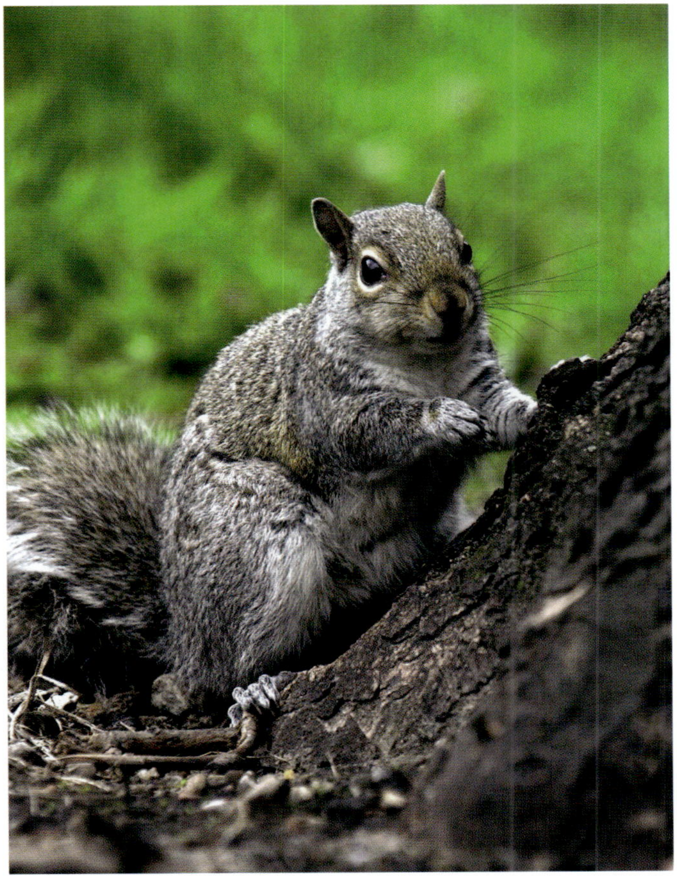

A grey squirrel in the Yorkshire Museum Gardens in York.
(YPP20055)

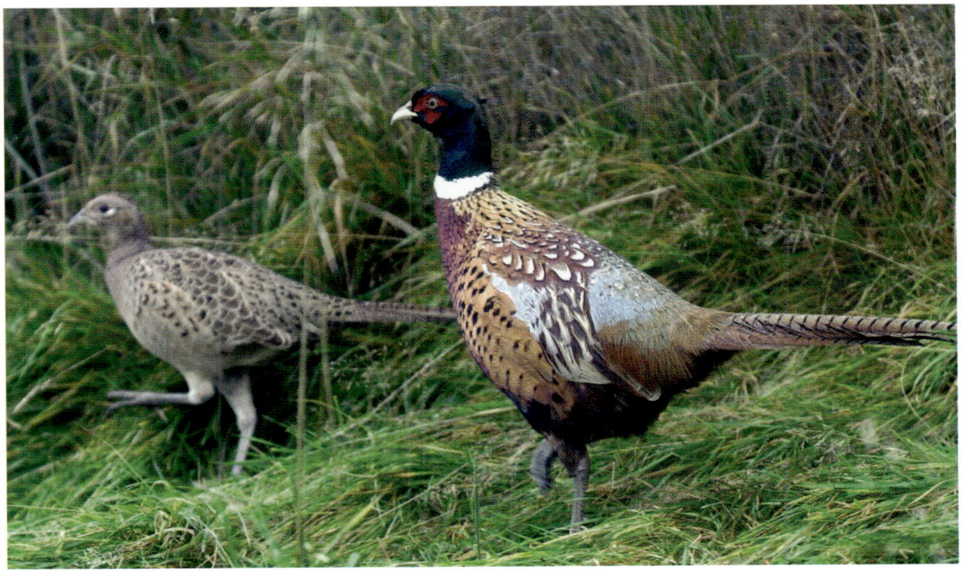

A cock pheasant, all dressed up in brilliant attire for the mating season, and a hen, conspicuously inconspicuous so as to escape attention when sitting on her eggs.
(YPP2056)

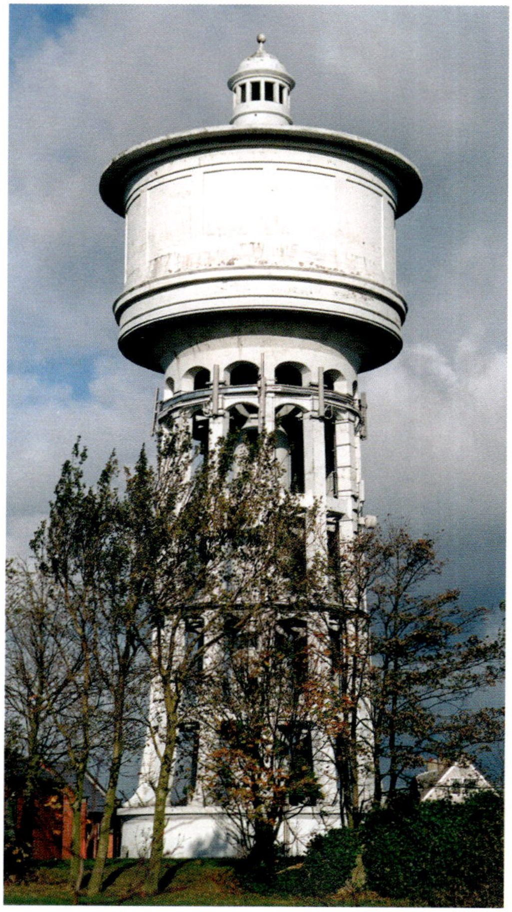

The Yorkshire Water reservoir at Gawthorpe, West Yorkshire. The water tower overlooks the landscape of Gawthorpe, Ossett and surrounding areas. (YPP2057)

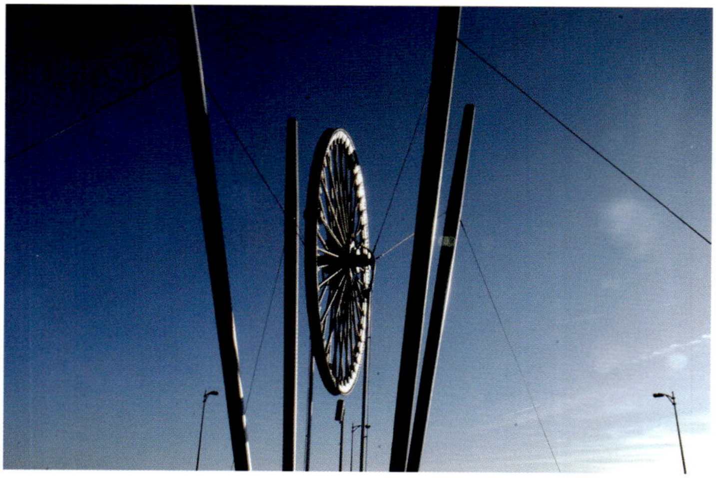

The Winding Wheel at Glasshoughton near Castleford The wheel is suspended from stainless steel cables and masts and symbolises both change and continuity. At night it is lit by 500 individual colour changing LED's. (YPP2058)

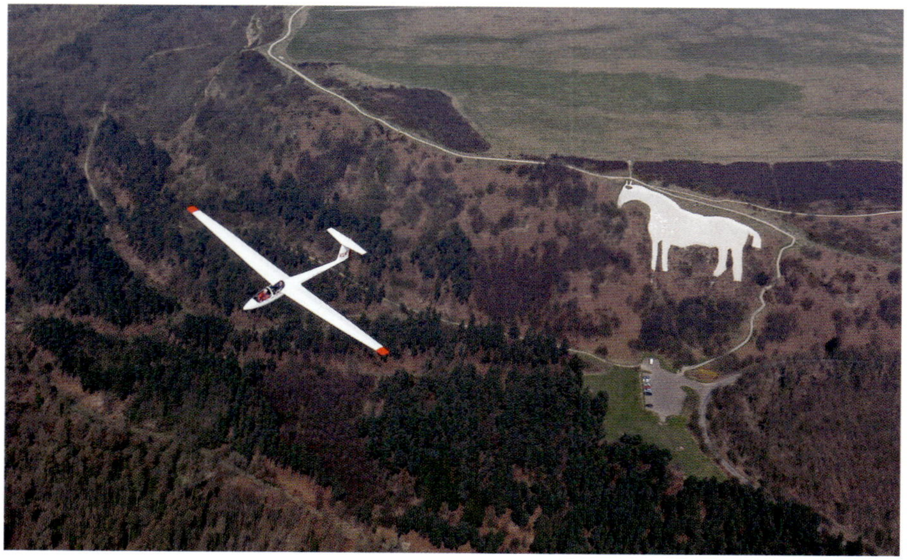

A glider flys over the White Horse of Kilburn. (YPP2059)

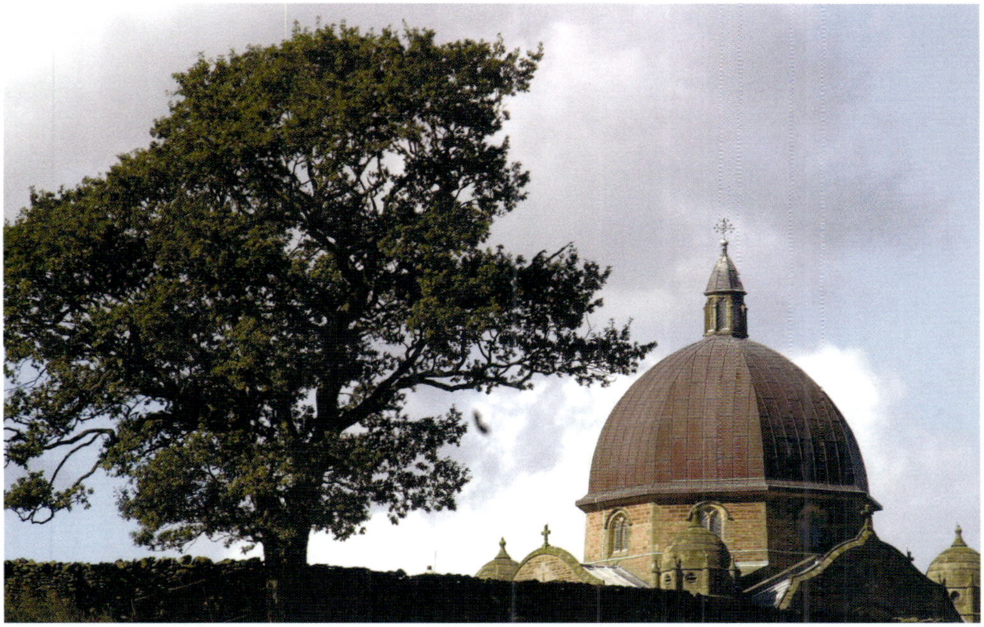

The dome of Giggleswick Chapel gives a Florintine look to this view in the Dales. (YPP2060)

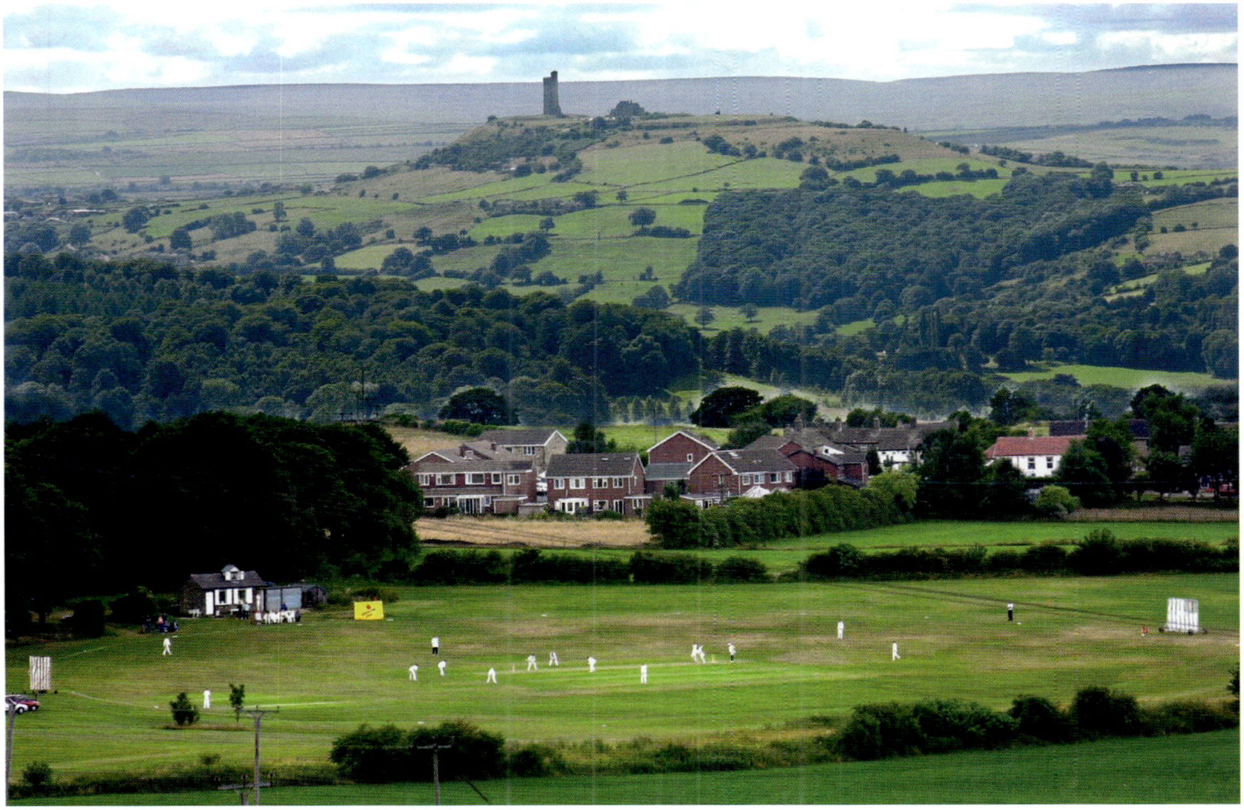

Village cricket at Lepton near Huddersfield in the shadow of Almondbury Hill Fort. (YPP2061)

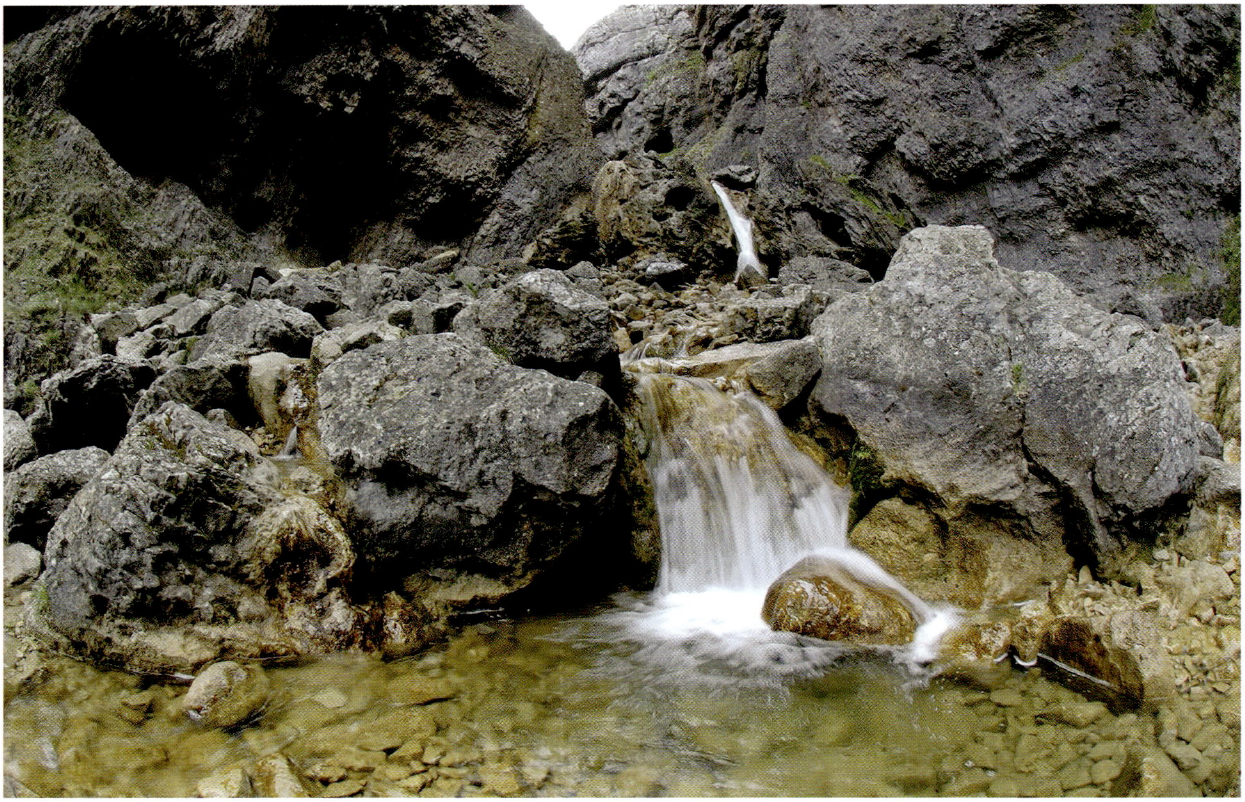

Cascading water splashes around the rocks strewn across Gordale Scar in Upper Wharfedale. (YPP2062)

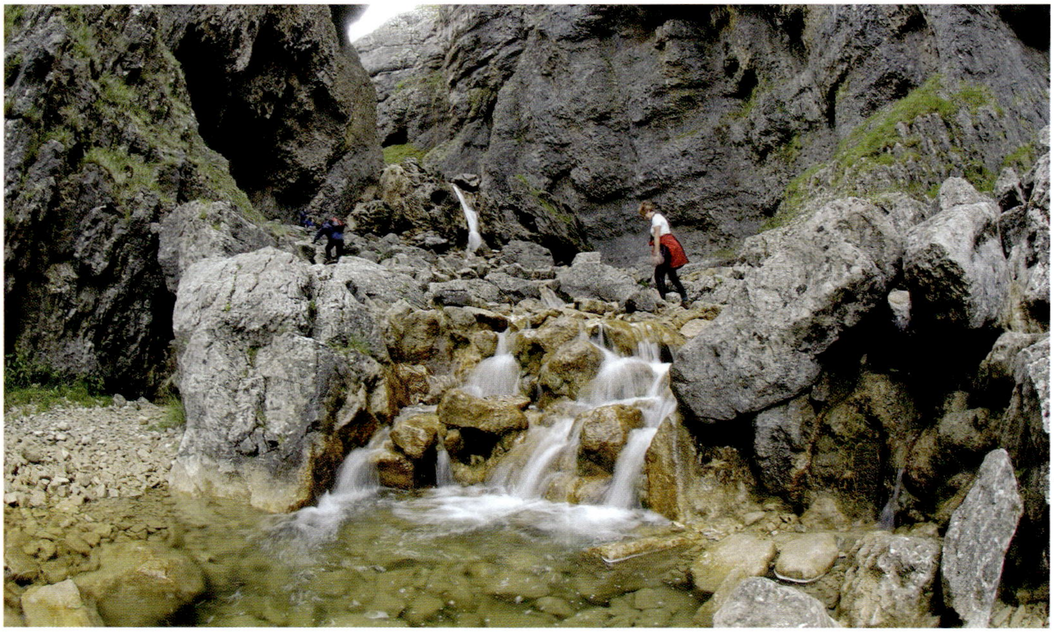

A walker, dwarfed by the towering limestone walls, picks his way across the rushing water. (YPP2063)

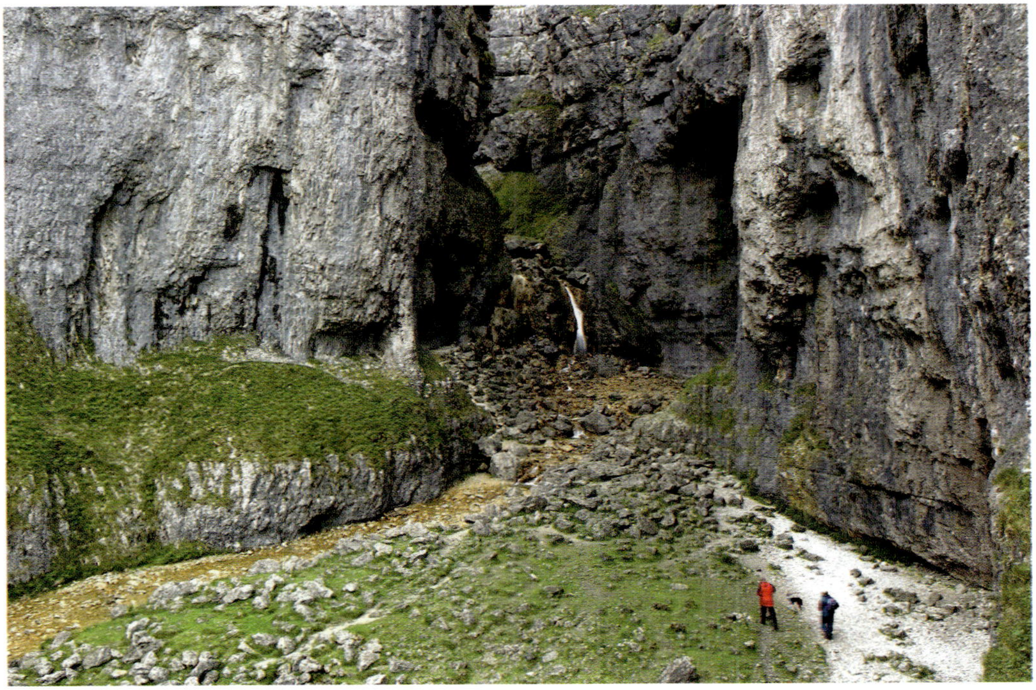

The Scar's extraordinary limestone architecture is a powerful draw to visitors. (YPP2064)

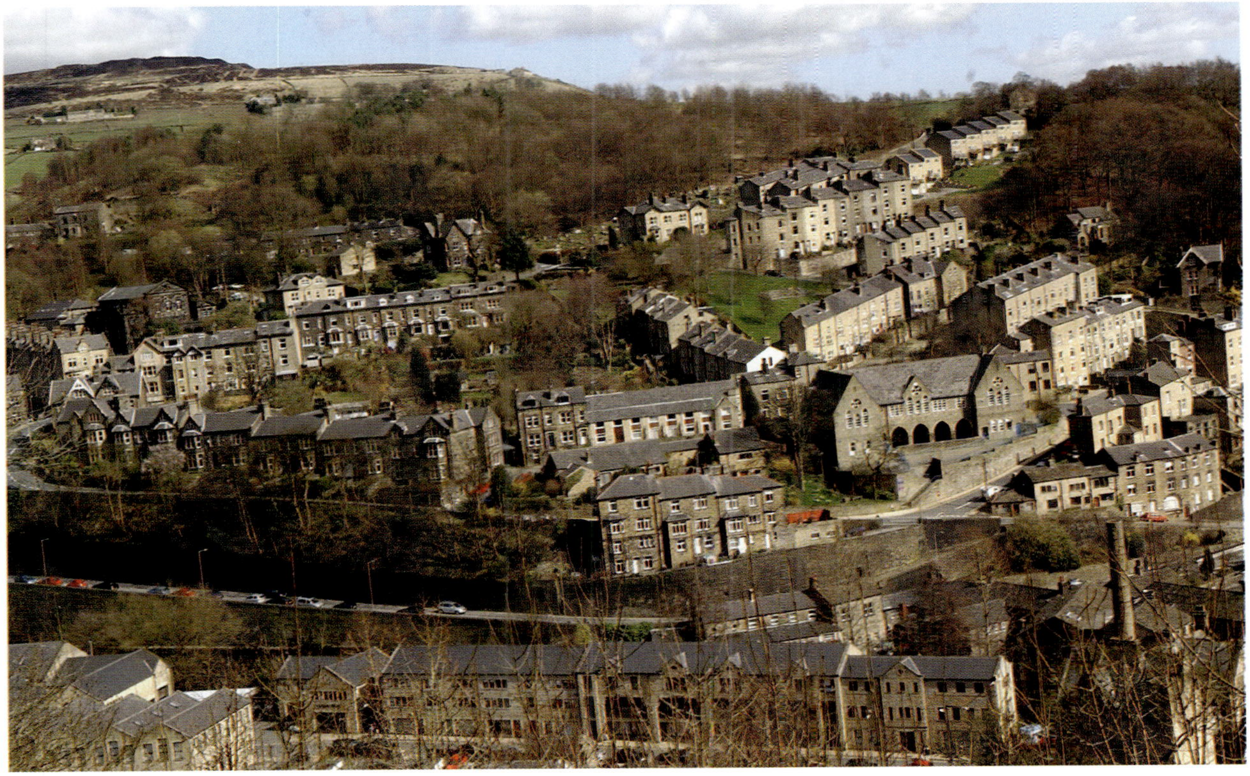

Hebden Bridge taken from the road leading up to Heptonstall. Stubbings Infants School can be clearly seen with its distinctive archways to the right of the picture. (YPP2065)

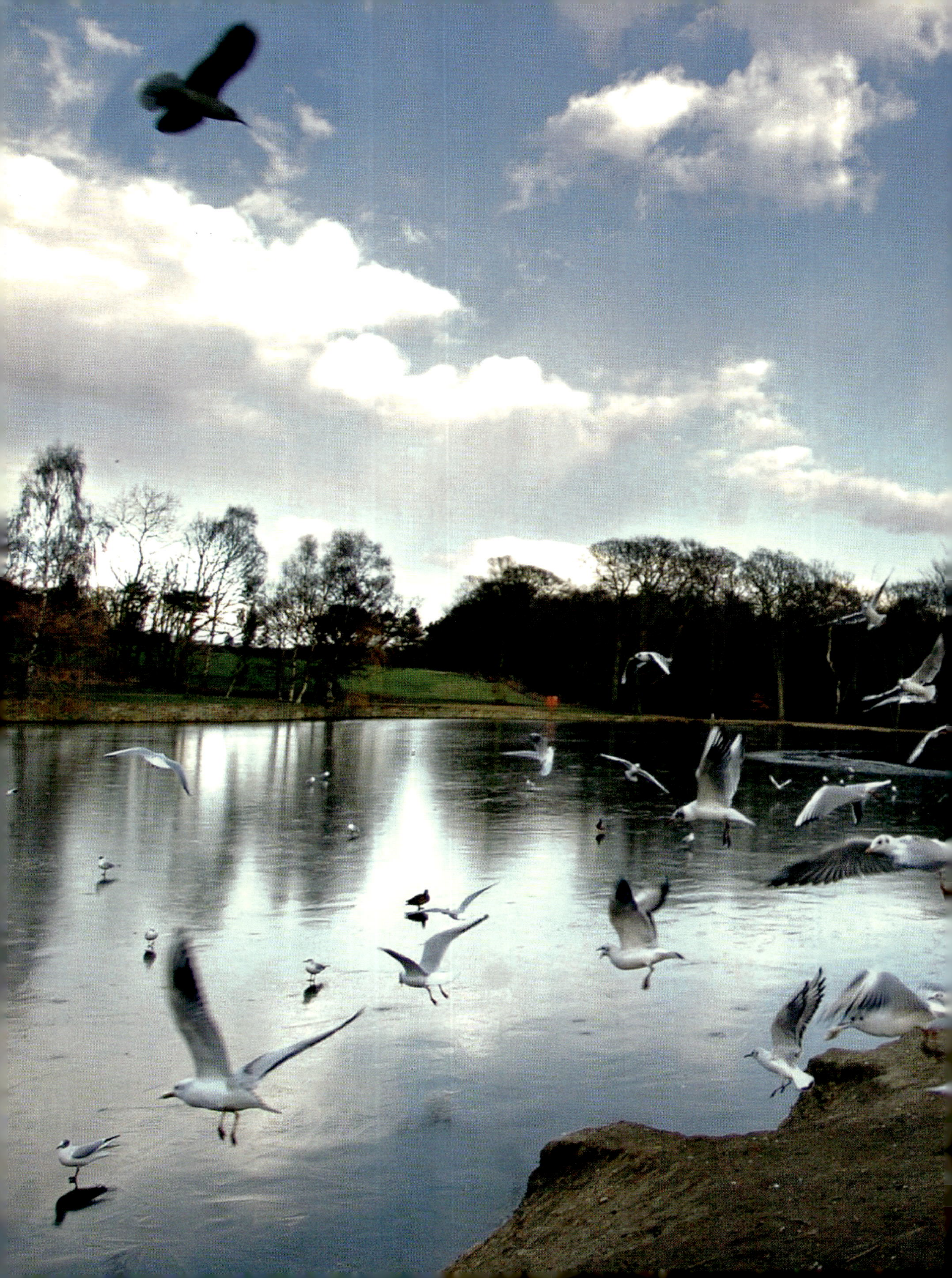

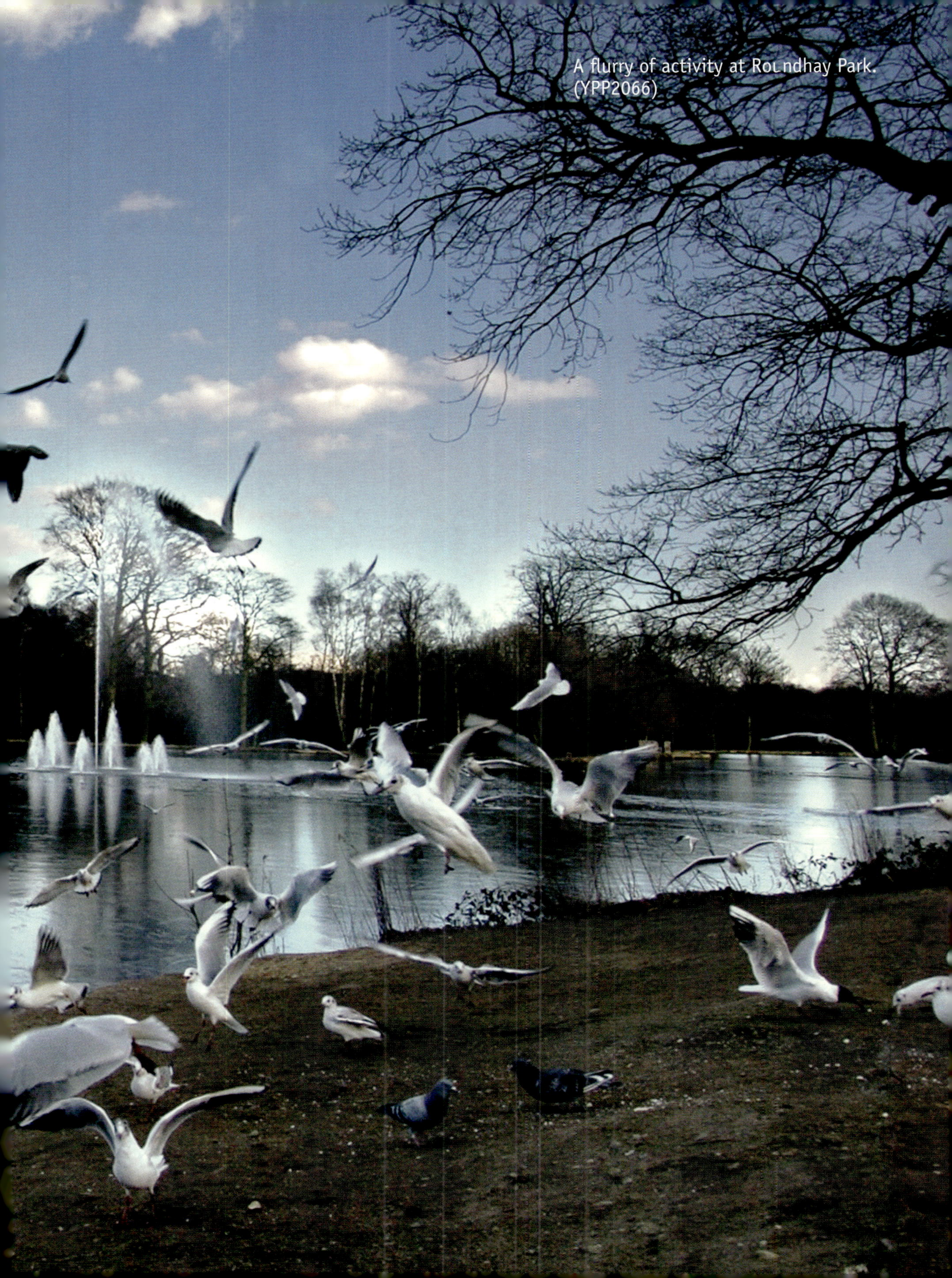

A flurry of activity at Roundhay Park. (YPP2066)

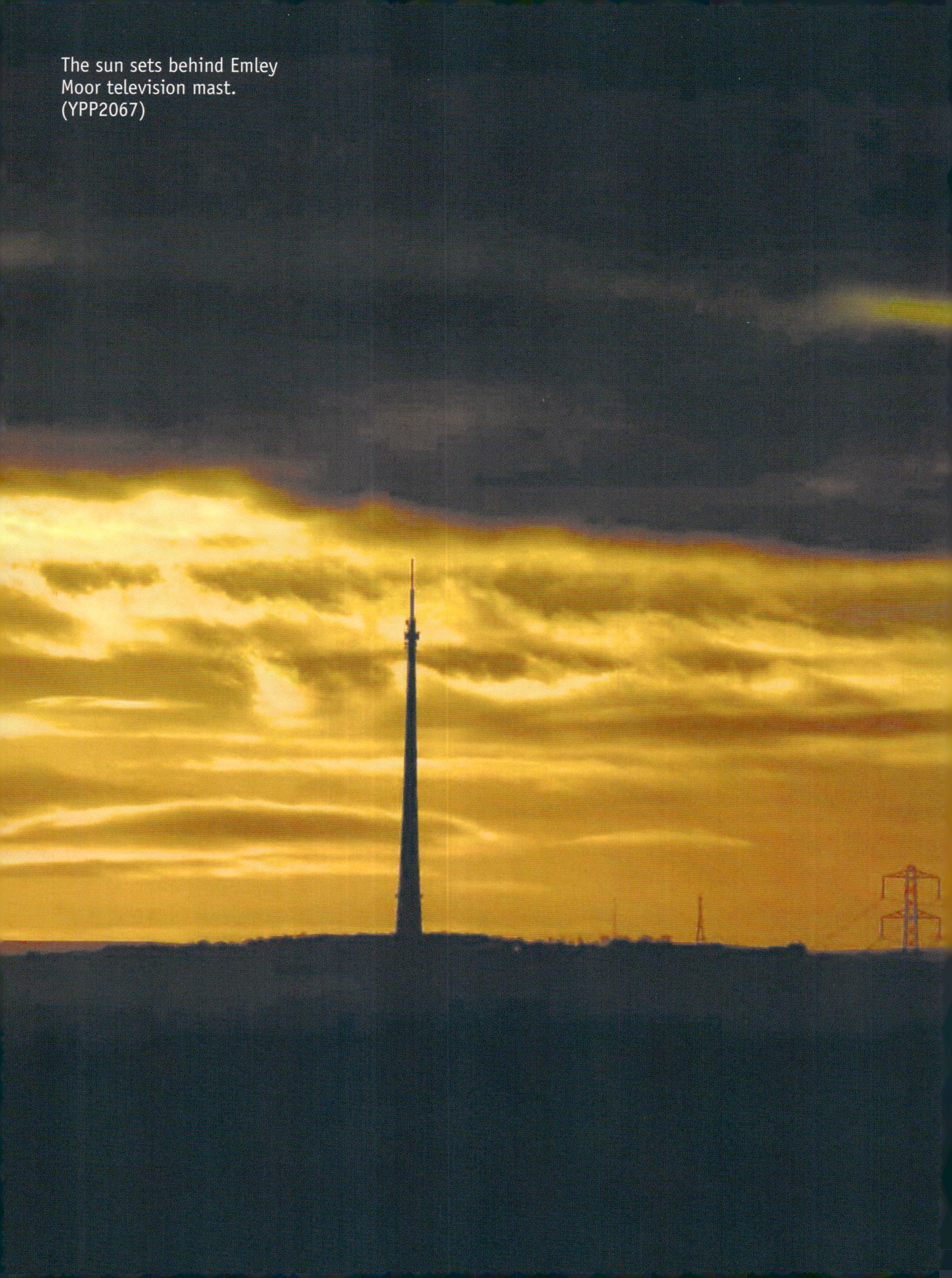

The sun sets behind Emley Moor television mast. (YPP2067)

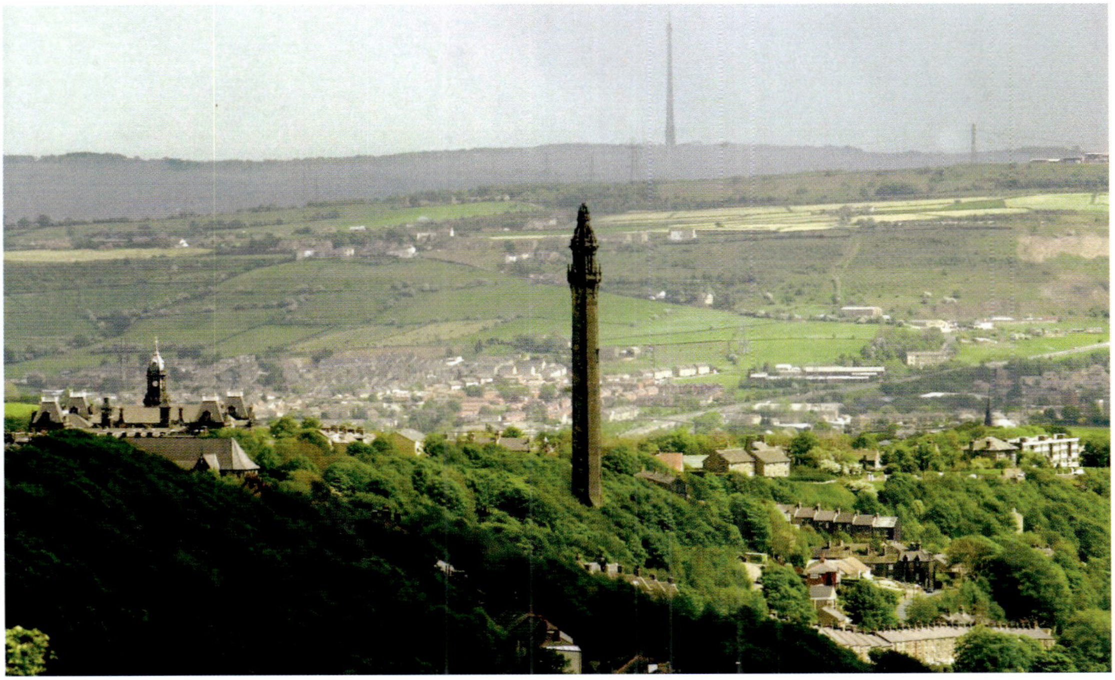

Dominating the skyline above Halifax is the Wainhouse Tower whilst on the horizon towering above everything is the Emley Moor Tower. (YPP2068)

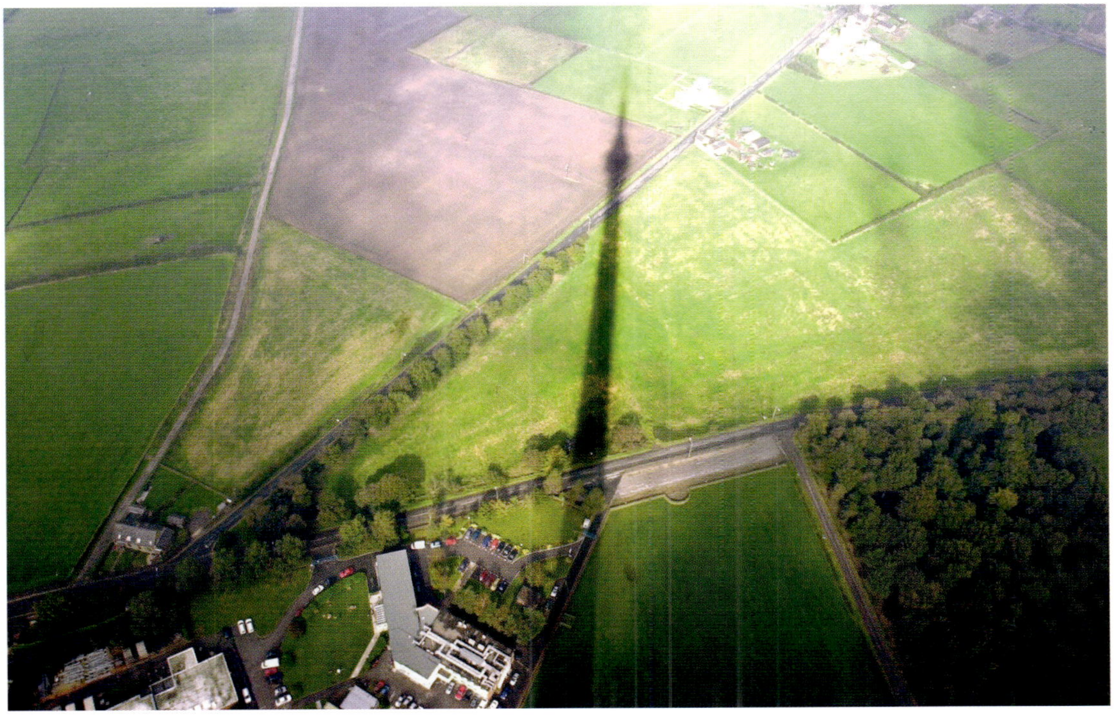

The shadow of Emly Moor TV mast, its top made hazey by whispy clouds, lies stretched across the surrounding patchwork of fields. (YPP2069)

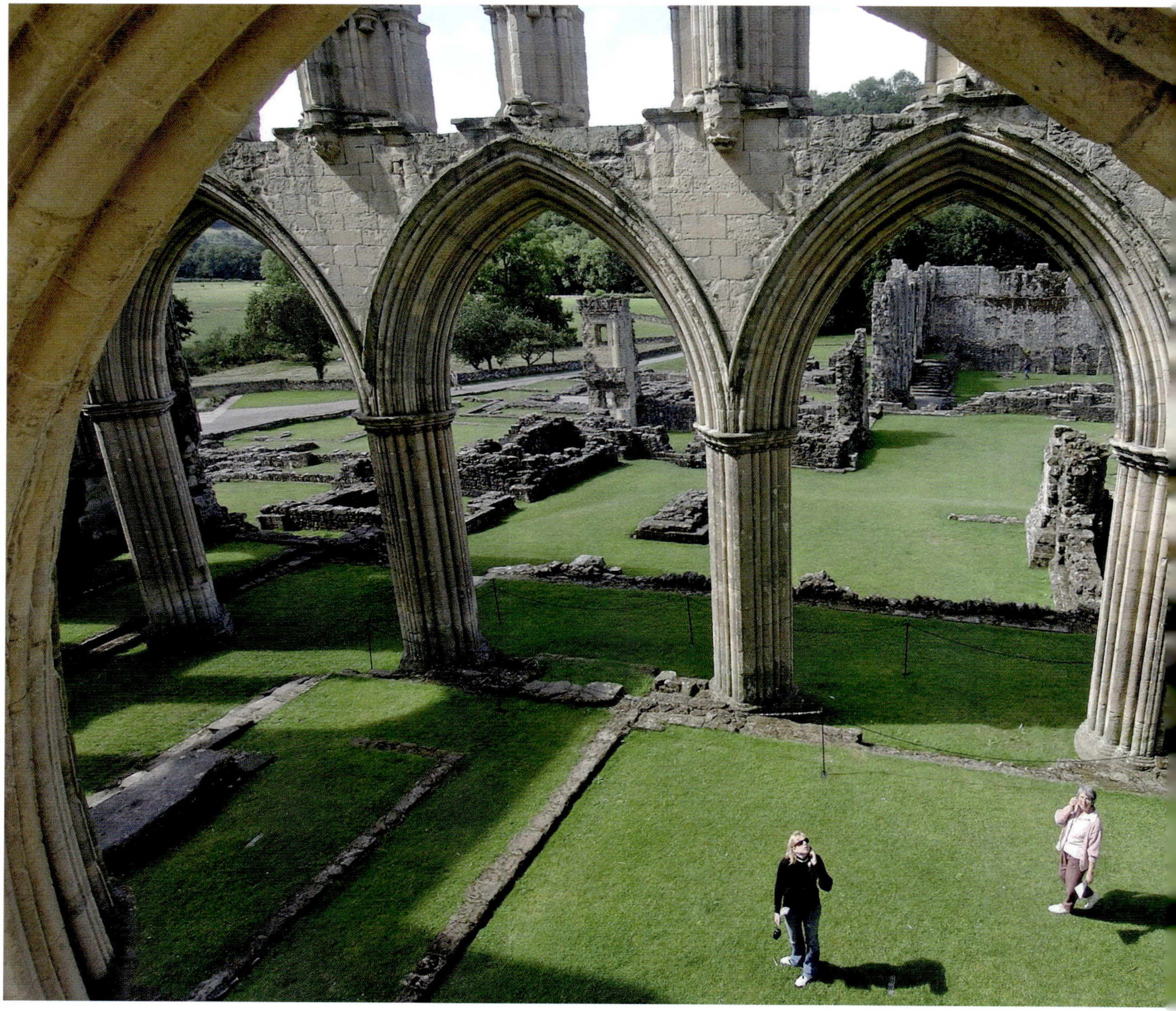

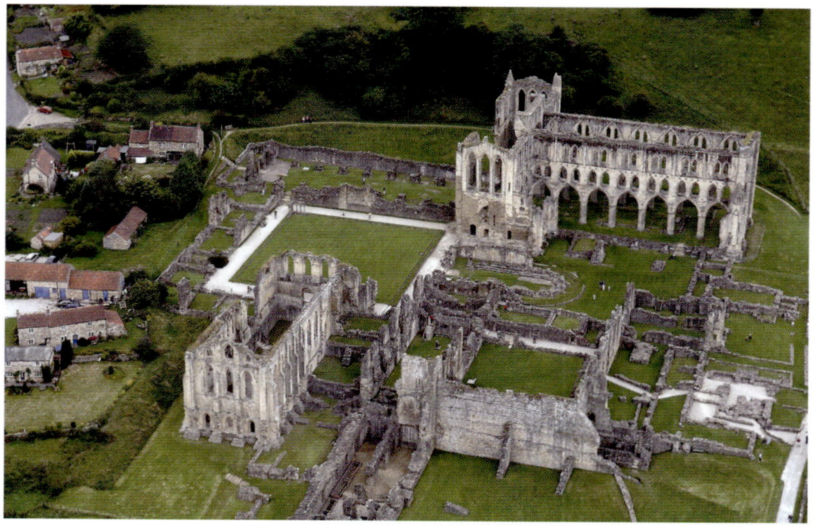

An aerial view of the abbey and monastic buildings. (YPP2071)

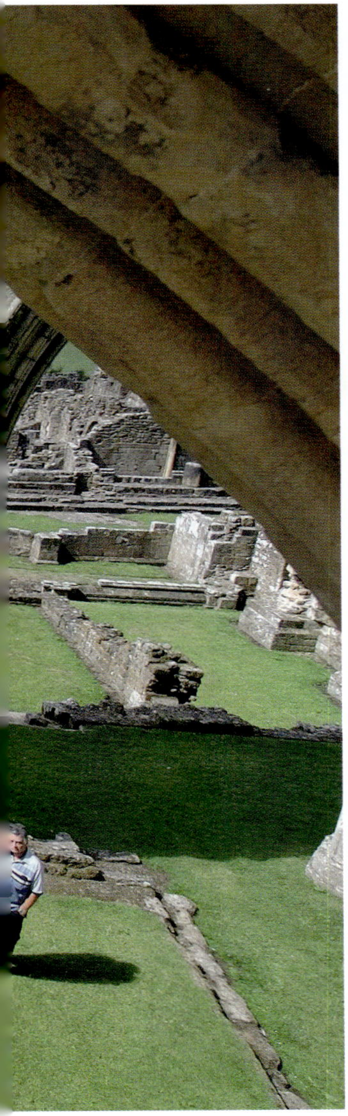

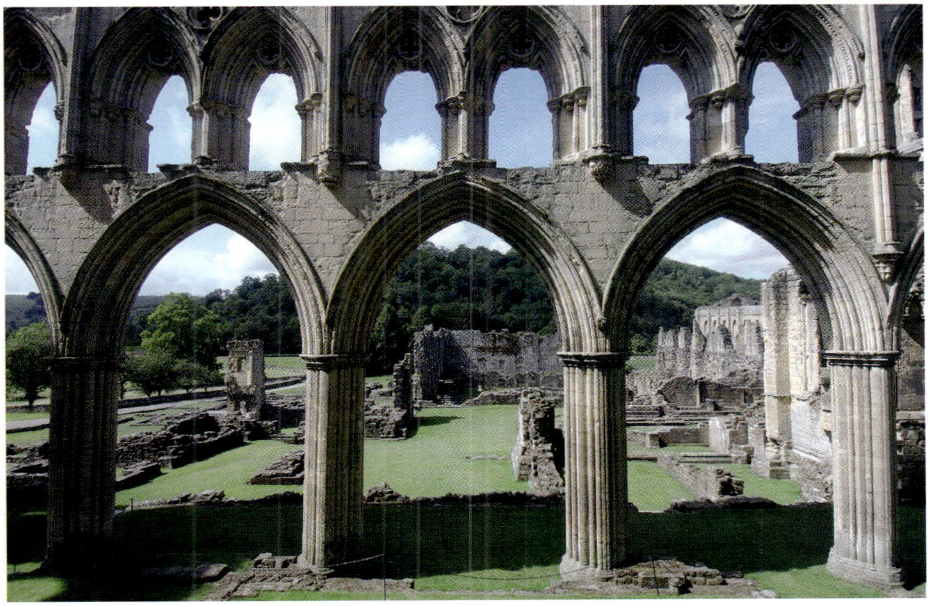

Columns and arches at Rievaulx, raised to the glory of God, remain elegant testimony to the skills of those who built them. (YPP2072)

Looking down into the ruined knave of Rievaulx Abbey, the 13th century Cistercian monastery near Helsmsley, North Yorkshire. (YPP2070)

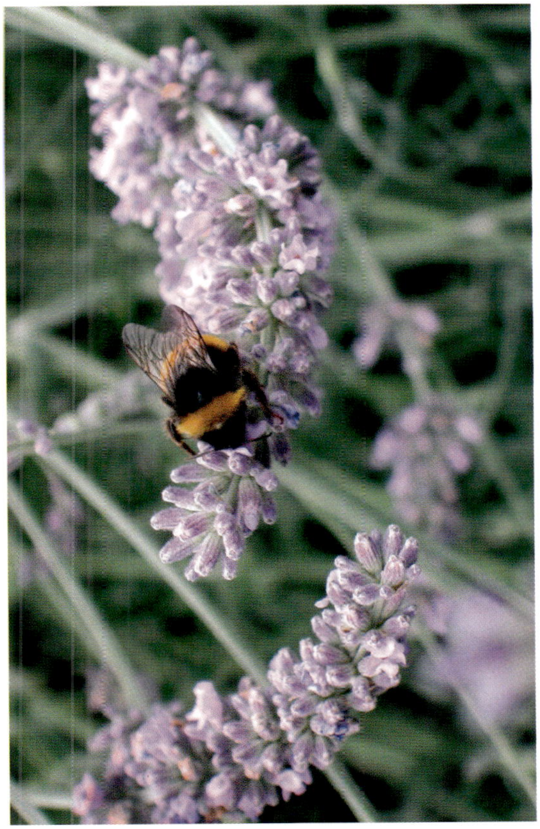

Temperatures are soaring, and a bee on her busy daily round visits a spike of lavender flowers. (YPP2073)

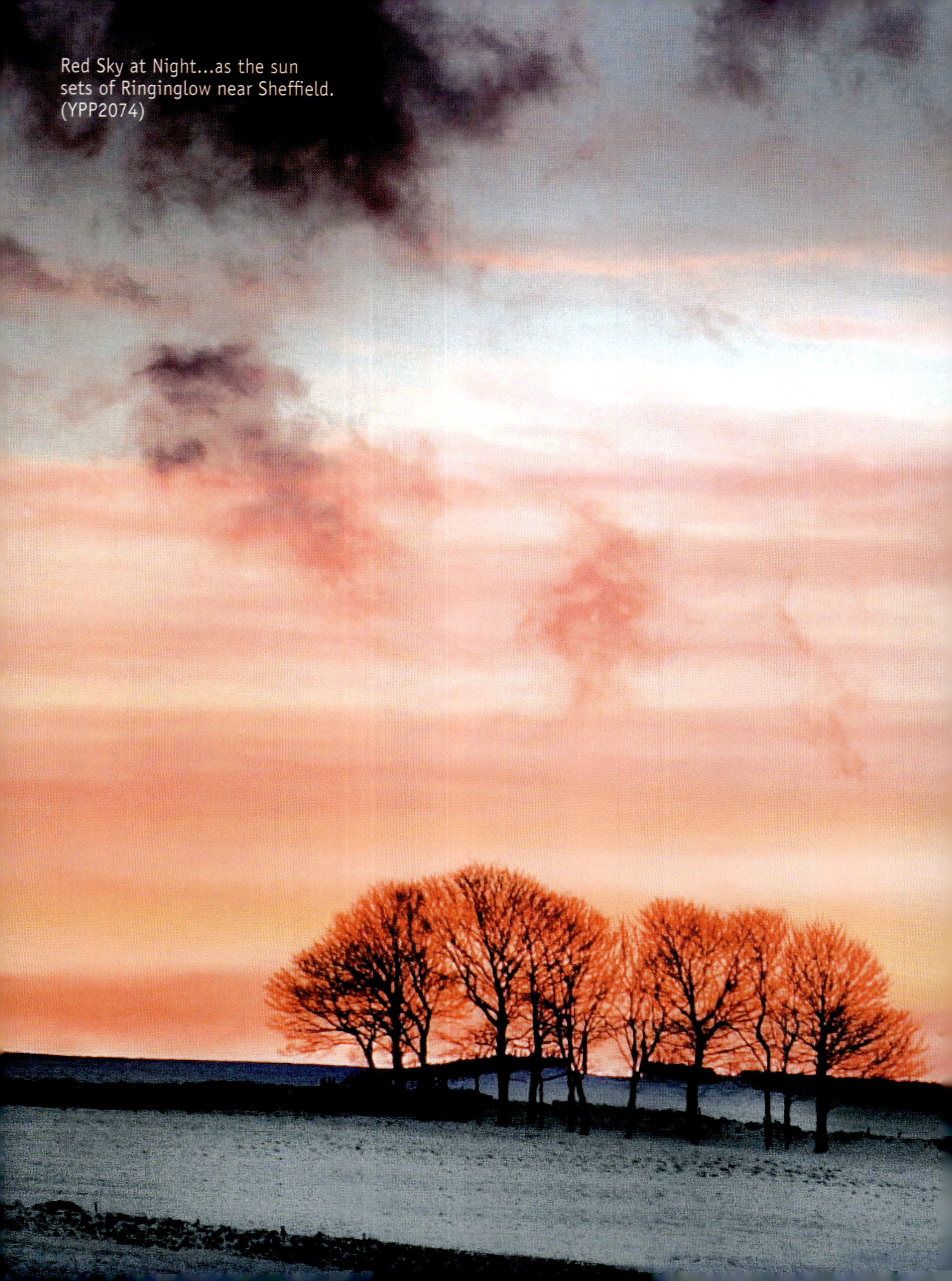

Red Sky at Night...as the sun
sets of Ringinglow near Sheffield.
(YPP2074)

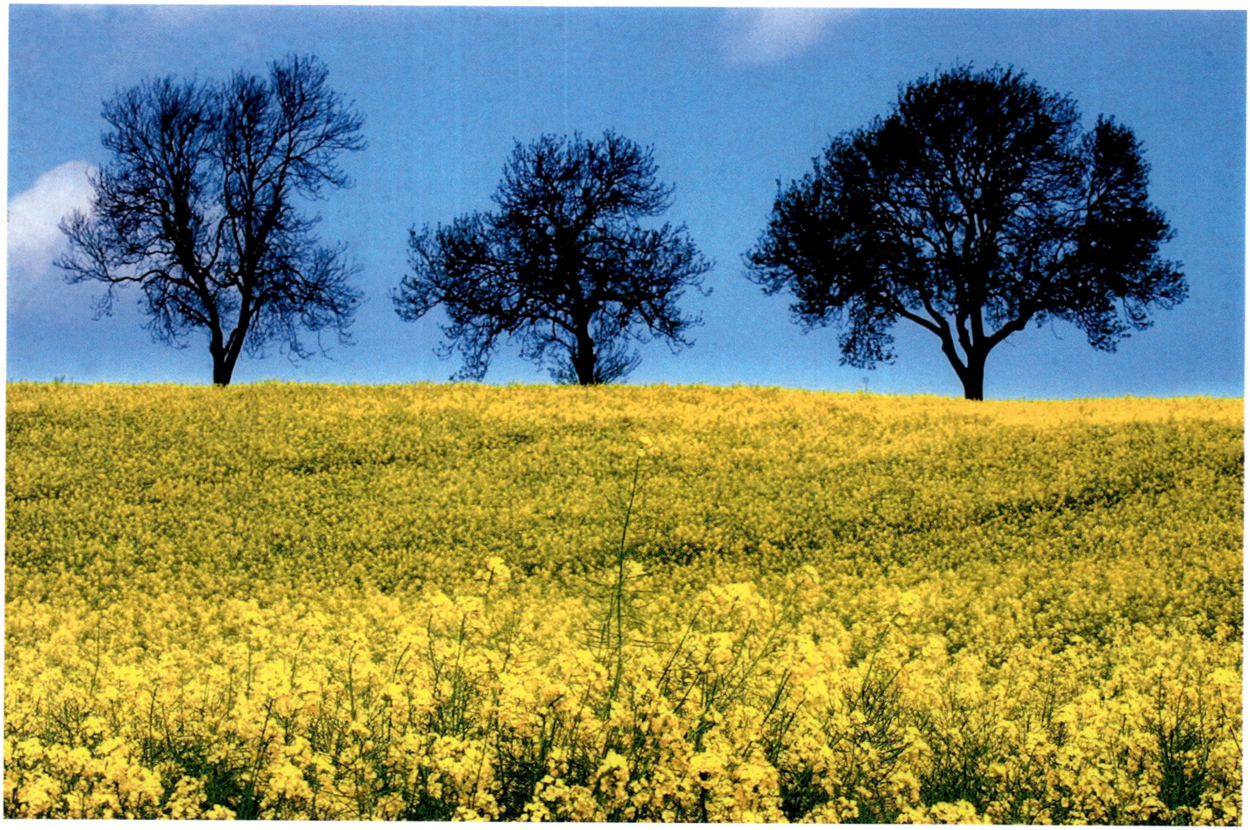

Rape seed fields at Thorner near Leeds.
(YPP2075)

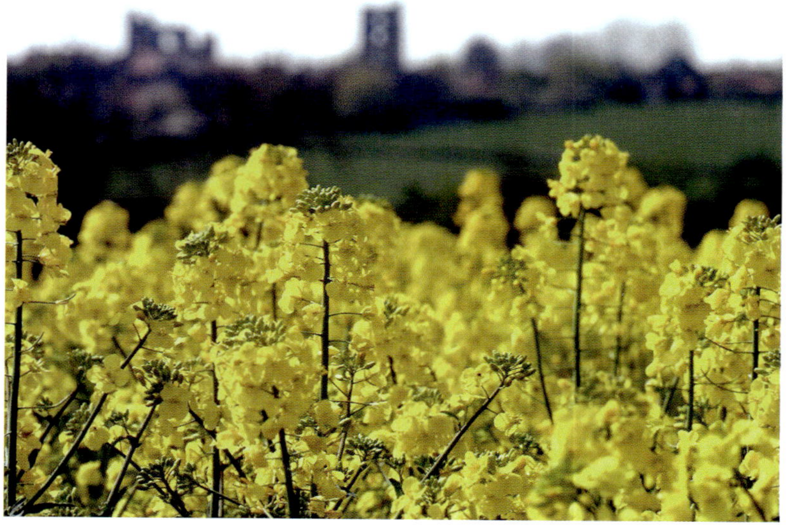

A field of oil seed rape with Sheriff Hutton Castle in the background.
(YPP2076)

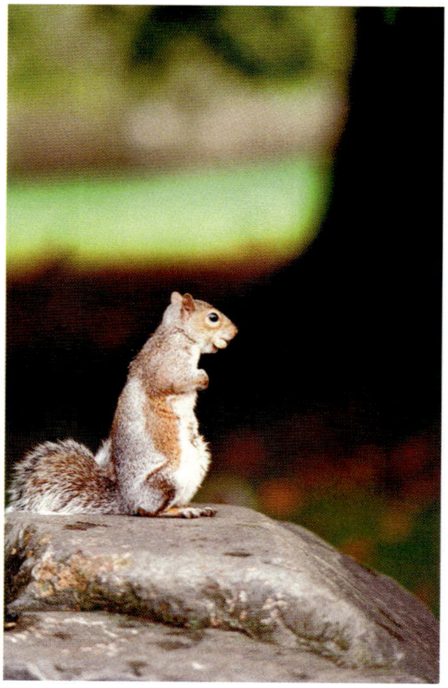

A squirrel prepares for his winter hibernation by gathering nuts in the Yorkshire Museum Gardens, York.
(YPP2077)

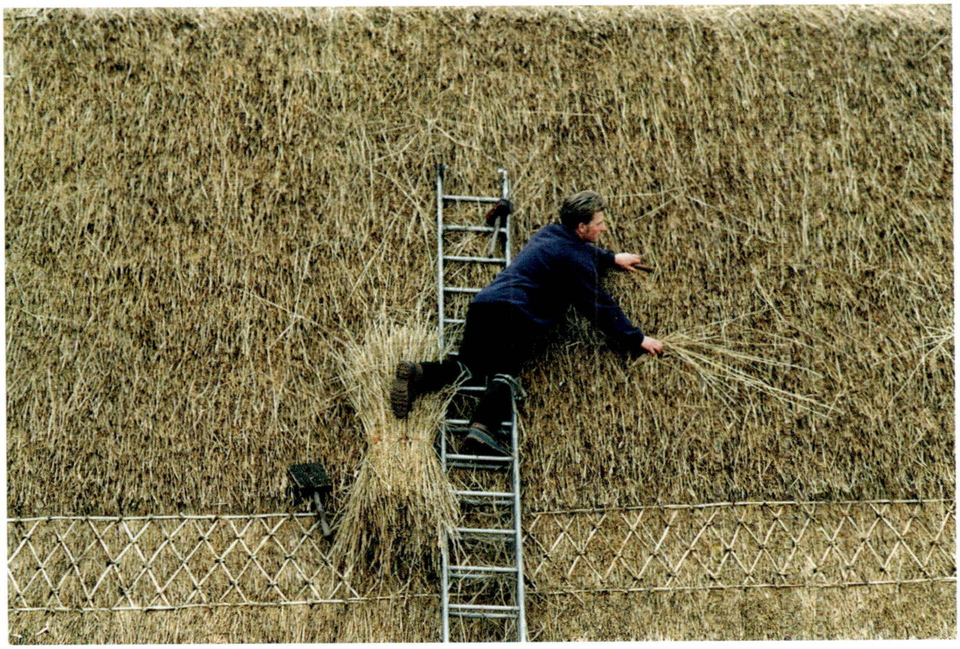

Thatcher Christopher Smart working on the roof of The Star Inn at Harome near Helmsley. (YPP2078)

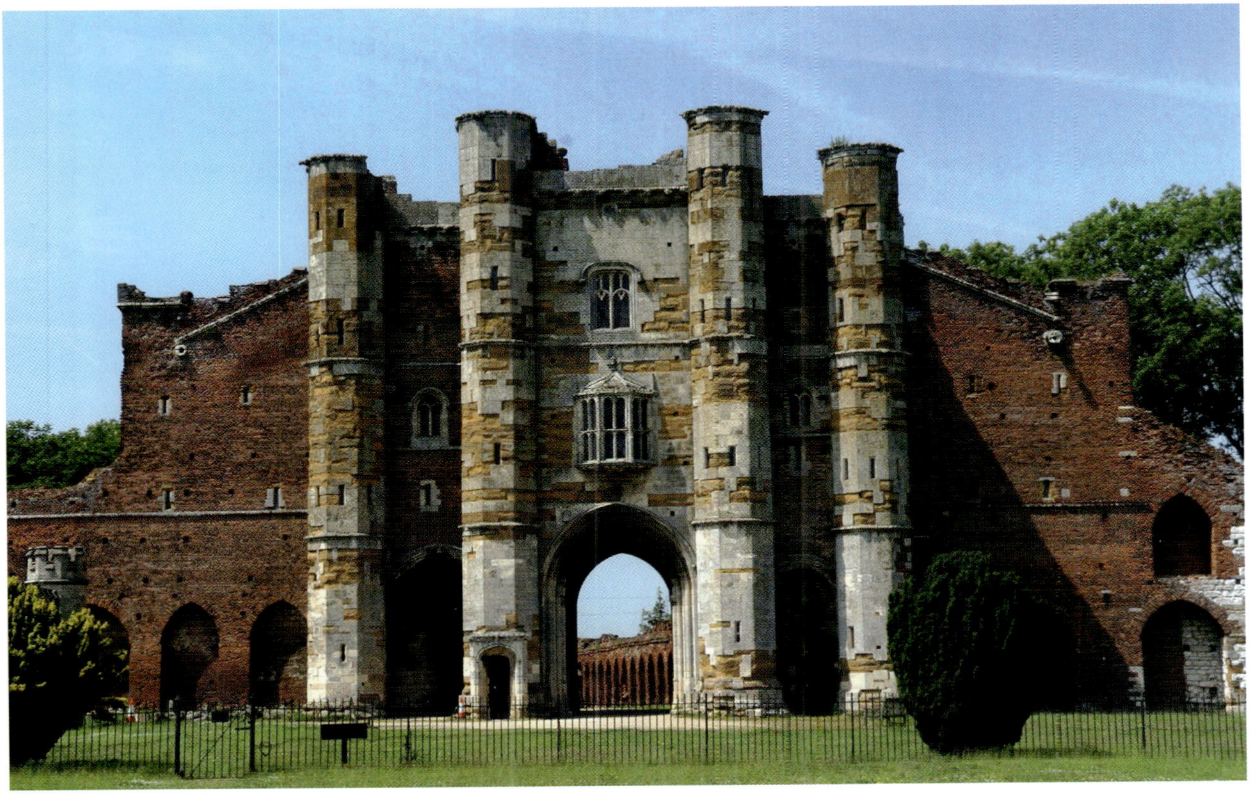

Thornton Abbey near Barton Upon Humber was founded as a priory in 1139 and was raised to the status of an abbey in 1148. (YPP2079)

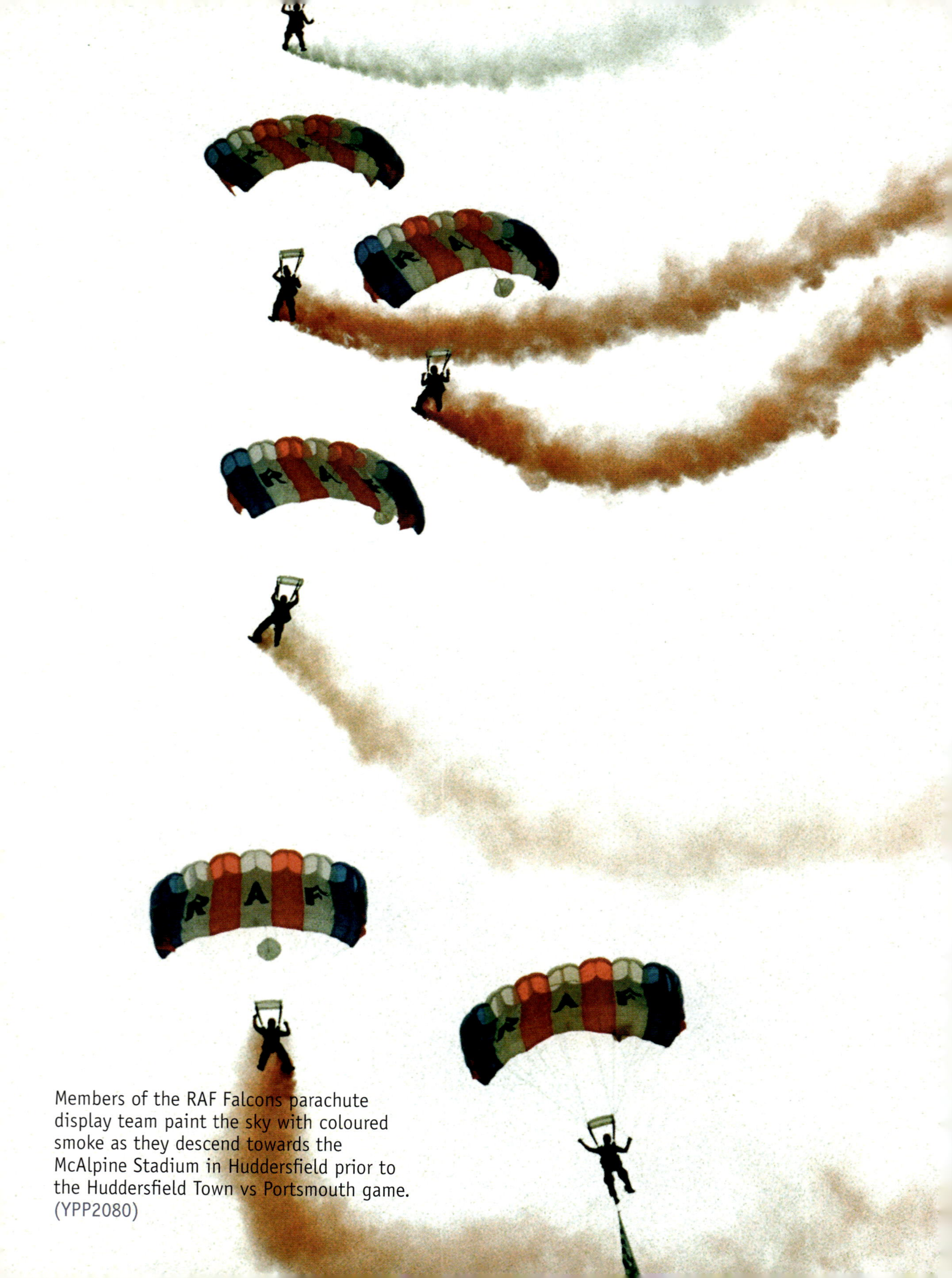

Members of the RAF Falcons parachute display team paint the sky with coloured smoke as they descend towards the McAlpine Stadium in Huddersfield prior to the Huddersfield Town vs Portsmouth game. (YPP2080)

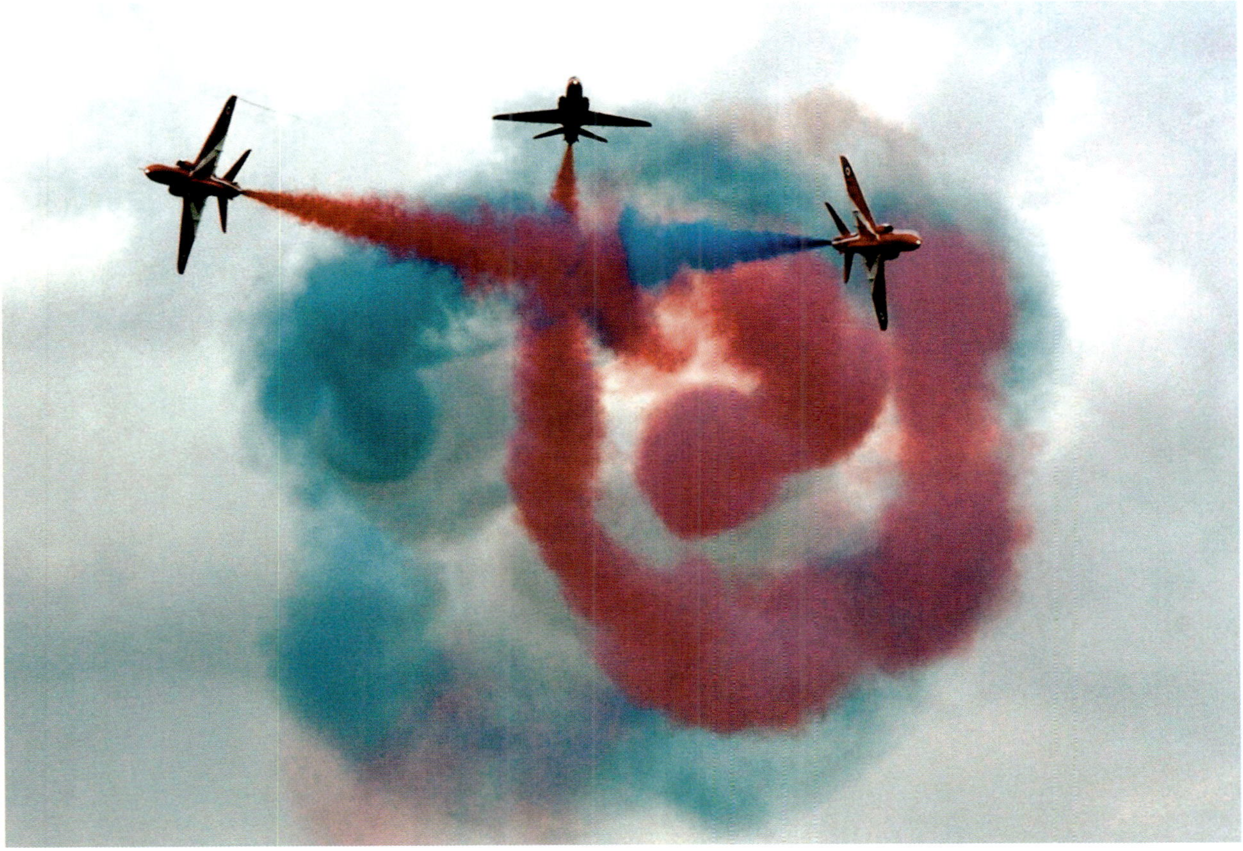

The Red Arrows display team in action at the Yorkshire Air show at Elvington sponsered by the Yorkshire Post. (YPP2081)

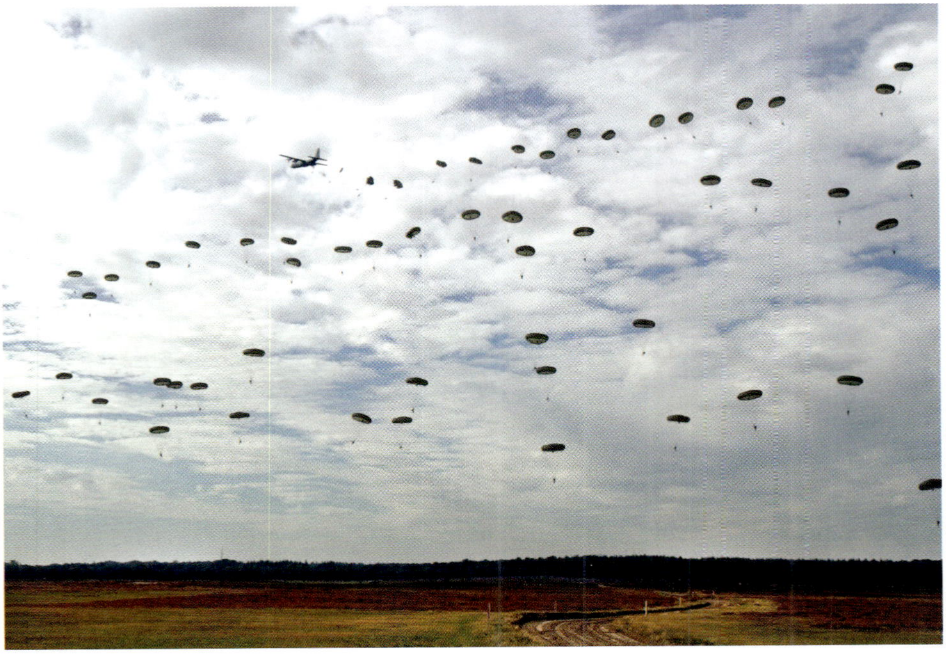

Parachutists pepper the sky above elvington (YPP2082)

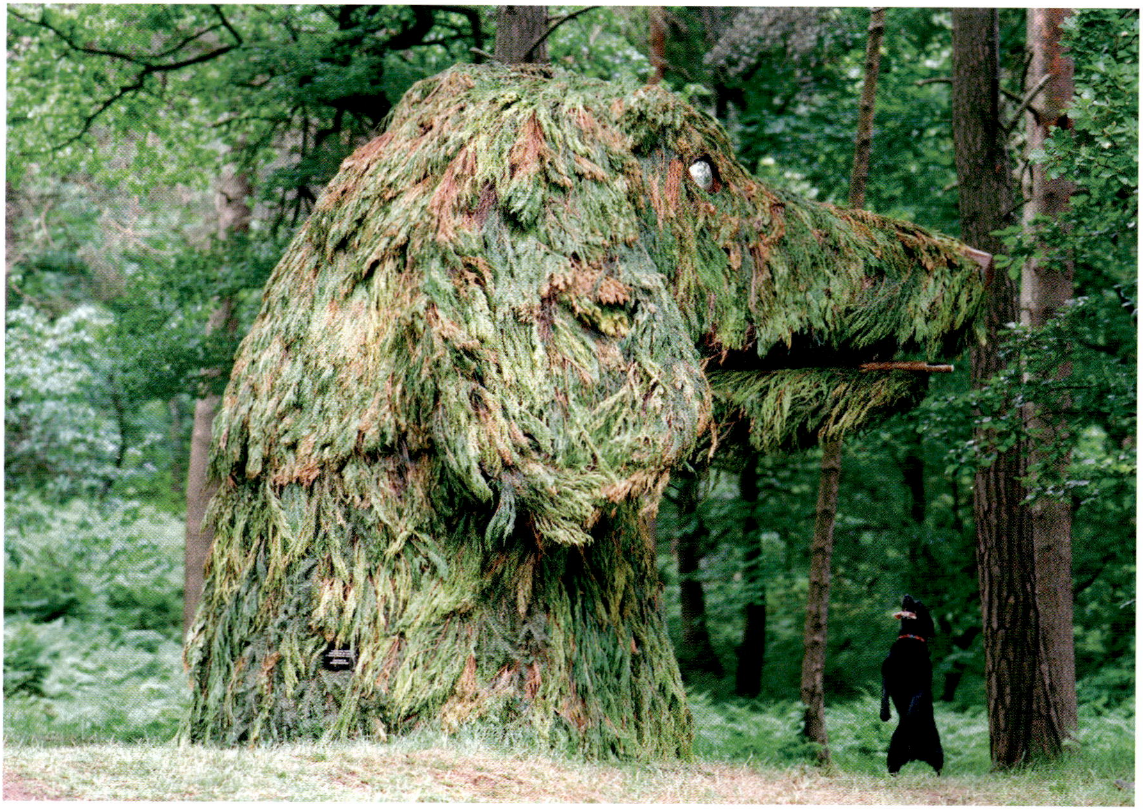

Something seems to have caught the interest of "Cabot's Dog", a sculpture created by Robert Bradford for the Hebden Bridge Sculpture Trail at Hardcastle Craggs; and "Cabot's Dog" has caught the interest of Rosie, the black labrador owned by William Prior of Hebden Bridge. (YPP2083)

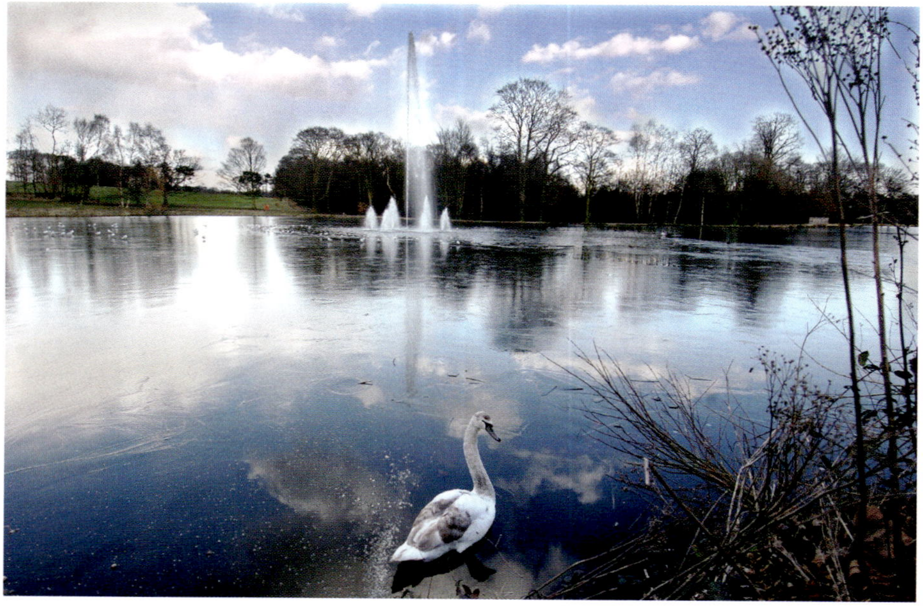

This tranquil summer-time scene bears no resemblance to the swans misfortune in the winter months. A rescue attempt had to be made when a swan at Roundhay Park became stuck on the upper lake that had iced over. The swan managed to free itself after people went out on a boat to rescue it. (YPP2084)

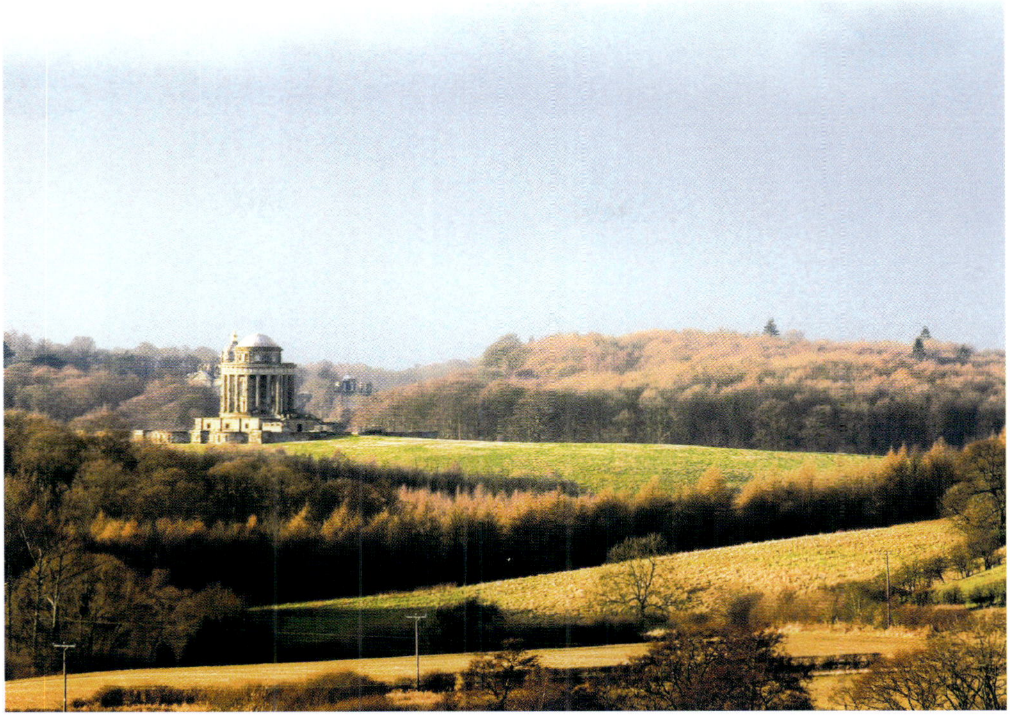

The Mausoleum in the grounds of Castle Howard, lit by a late afternoon winter's sun. (YPP2085)

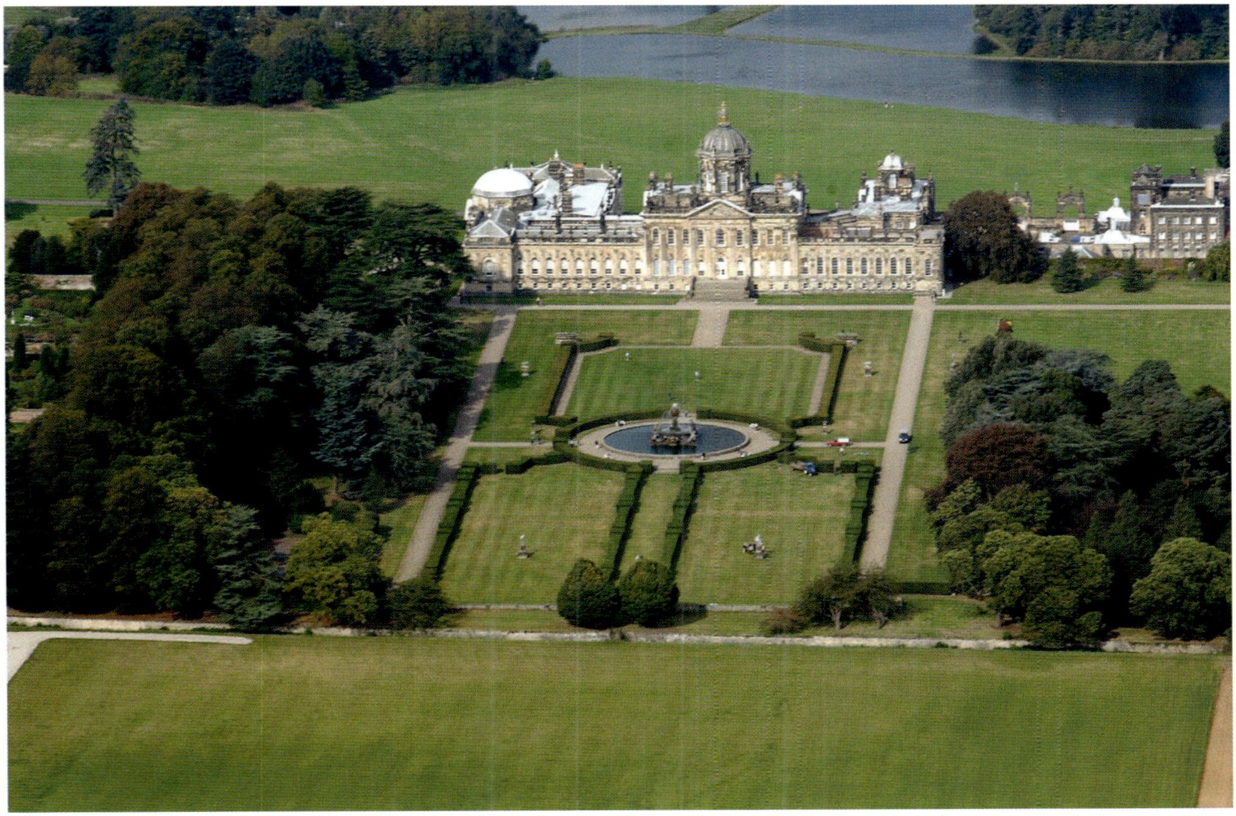

An aerial view of Castle Howard. (YPP2086)

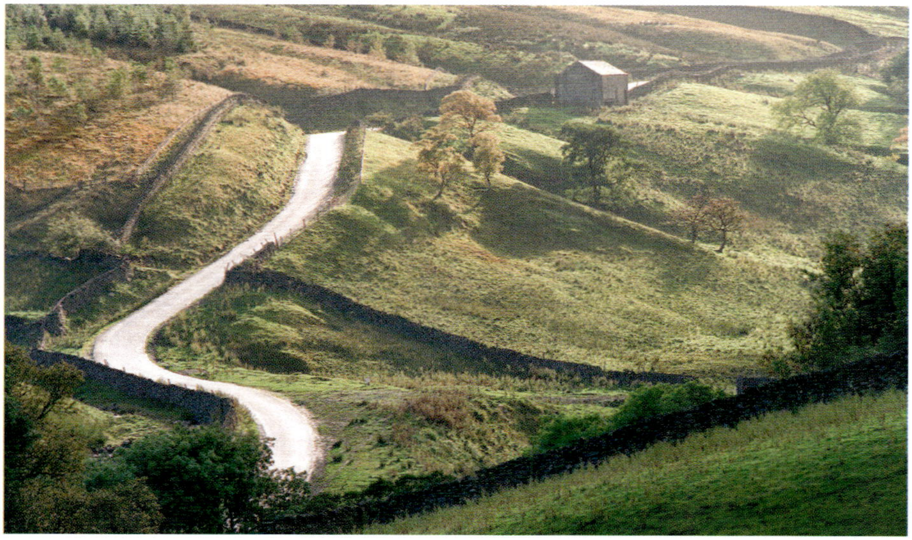

Autmun sunlight bathes the countryside near Woodale in Coverdale. (YPP2087)

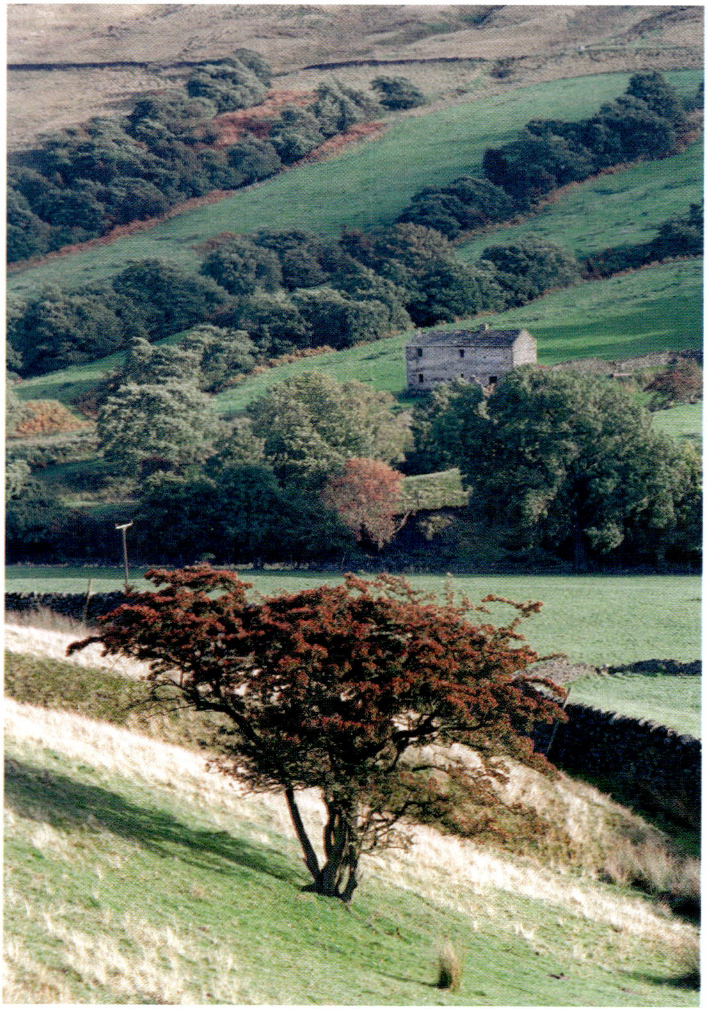

Autmun colours glow in the upper reaches of Coverdale. (YPP2088)

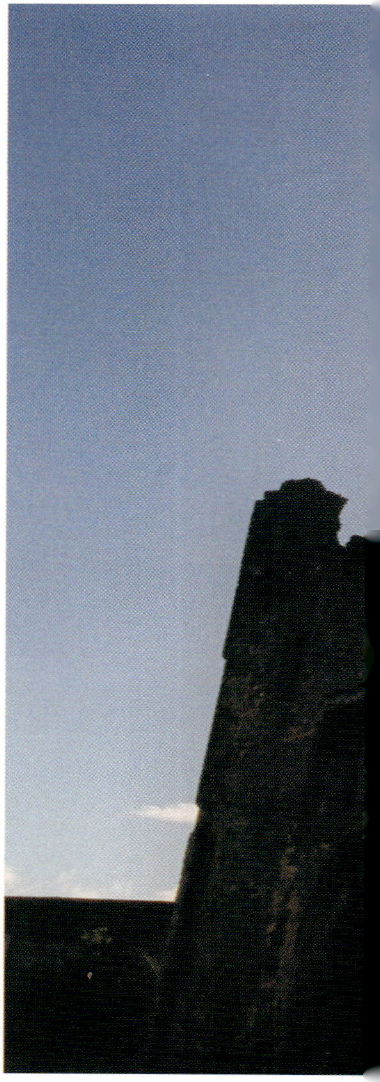

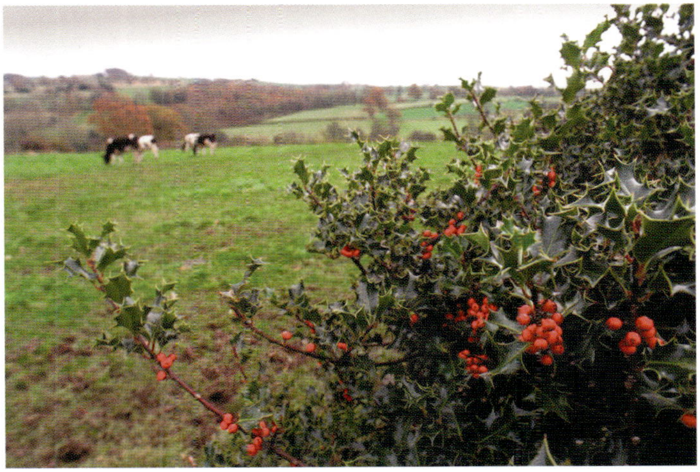

A glossy leafed holly bush laden with a glut of berries. (YPP2089)

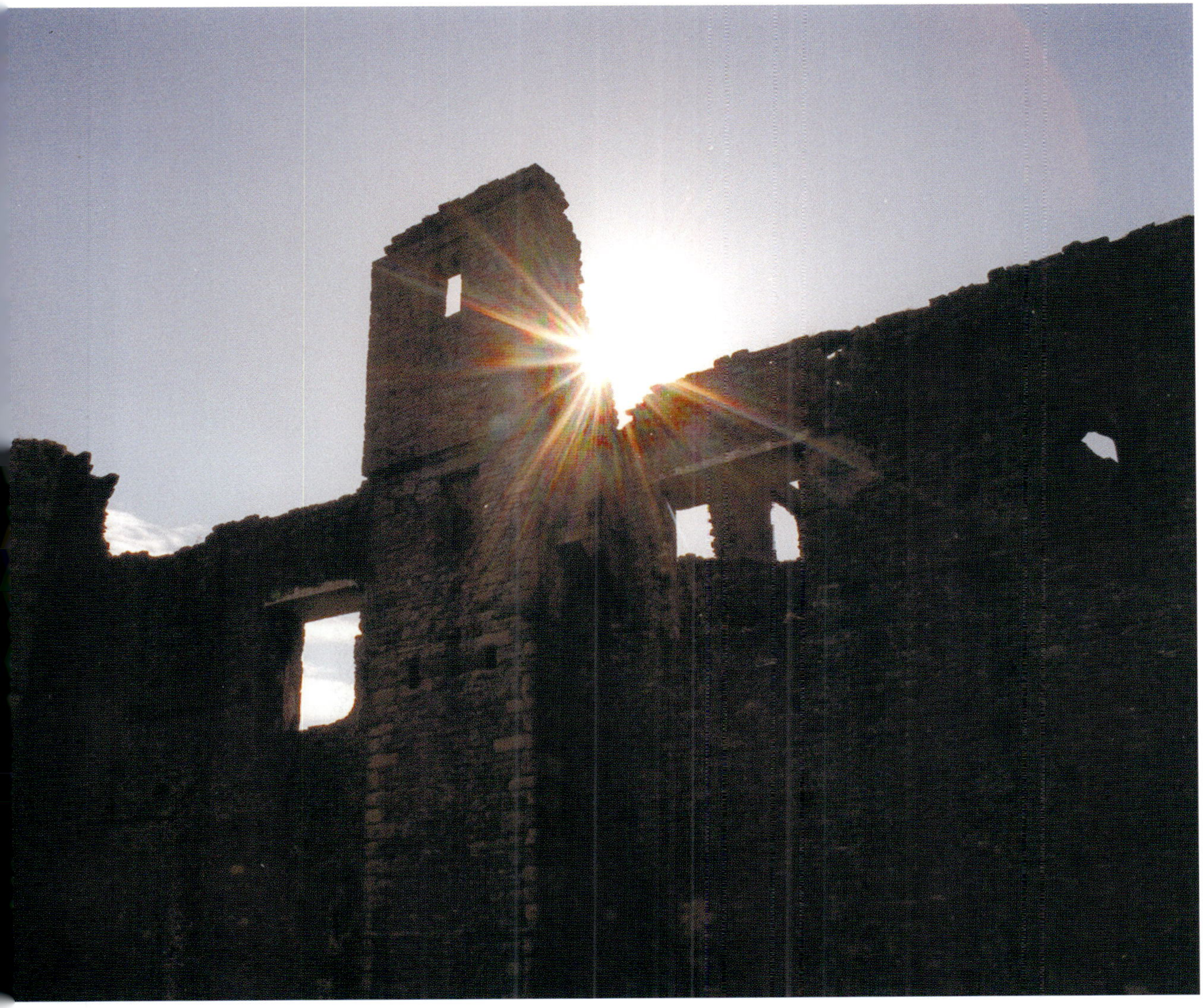

Sunlight explodes from behind the stark silhouette of the ruins of Middleham Castle. (YPP2090)

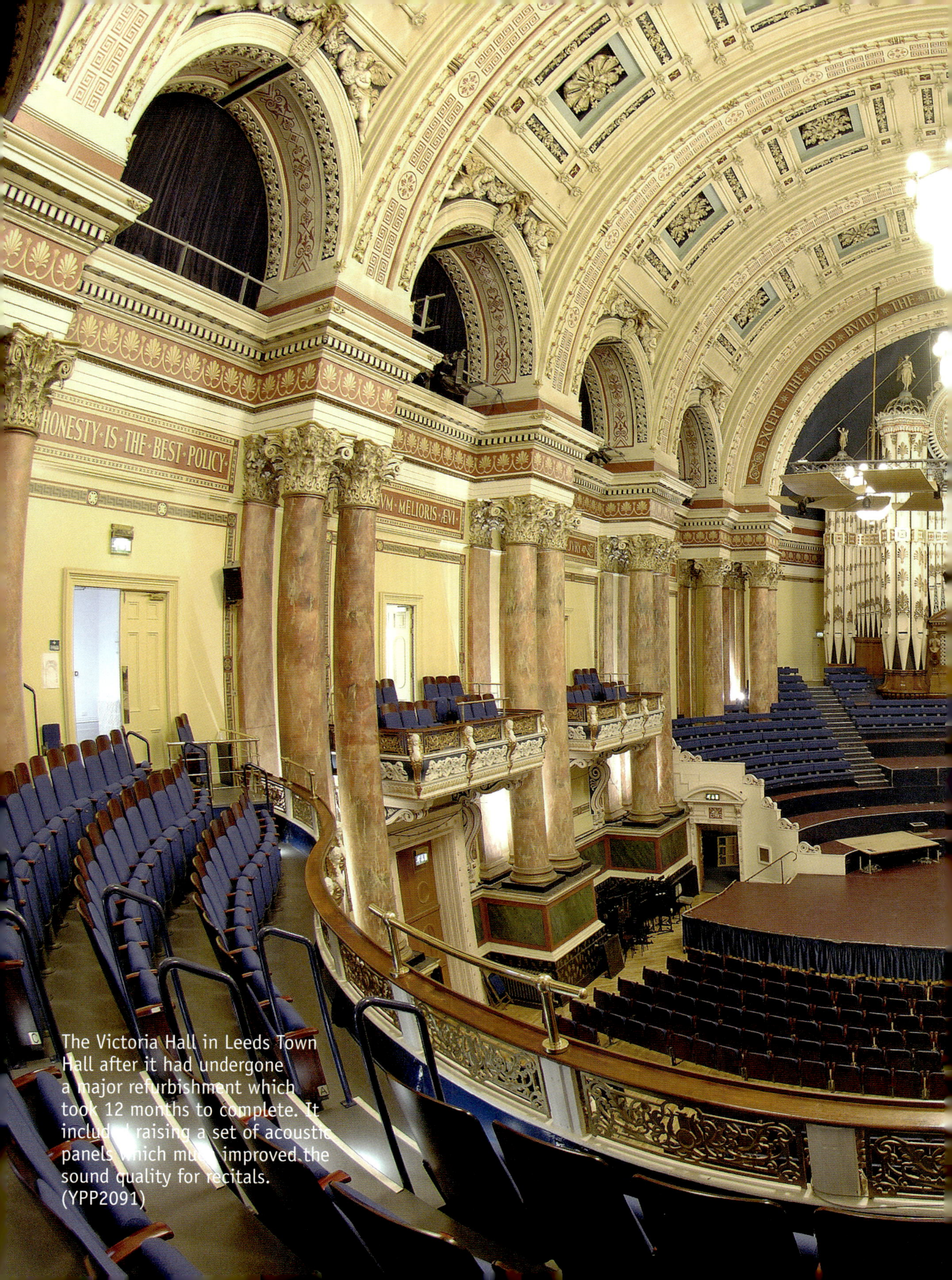

The Victoria Hall in Leeds Town Hall after it had undergone a major refurbishment which took 12 months to complete. It included raising a set of acoustic panels which much improved the sound quality for recitals. (YPP2091)

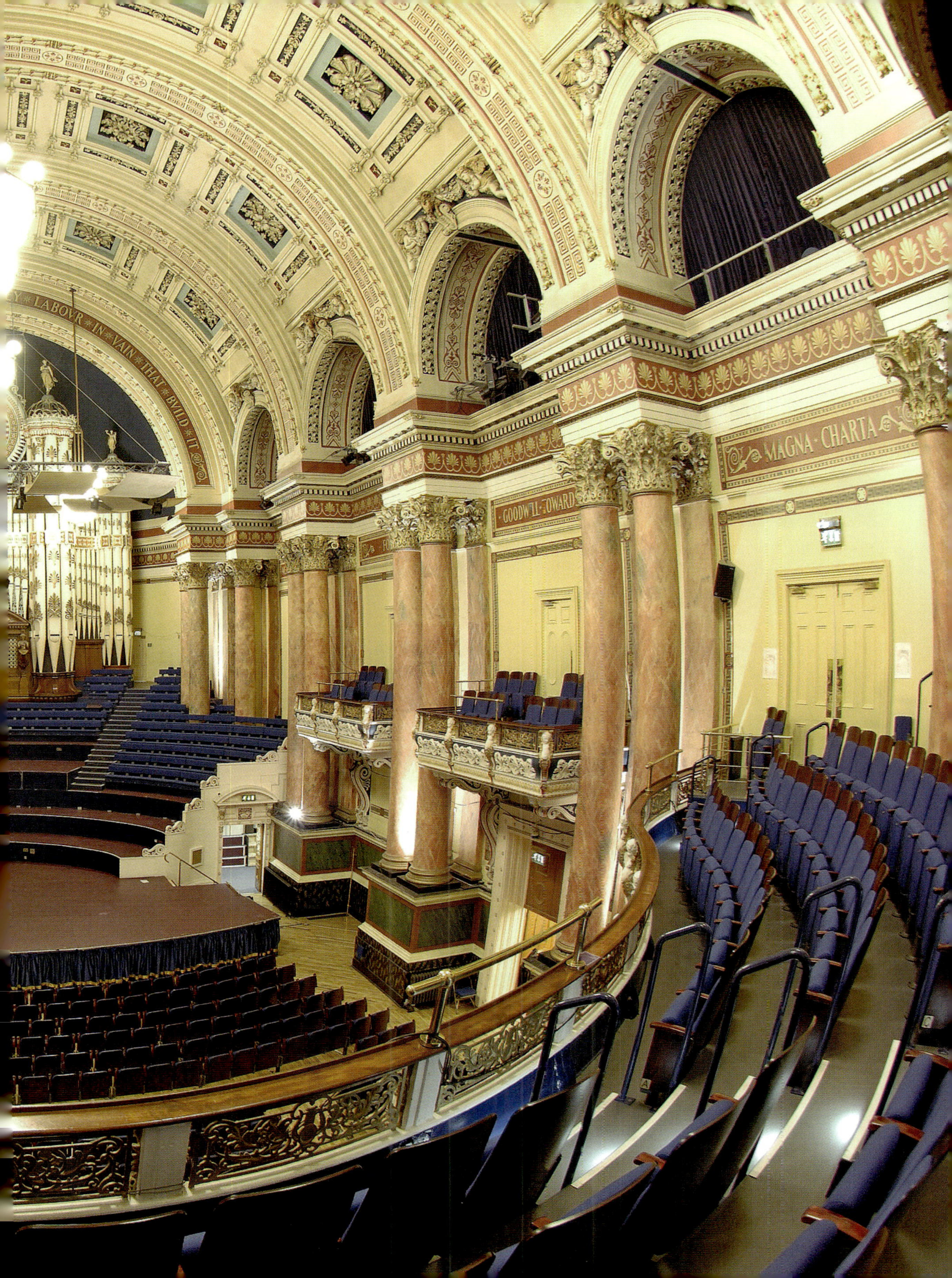
LABOVR IN VAIN THAT BVILD IT
GOODWILL TOWARD
MAGNA · CHARTA

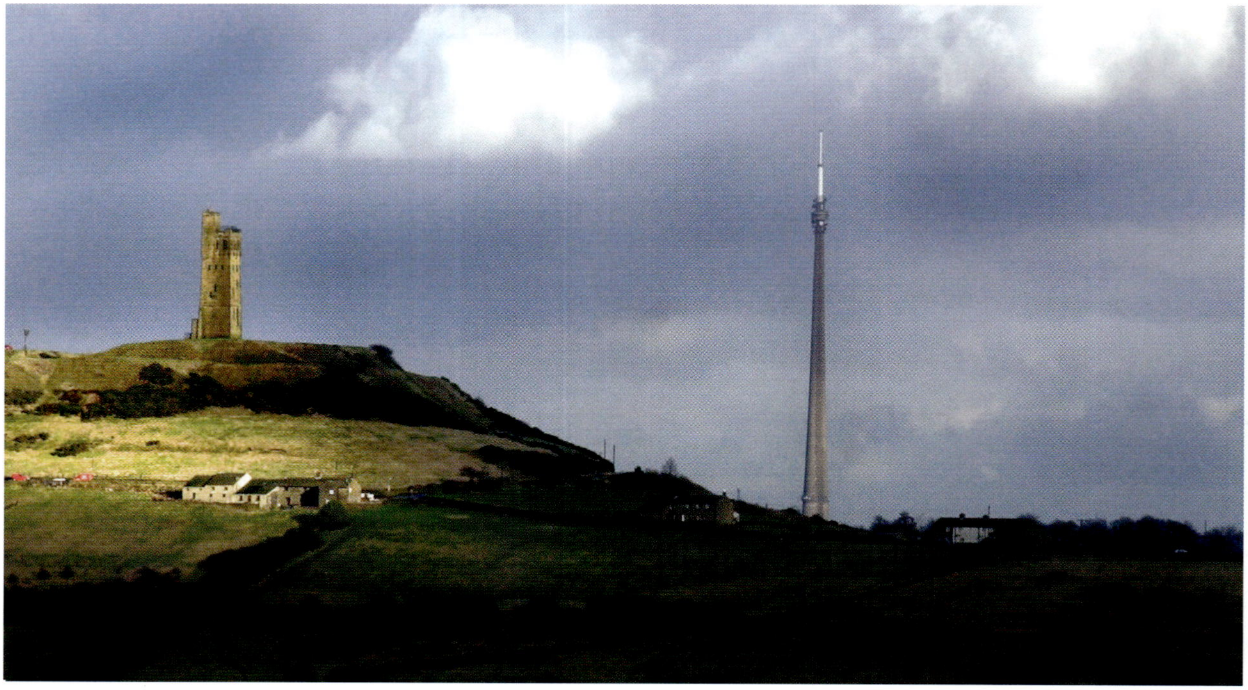

Sunlight falls on Castle Hill above Huddersfield, and in the distance is the 1,084 ft high Emley Moor transmission mast which replaced it as the most prominent landmark for miles around.
(YPP2192)

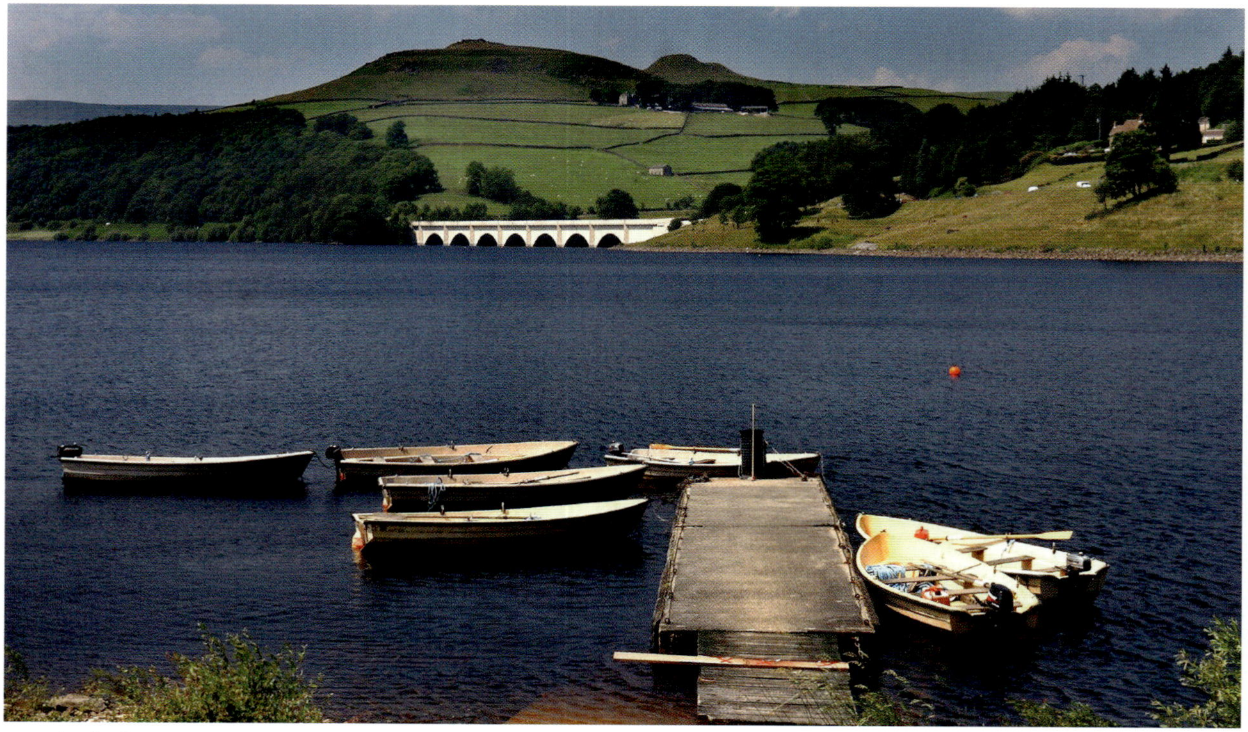

Angler's boats wait for anglers at Derbyshire's Ladybower reservoir.
(YPP293)

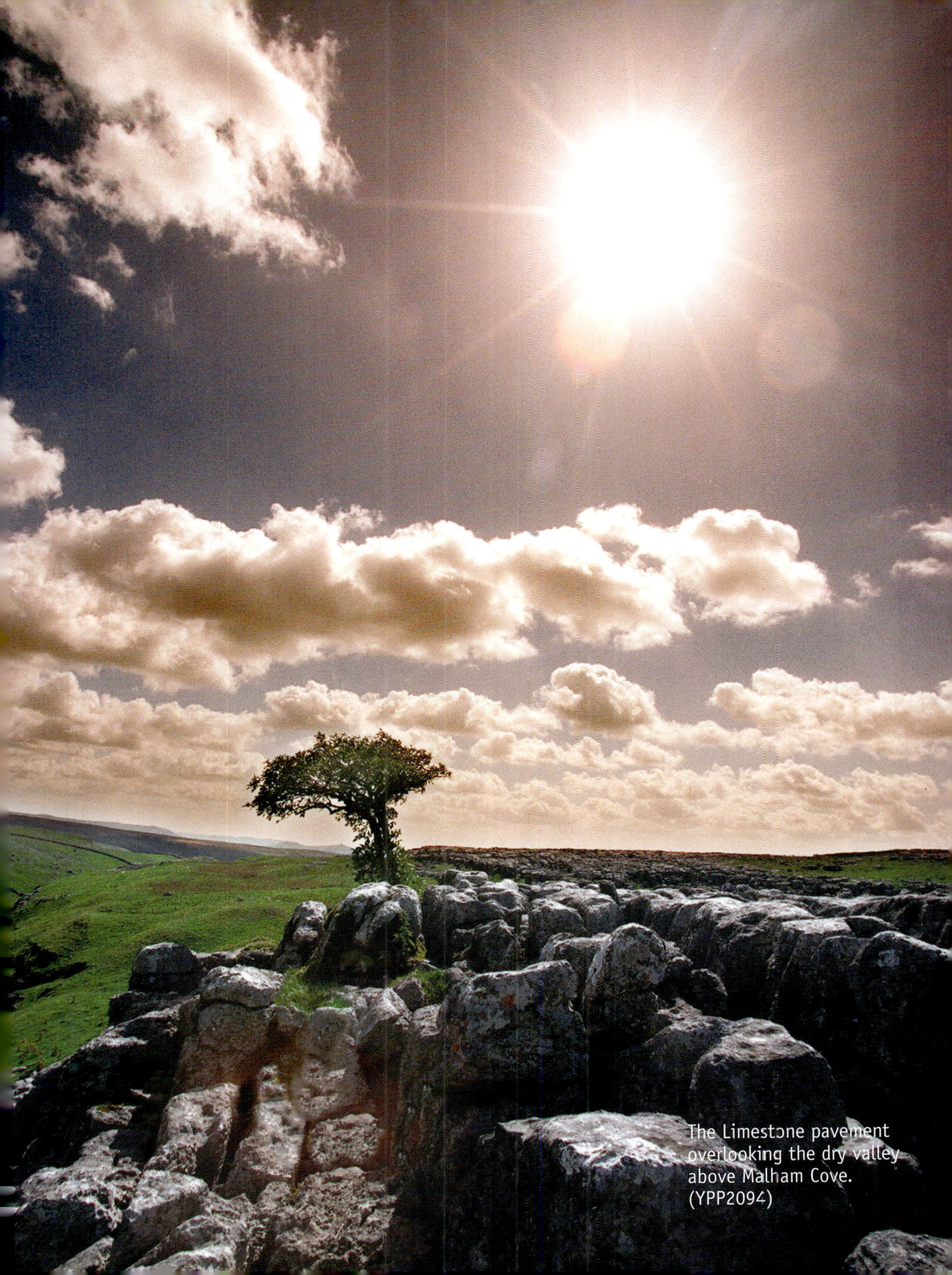

The Limestone pavement overlooking the dry valley above Malham Cove. (YPP2094)

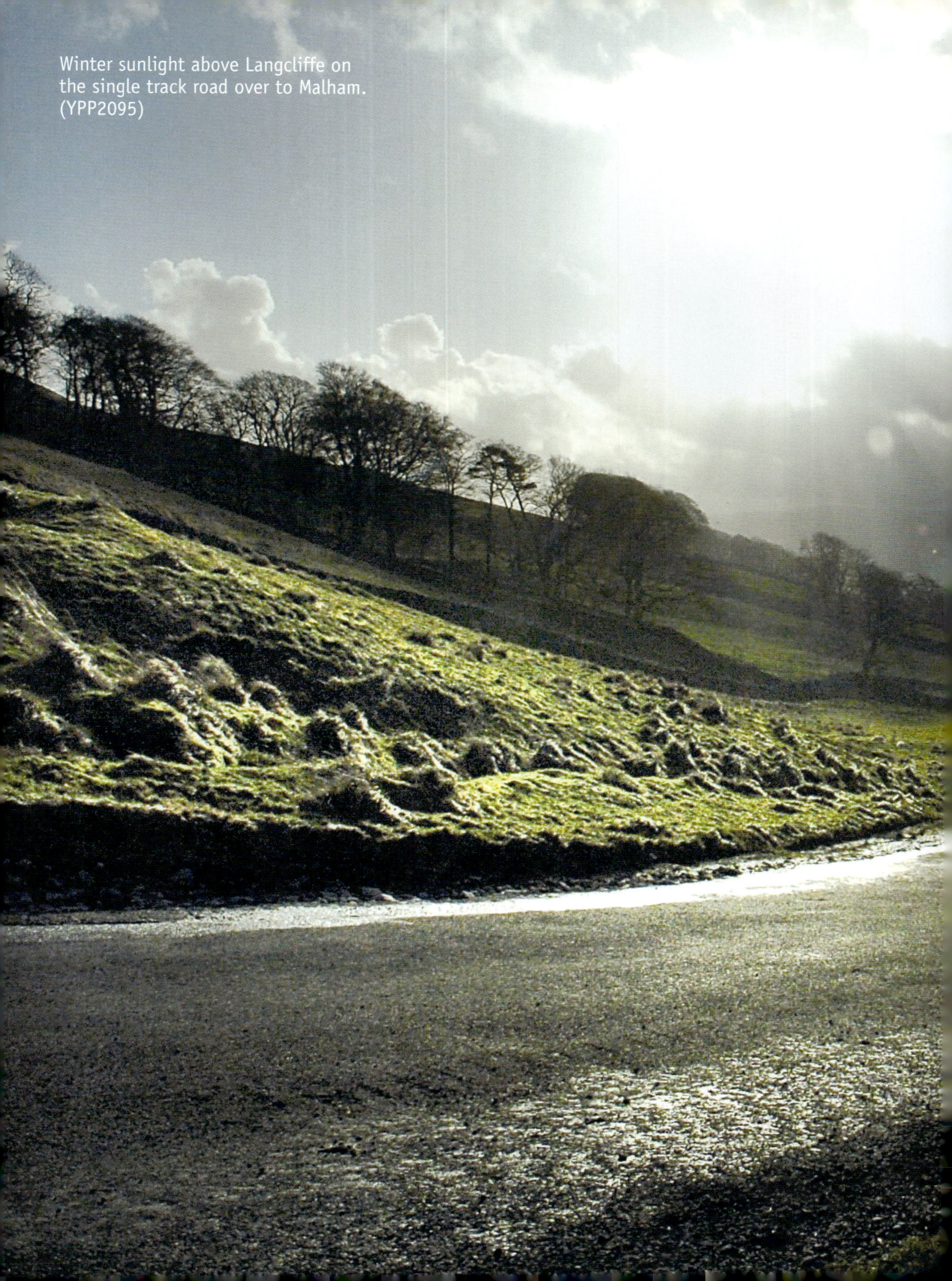

Winter sunlight above Langcliffe on the single track road over to Malham. (YPP2095)

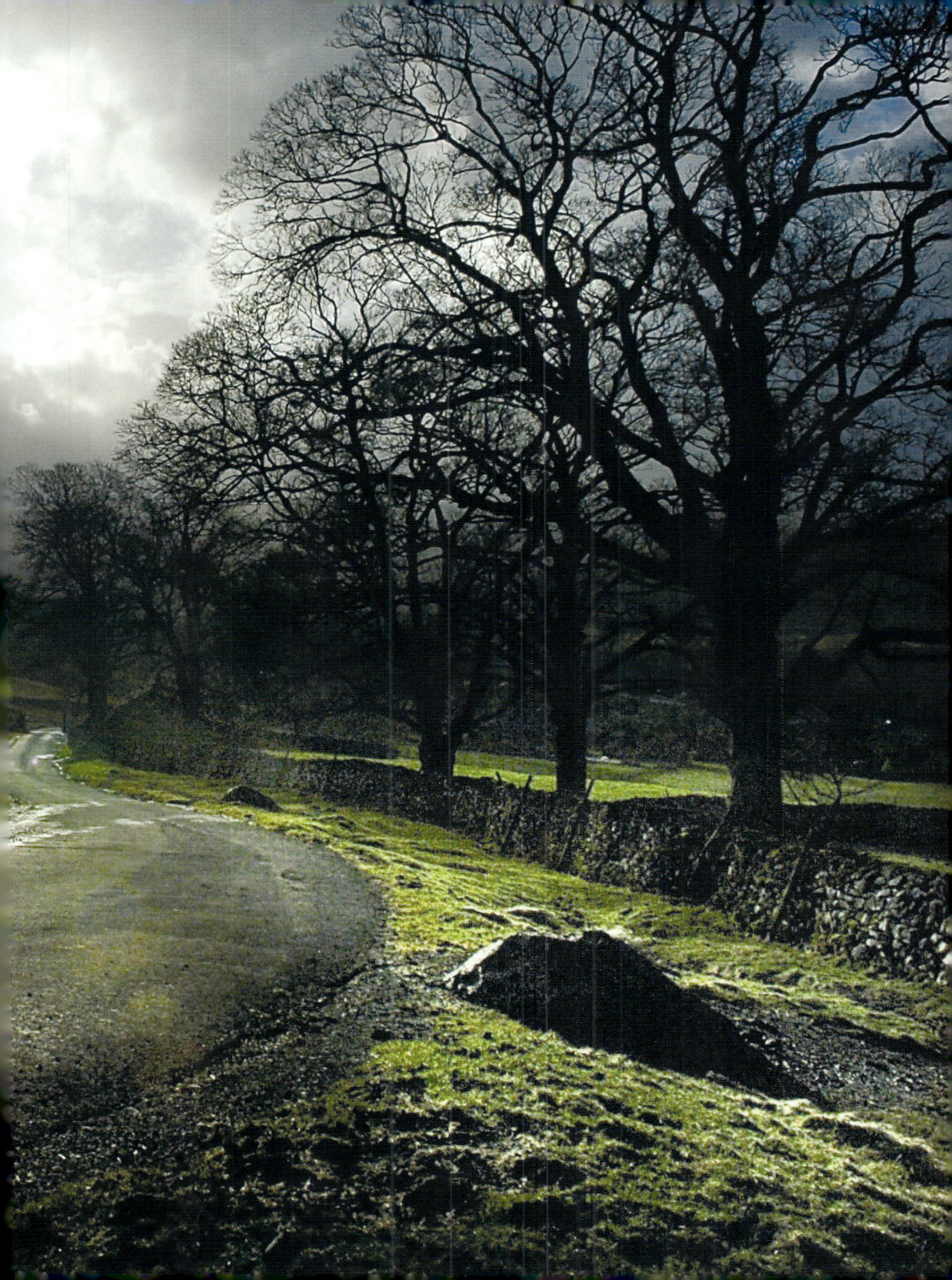

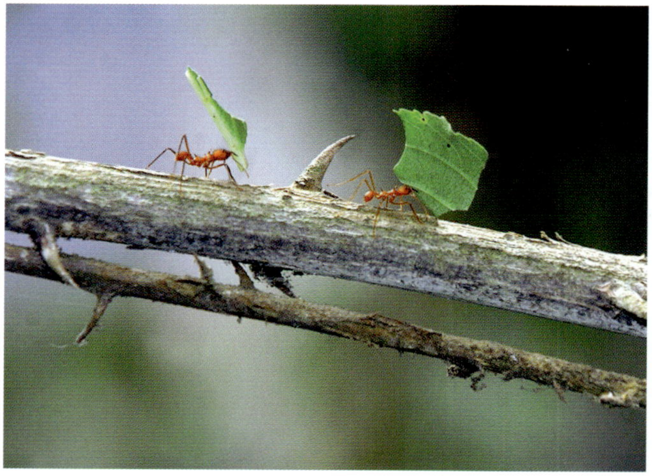

Leaf Cutter Ants carry parts of leaves along a branch back to their nest inside the Tropical Butterfly House in Sheffield. (YPP2096)

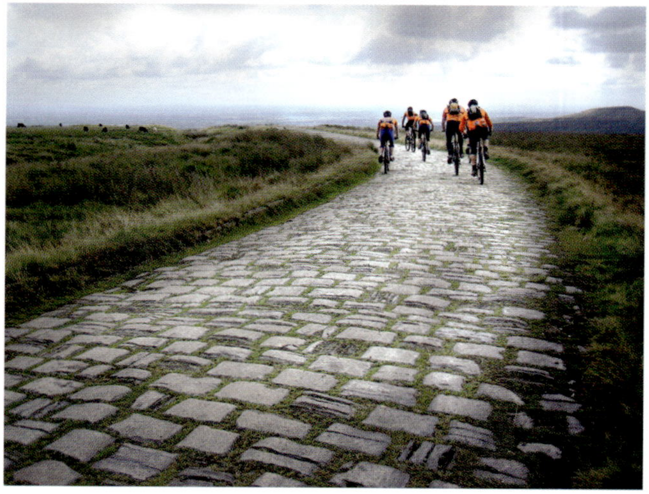

Mountain Bikers head south high above Rossendale on the Rooley Moor Road near 'Top of Leach'. (YPP2097)

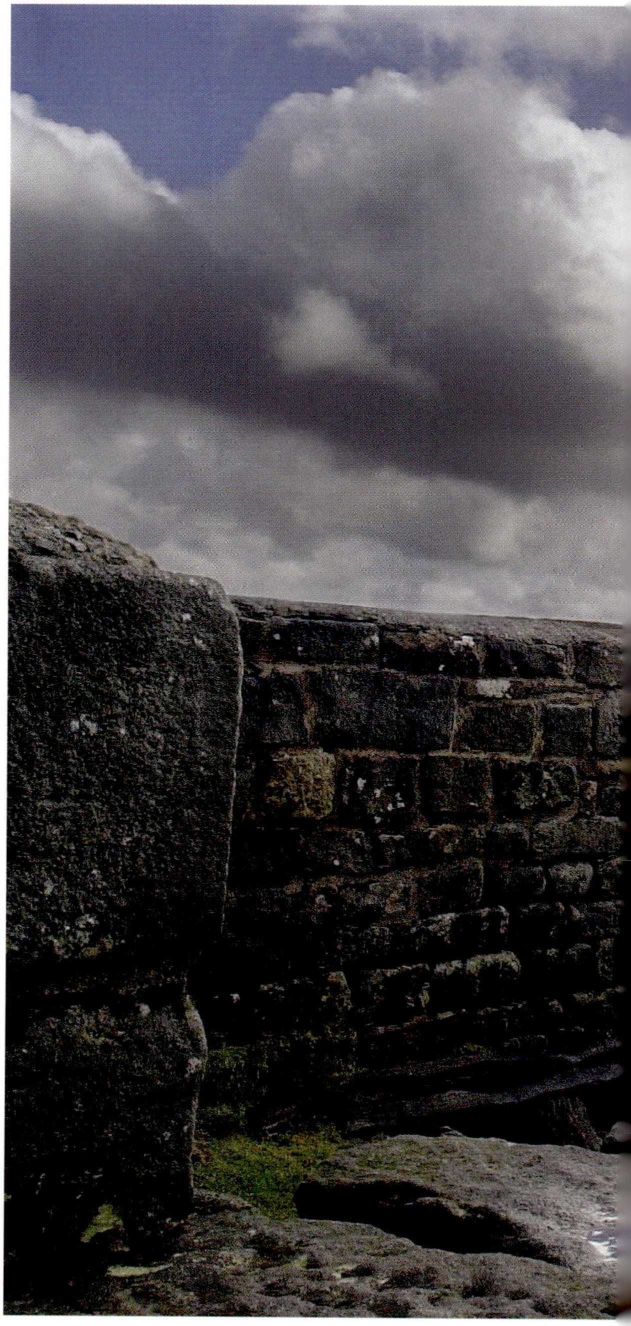

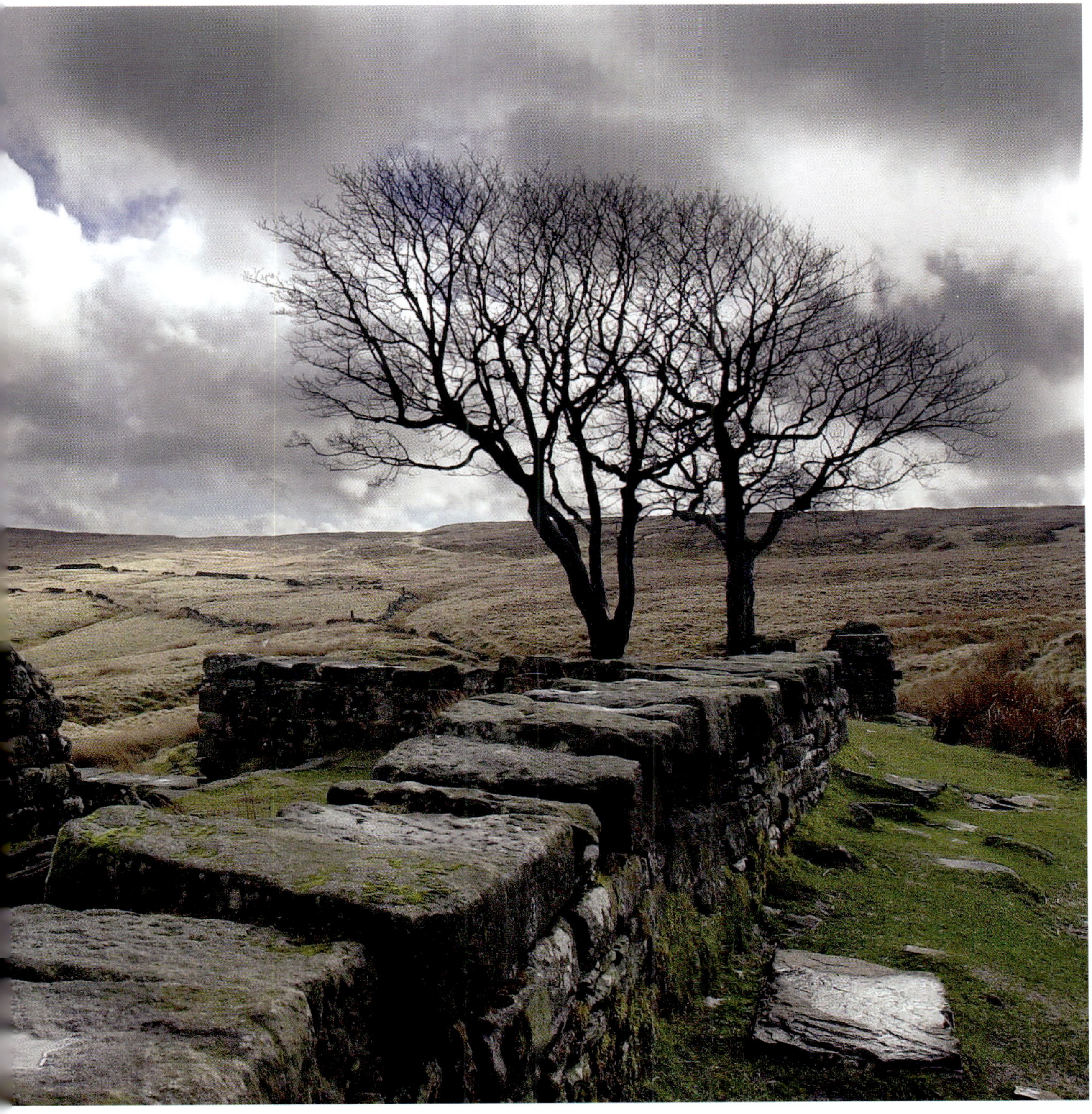

The ruins of Top Withens, high on the Pennine moors above Haworth, have long been associated with Emily Bronte's novel "Wuthering Heights.". Even though the building bore no resemblance to the farm she described as belonging to the Earnshaws, its situation may have been in her mind when she wrote of the Height's remote moorland setting. (YPP2098)

Conisbrough Castle sits proudly on the hill in the middle of the town. (YPP2099)

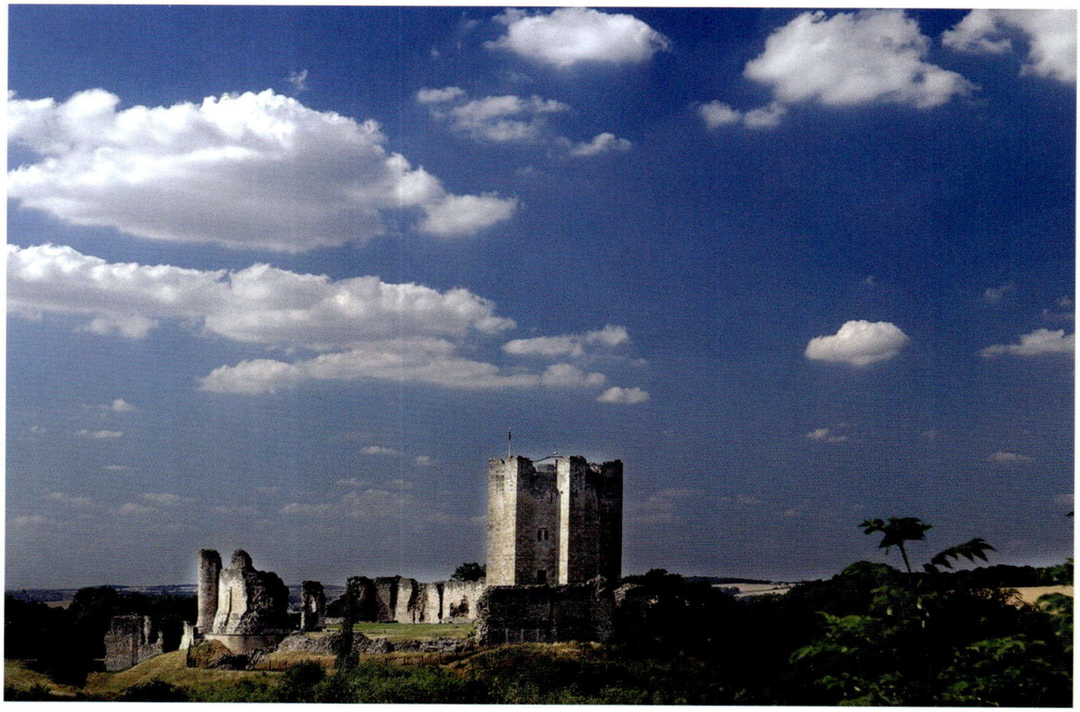

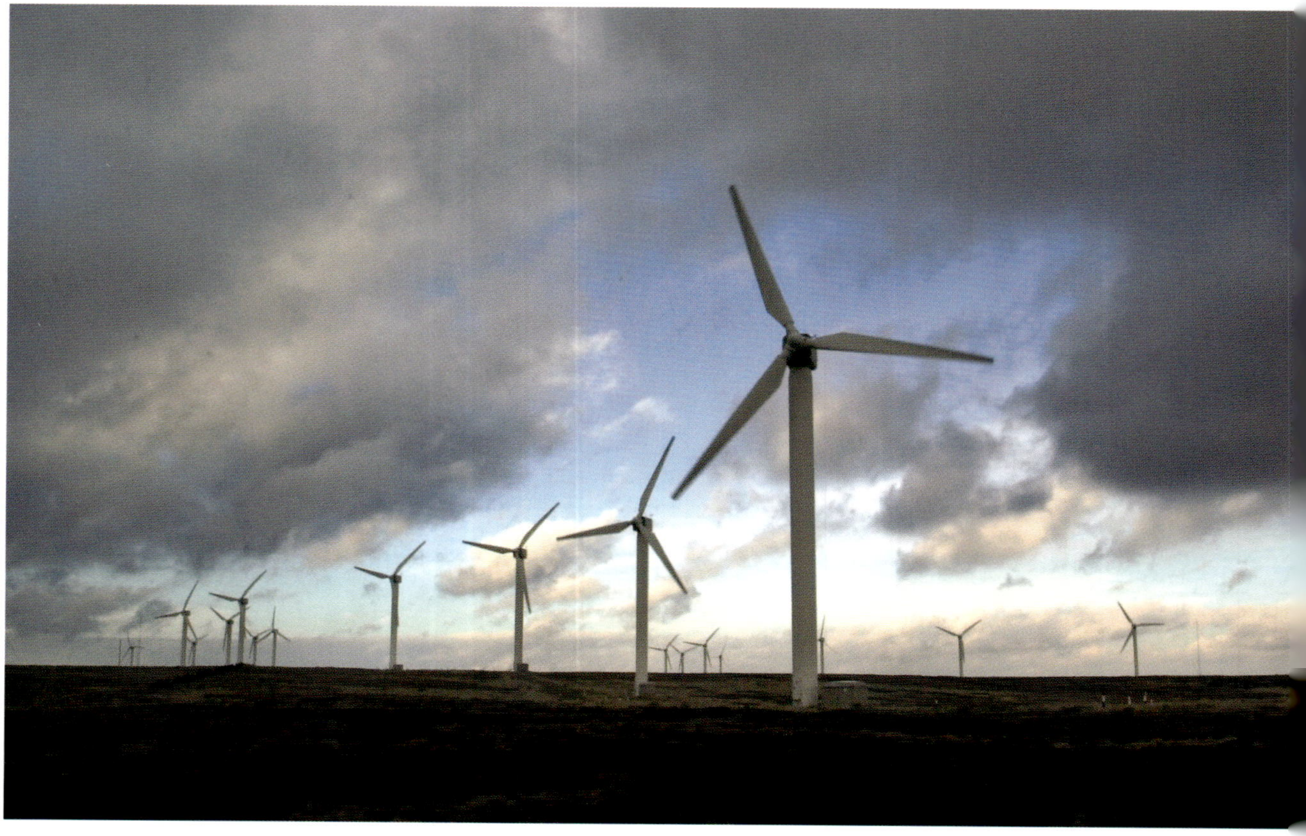

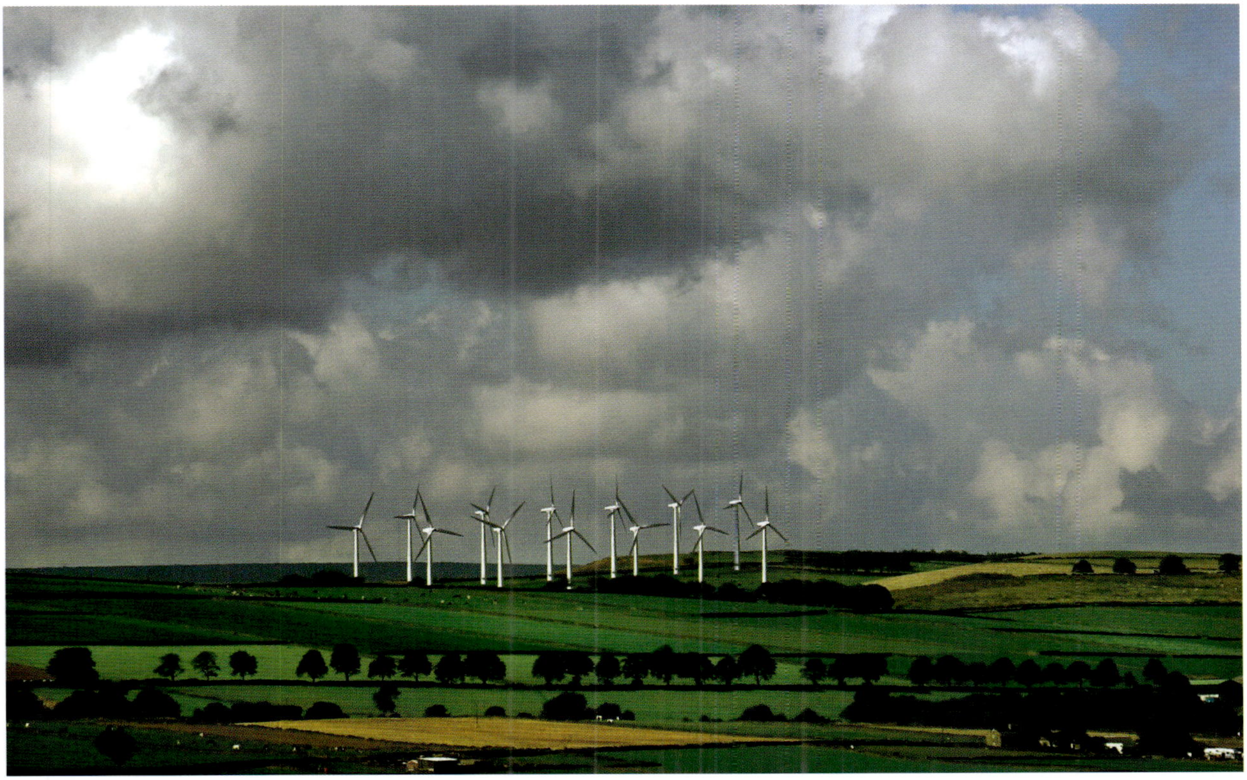

Giant wind turbines look like mechanical flowers sprouting from moorland at Royd Edge, above Penistone near Barnsley. (YPP2101)

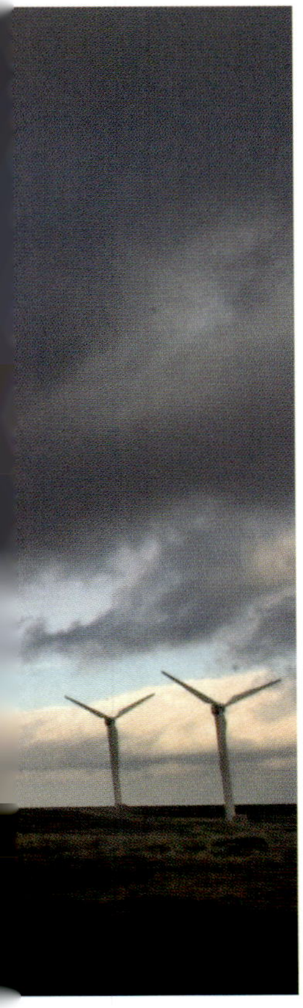

Ovenden Moor Wind Farm near Halifax which has 23 turbines.The farm generates enough electricity annually for 7,500 homes. Ovenden Moor is 1,411 feet above sea level which makes it an ideal site for a wind farm. (YPP2100)

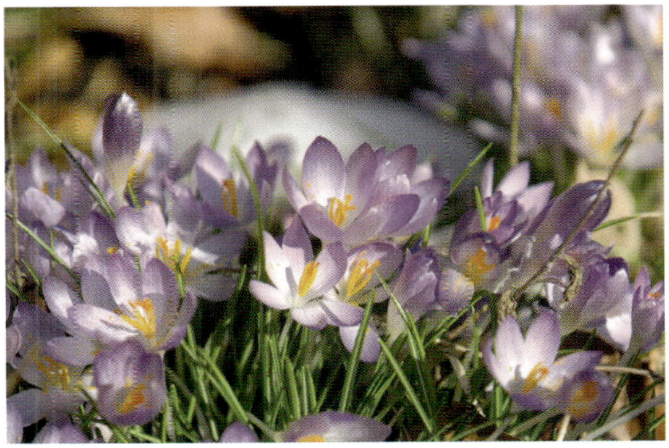

Crocuses opening up through the snow in Becketts Park, Headingley showing that spring is on the way. (YPP2102)

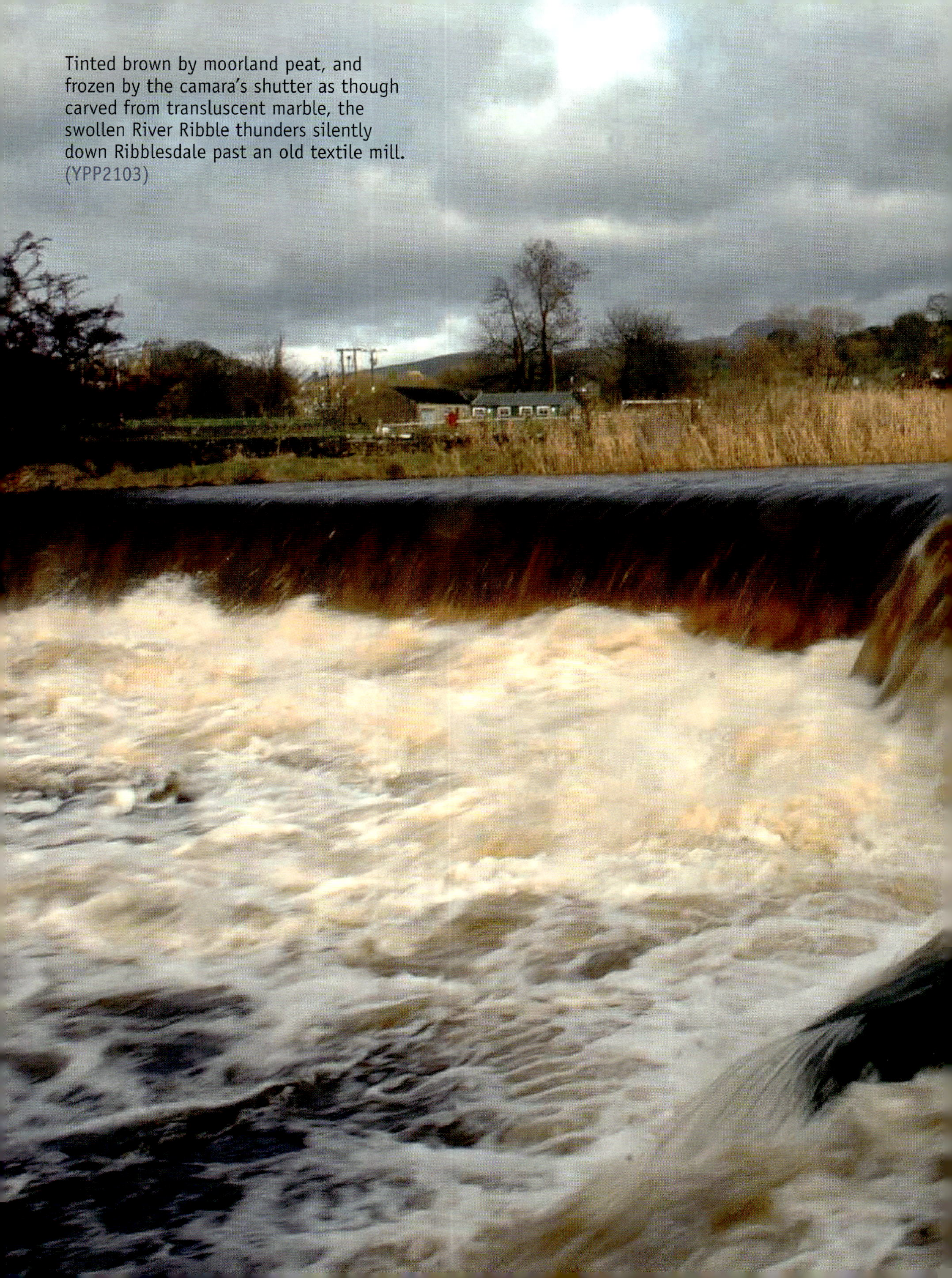

Tinted brown by moorland peat, and frozen by the camara's shutter as though carved from transluscent marble, the swollen River Ribble thunders silently down Ribblesdale past an old textile mill. (YPP2103)

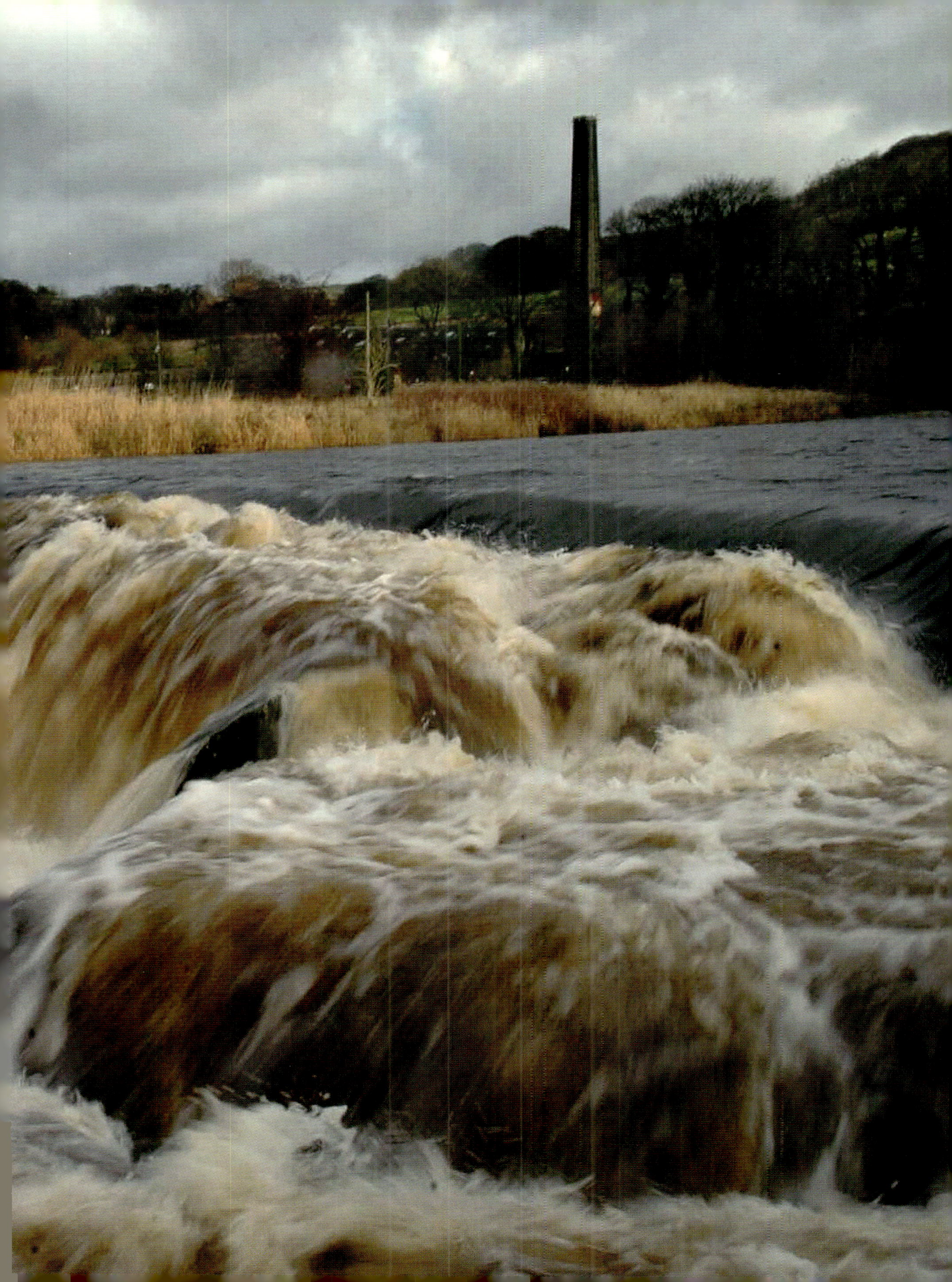

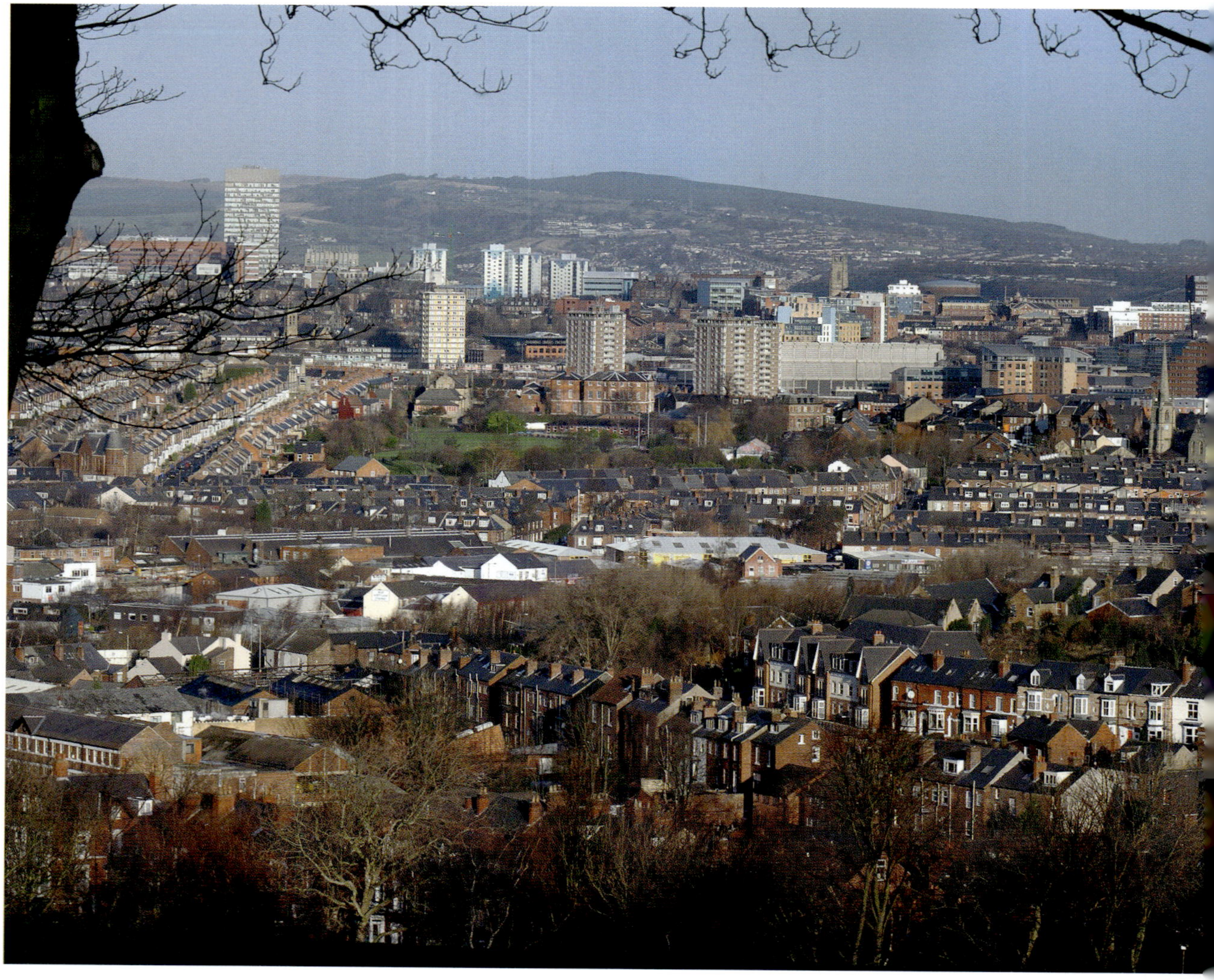

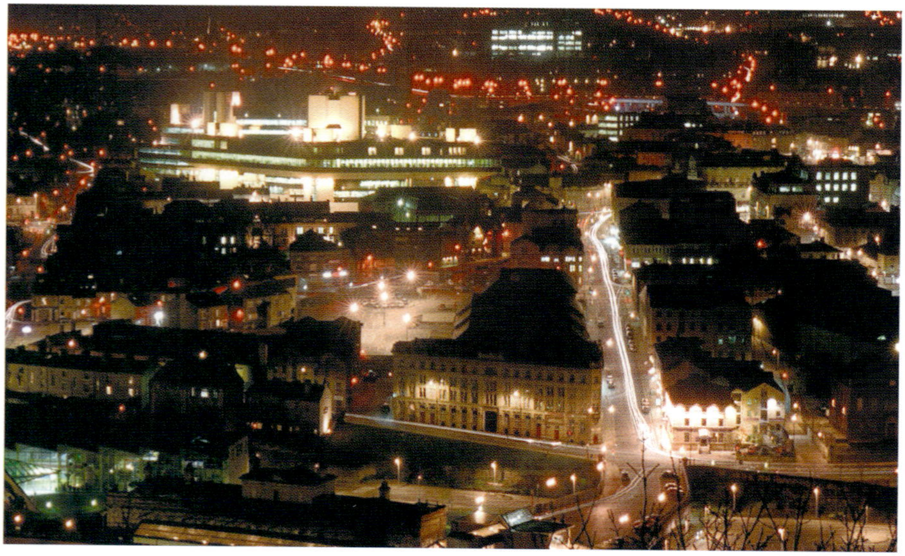

Halifax at night, ablaze with lights, its streets like neon strips. (YPP2105)

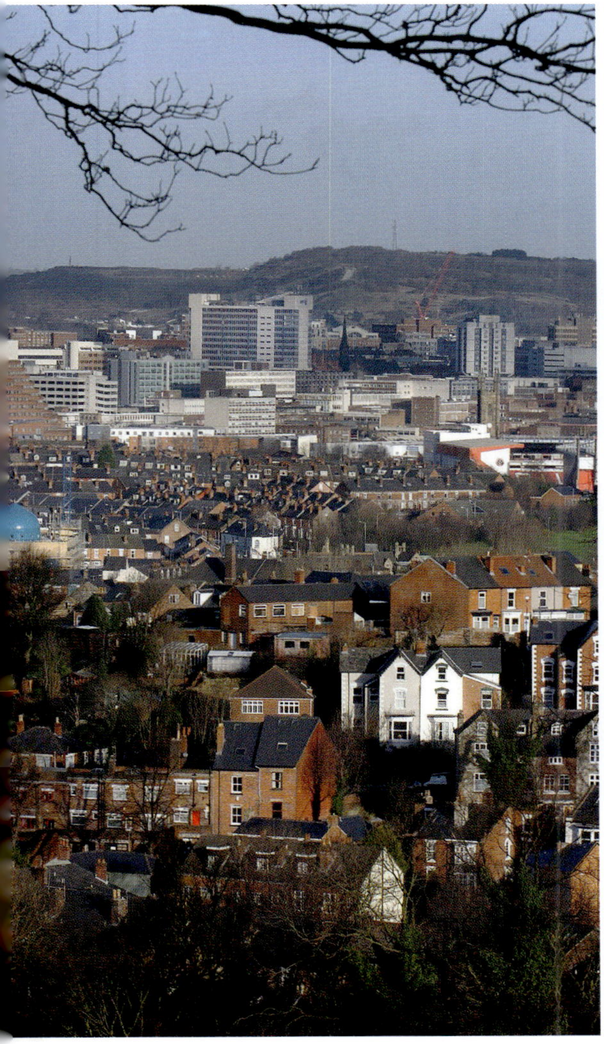

Old and not-so-old, and new and not-so-new layer this view of Sheffield from Meersbrook Park.
(YPP2104)

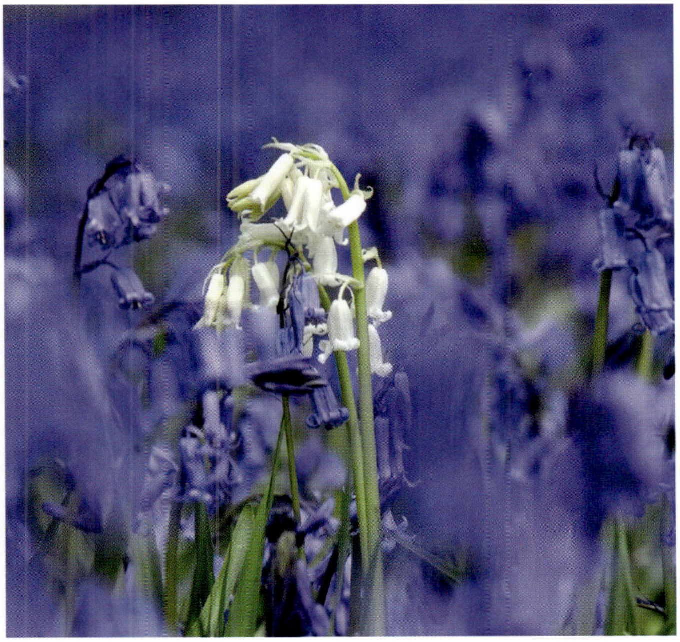

A solitary white bluebell amongst a sea of blue.
(YPP2106)

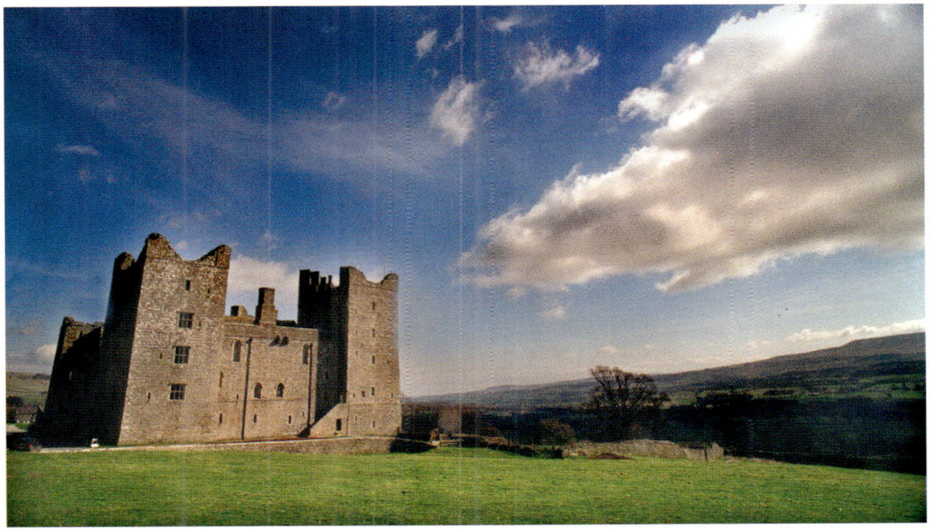

Bolton Castle at Castle Bolton near Leyburn, Wensleydale.
(YPP2107)

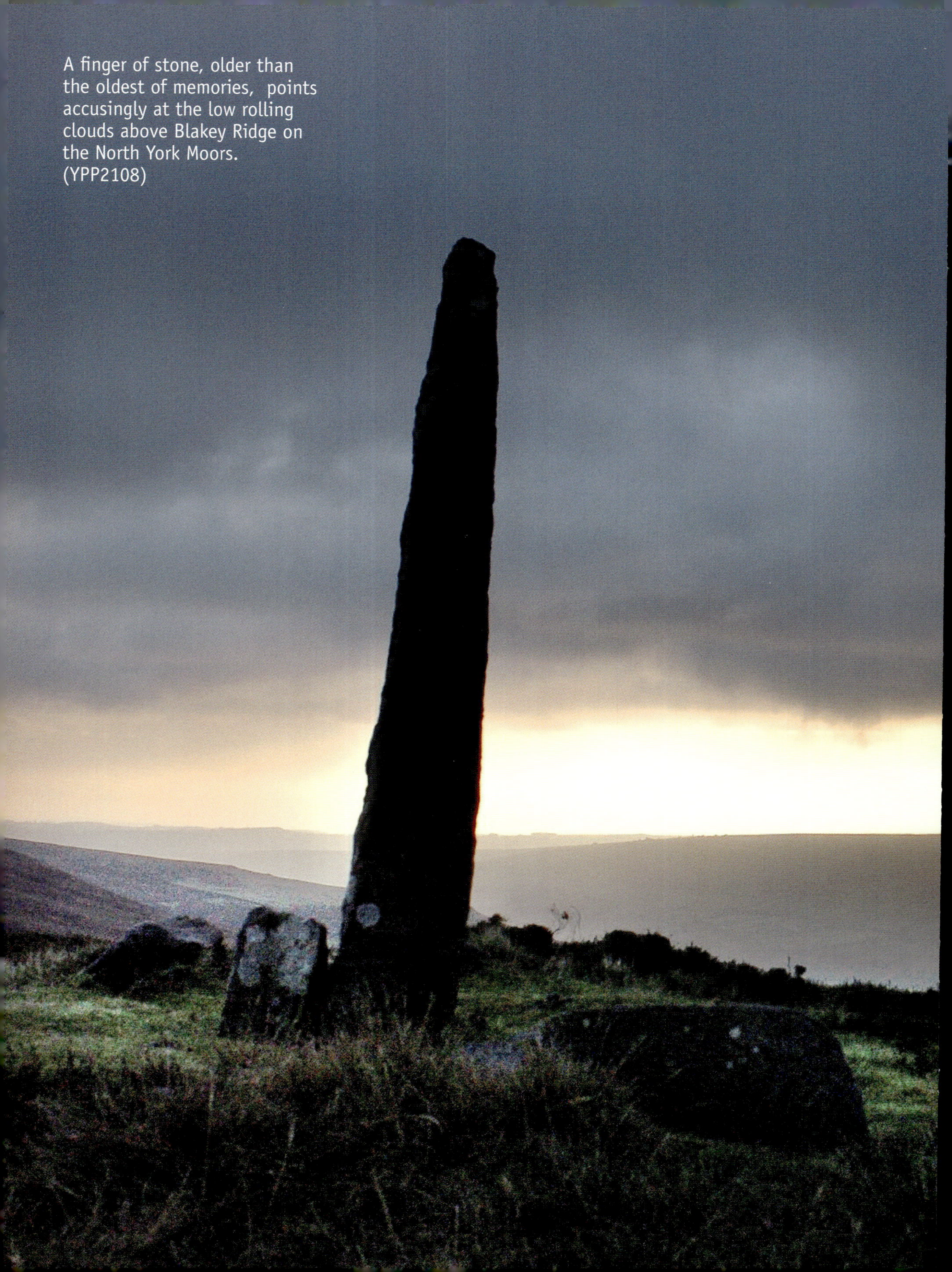

A finger of stone, older than the oldest of memories, points accusingly at the low rolling clouds above Blakey Ridge on the North York Moors. (YPP2108)

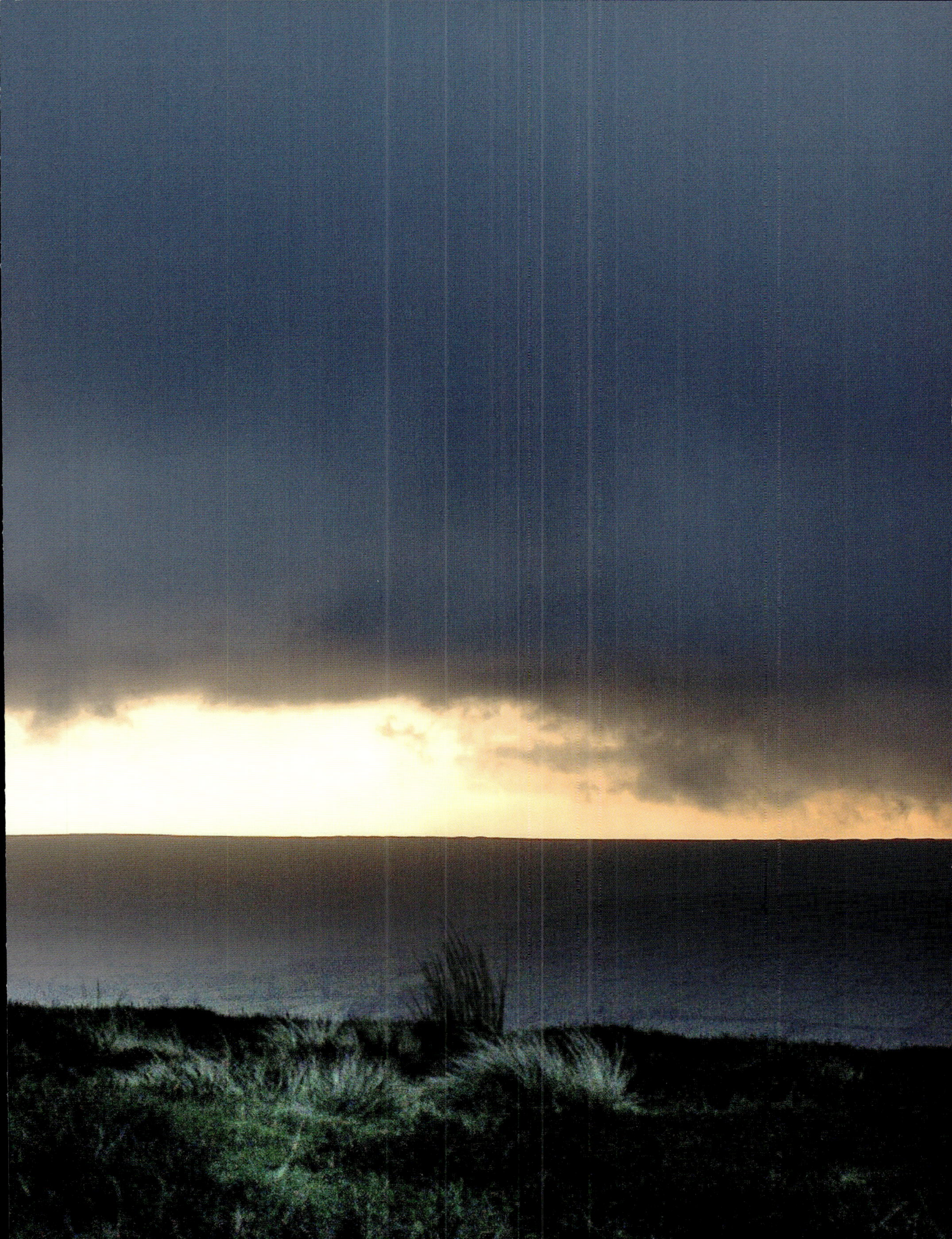

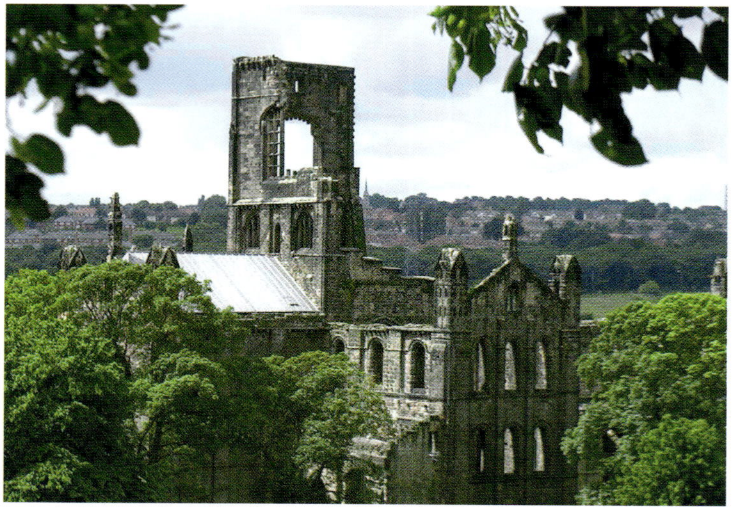

Sunlight strikes Kirkstall Abbey.
(YPP2109)

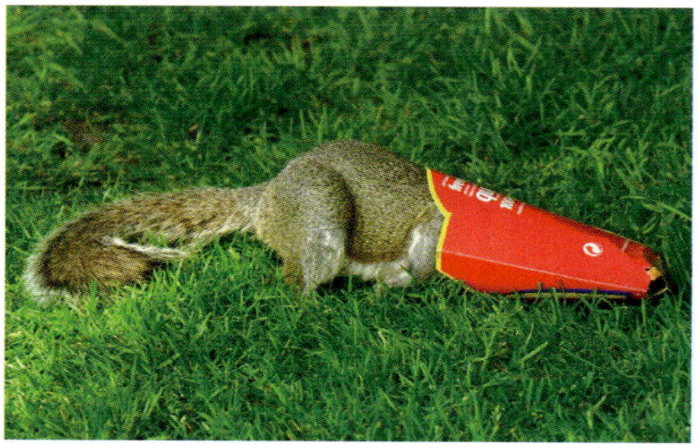

Having a problem getting the last french fry from the packet is one of the squirrels that inhabit the Yorkshire Museum Gardens in York.
(YPP2110)

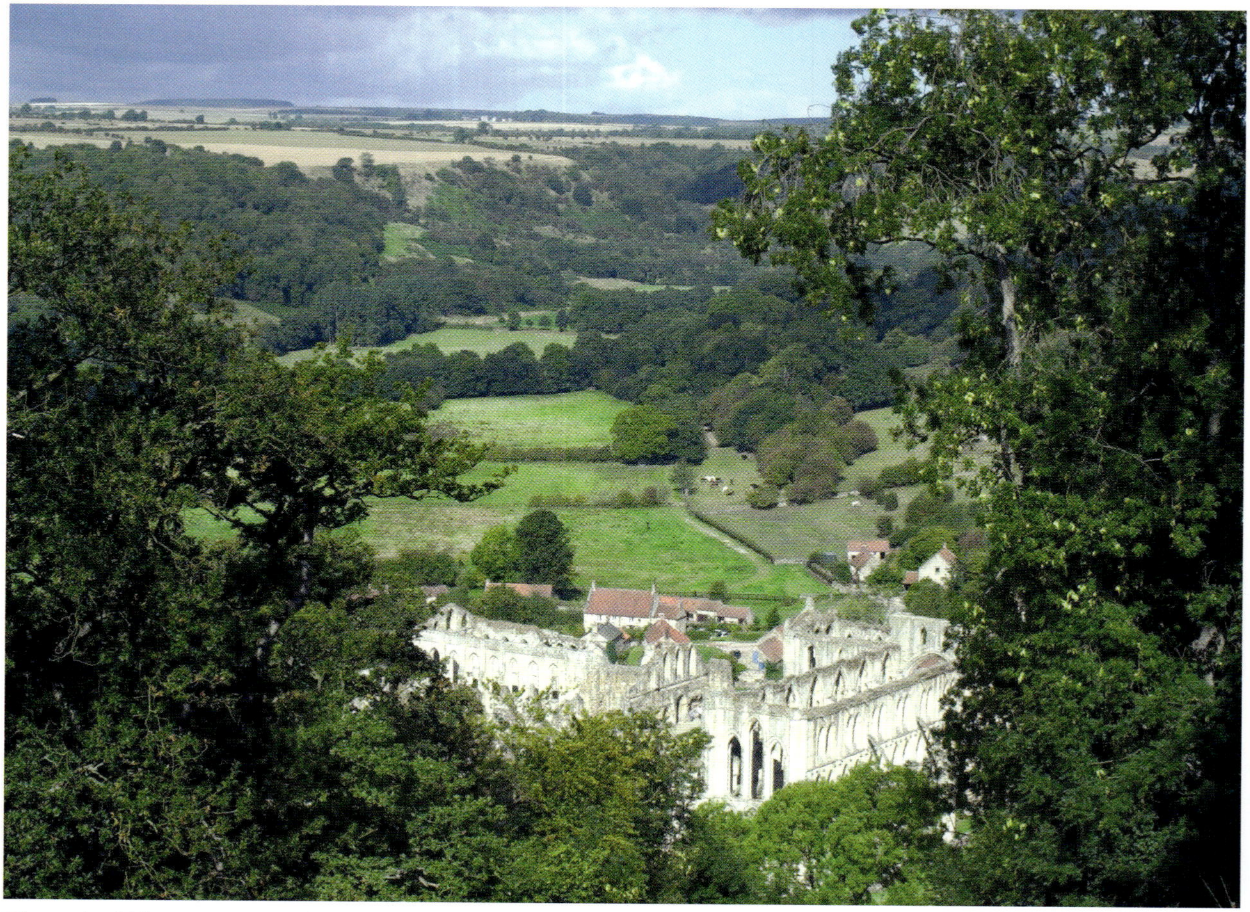

Rievaulx Abbey, now a splendid ruin, is unusual in that the church runs north to south owing to the narrowness of the valley in which it stands.
(YPP2111)

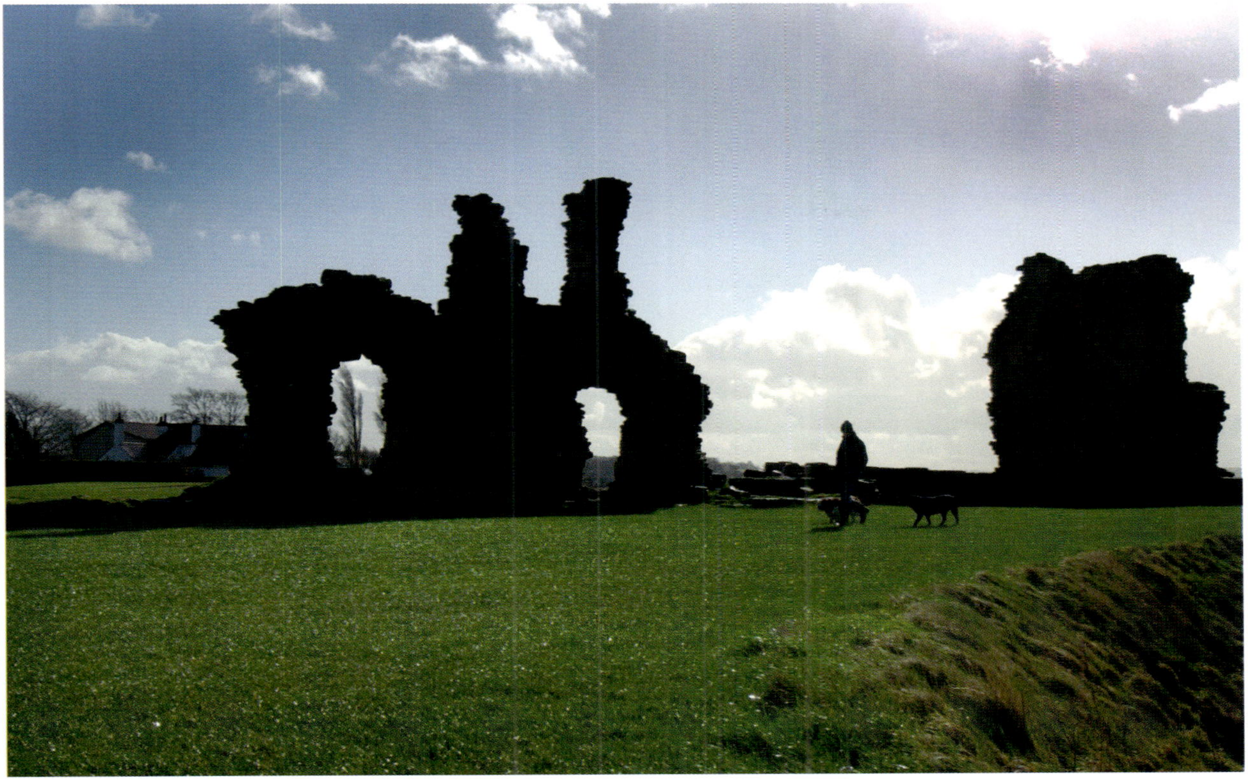

A man and his dogs take a walk by Sandal Castle.
(YPP2112)

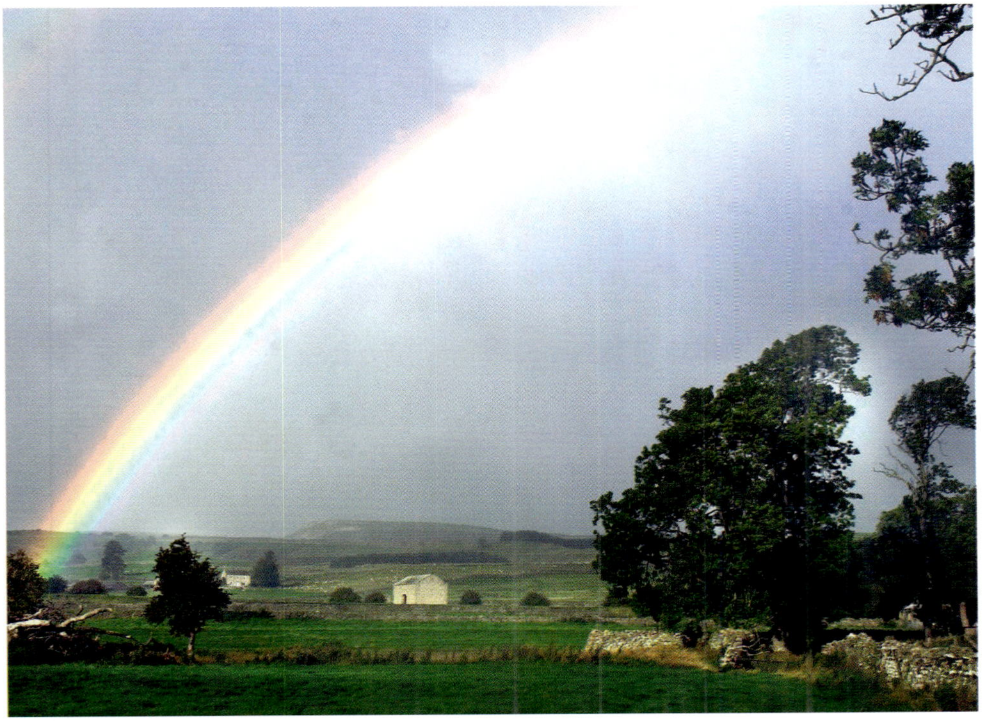

In the Dales a rainbow arches up from a pot of pure gold.
(YPP2113)

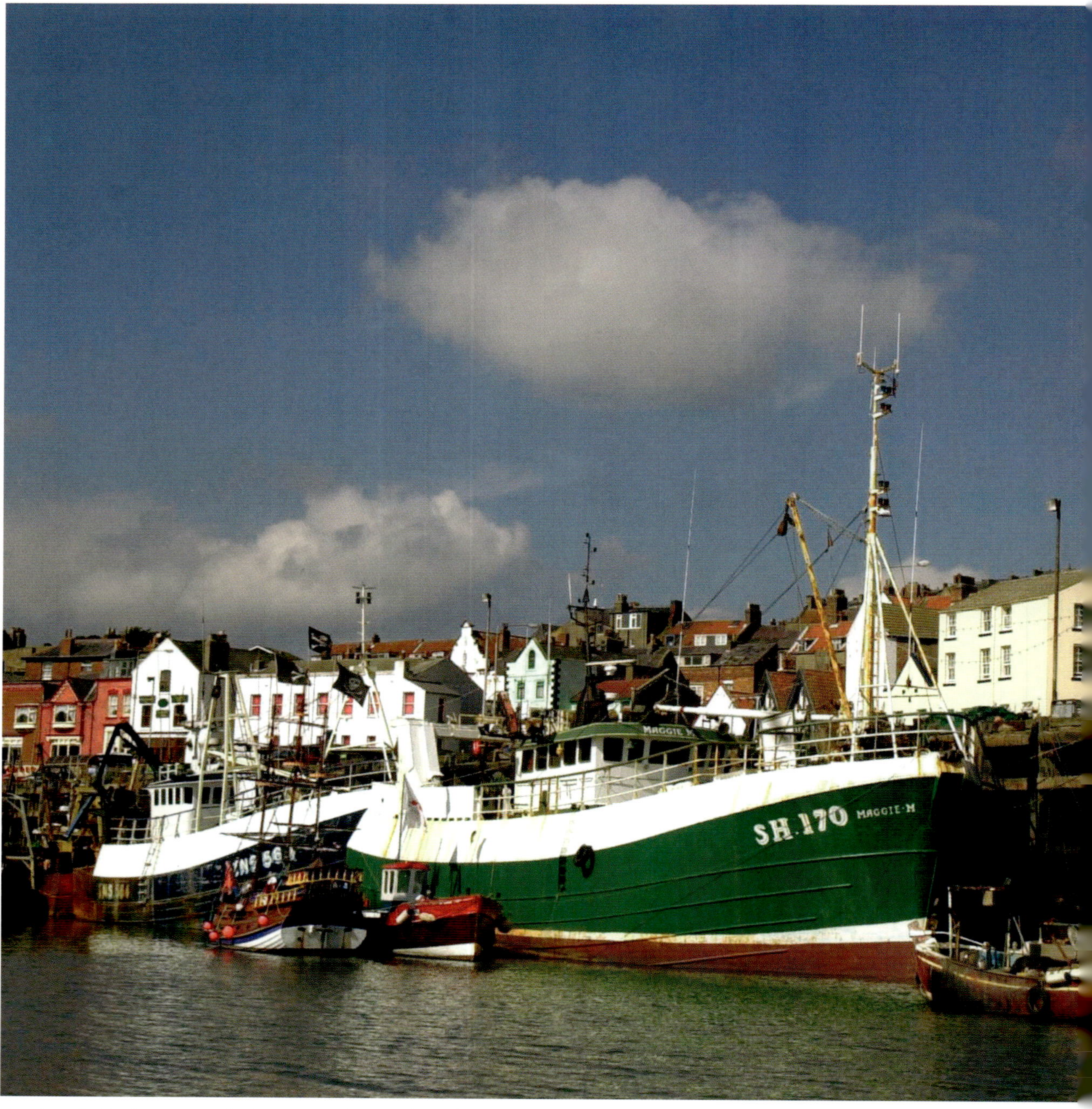

Boats of all shapes and sizes crowd the rim of Scarborough harbour.
(YPP2114)

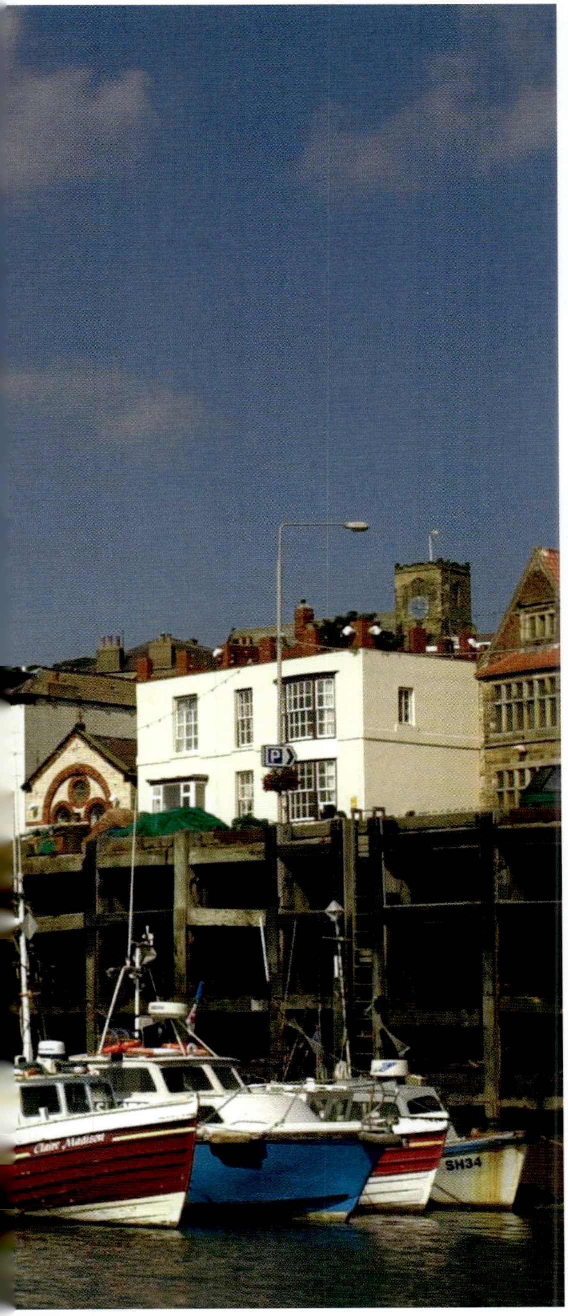

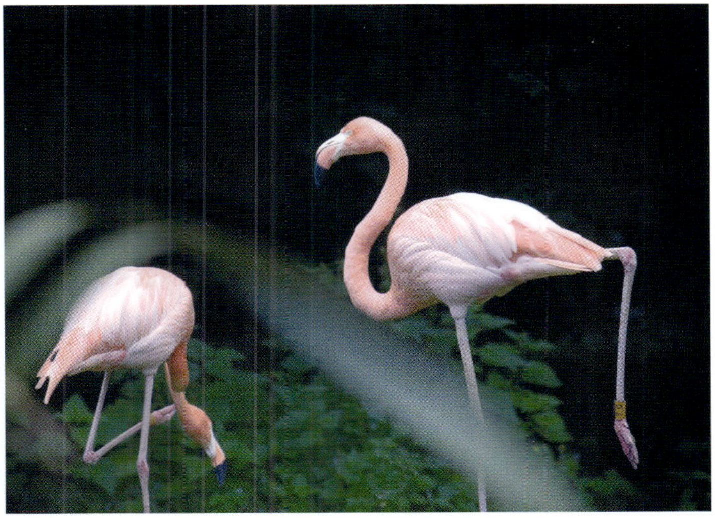

Caribbean Flamingoes at Lotherton Hall Bird Garden, near Garforth.
(YPP2115) Above
(YPP2116) Below

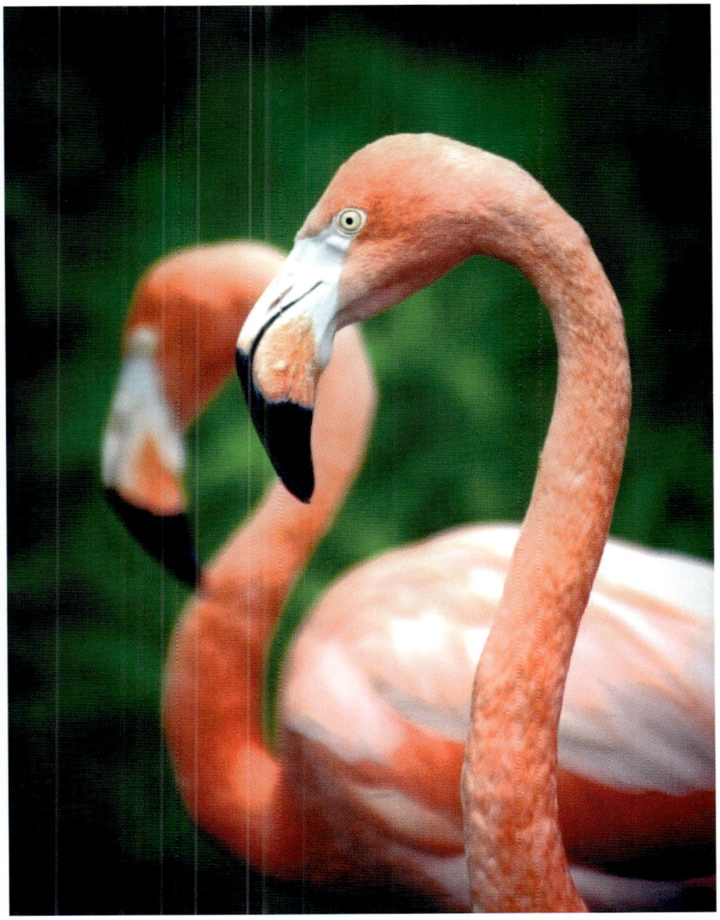

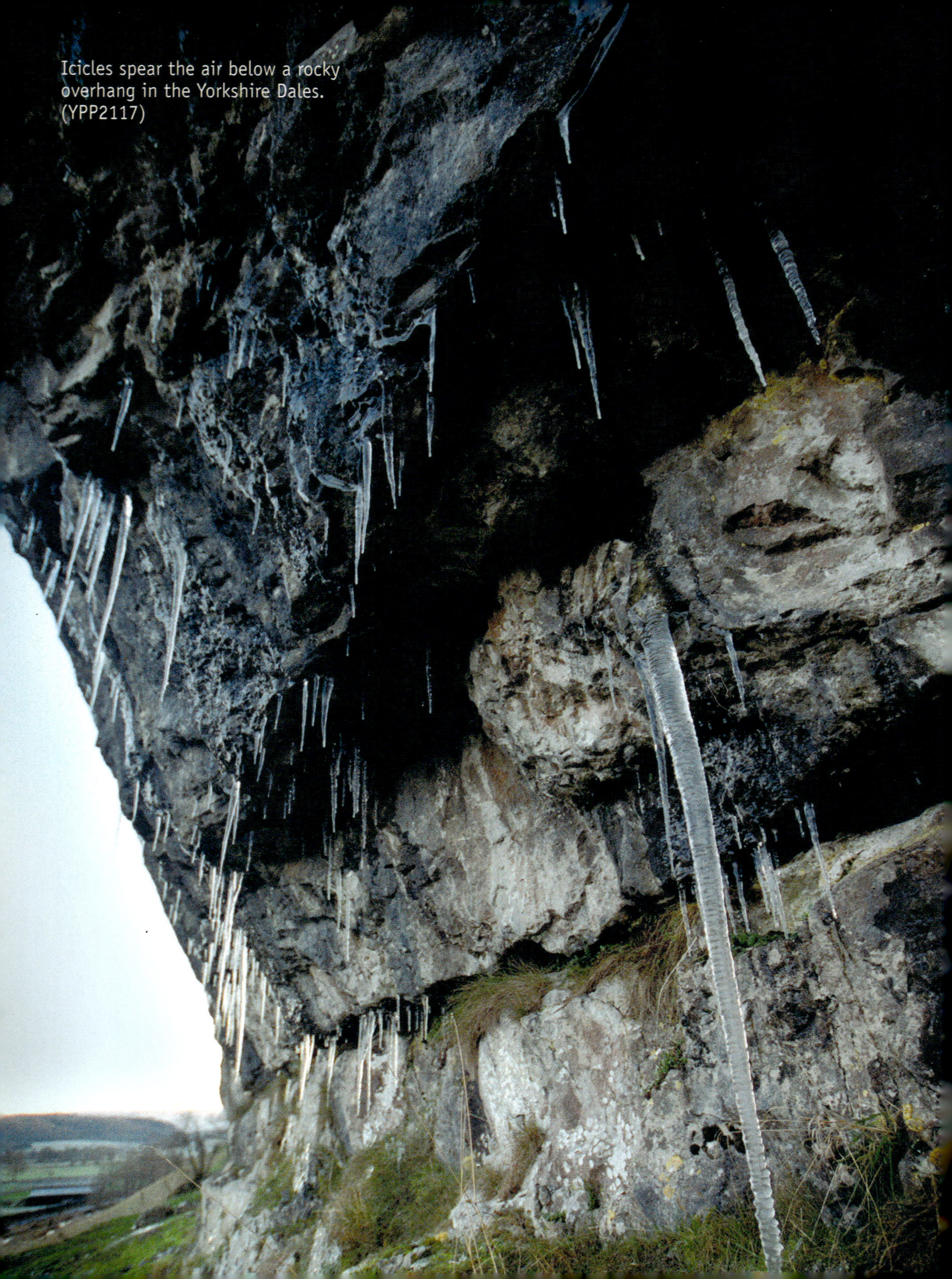

Icicles spear the air below a rocky overhang in the Yorkshire Dales. (YPP2117)

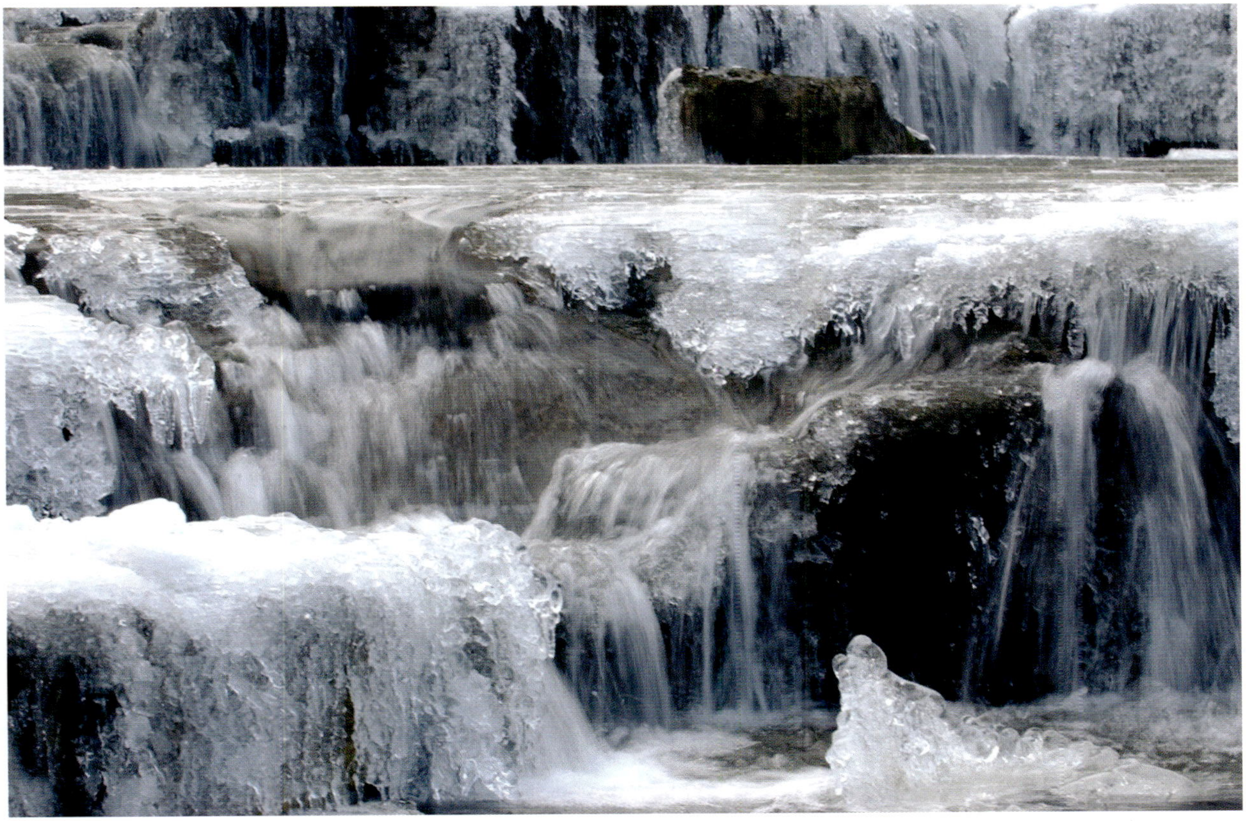

Falling into Wensleydale, a tributary of the Ure is cystalised in ice.
(YPP2118)

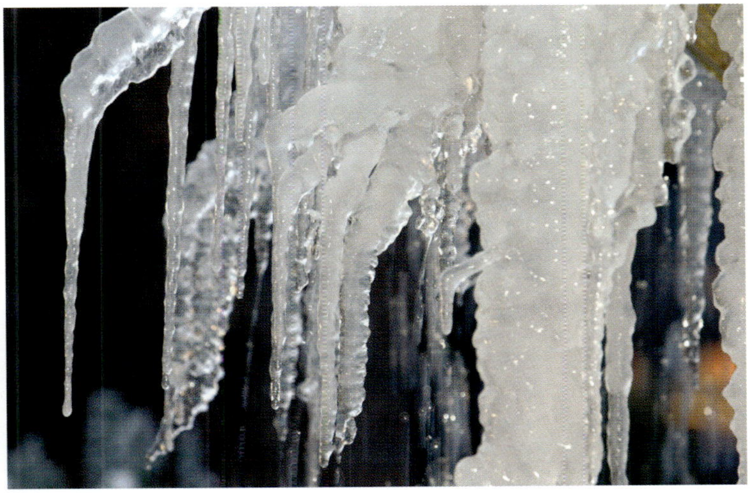

Icicles on the frozen fountain
at Aldwark Manor Hotel near York.
(YPP2119)

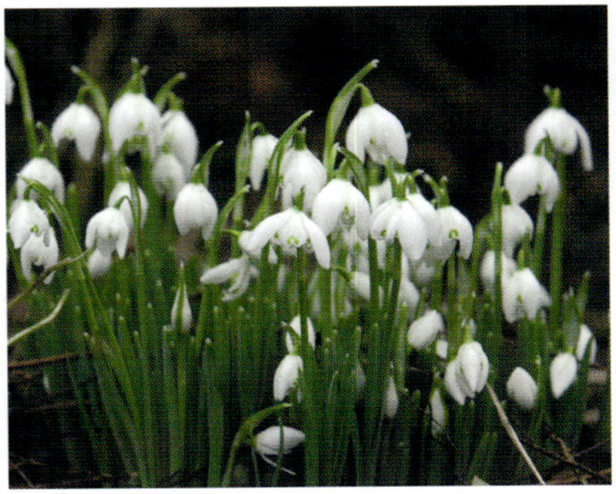

The first signs of spring as
snowdrops start to appear.
(YPP2120)

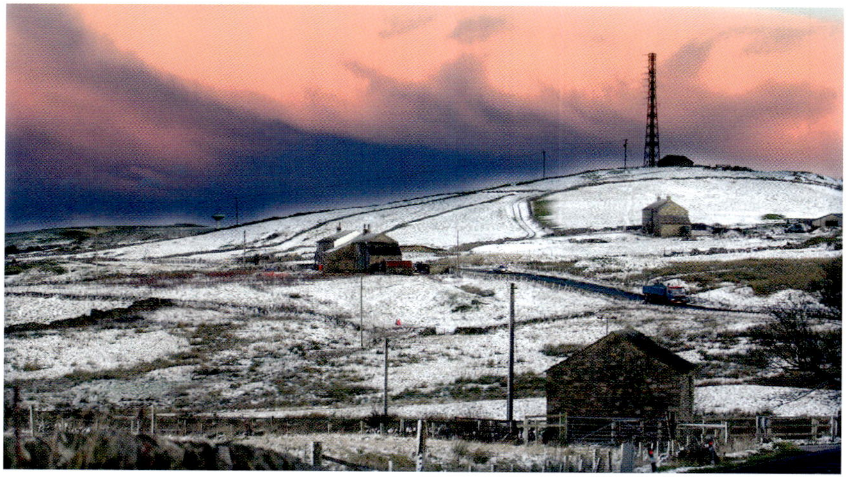

Snow on the hills above Greenhow village Nidderdale as the sun sets. (YPP2121)

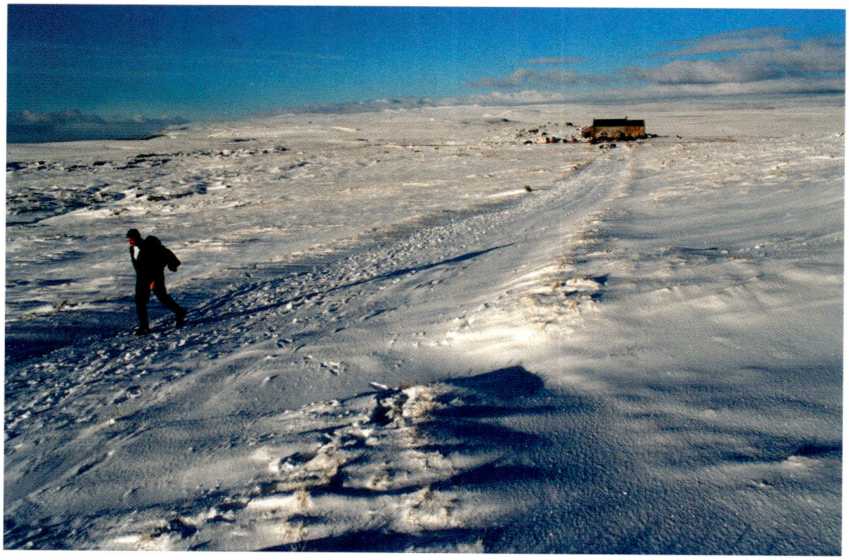

A lone walker on the Pennine Way against a snowscape backdrop of the Tan Hill Inn, Great Britain's highest inn at 1,732 feet above sea level. (YPP2122)

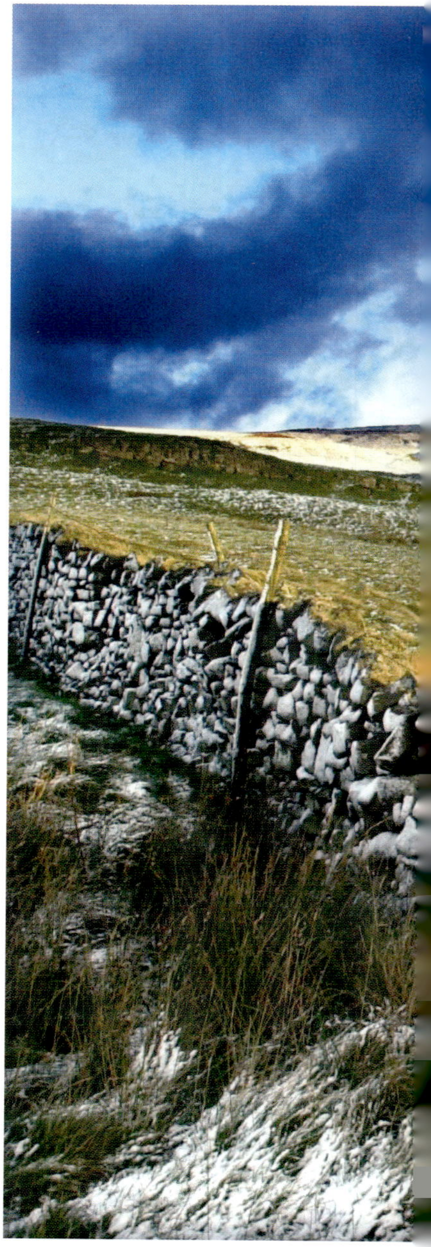

Snow covered hills in the Yorkshire Dales National Park on the road between Grassington and Kilnsey in Wharfedale. (YPP2123)

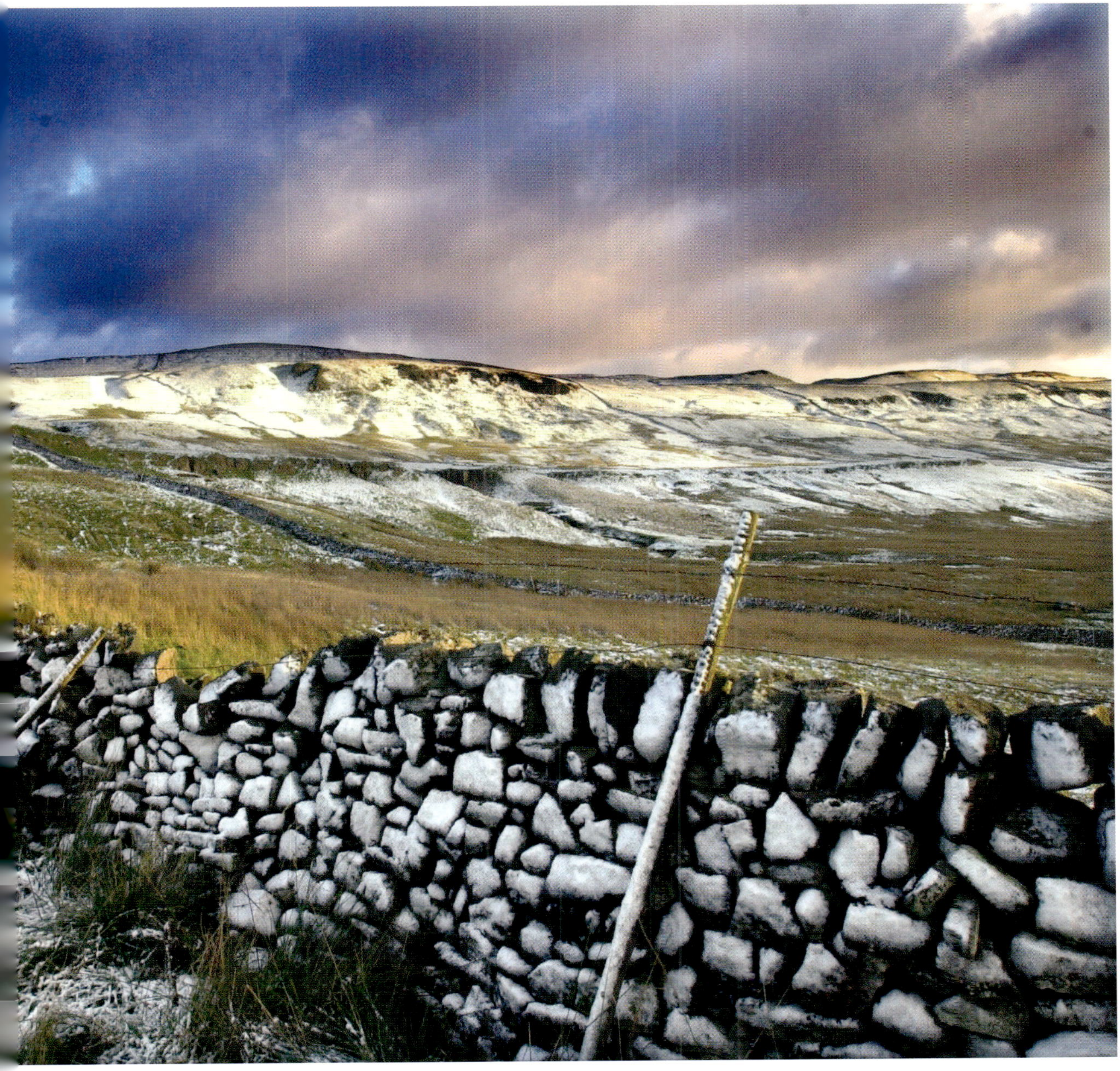

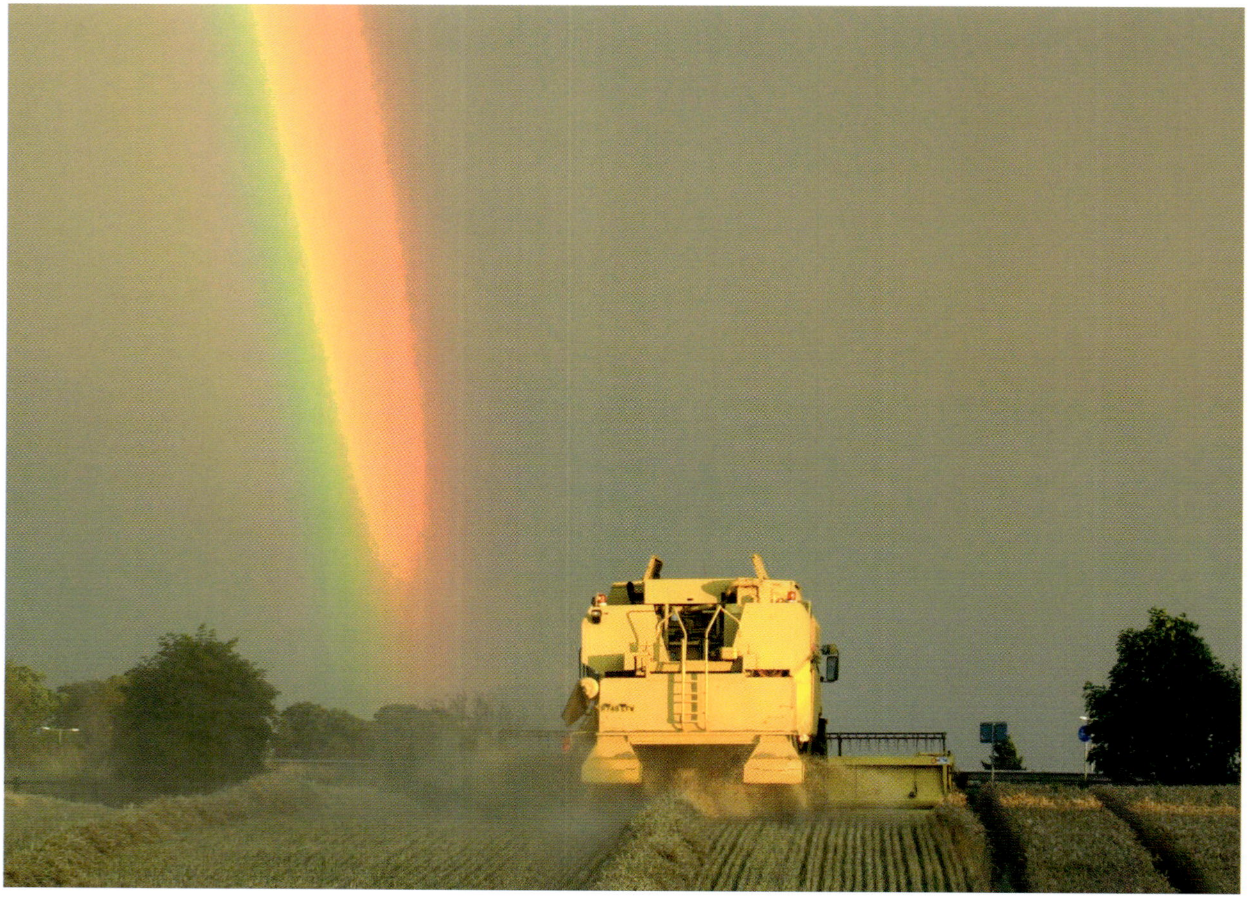

A combined harvester gathers up the barley in a field near Pickering while rain and sunlight create an exuberant display behind it (YPP2124)

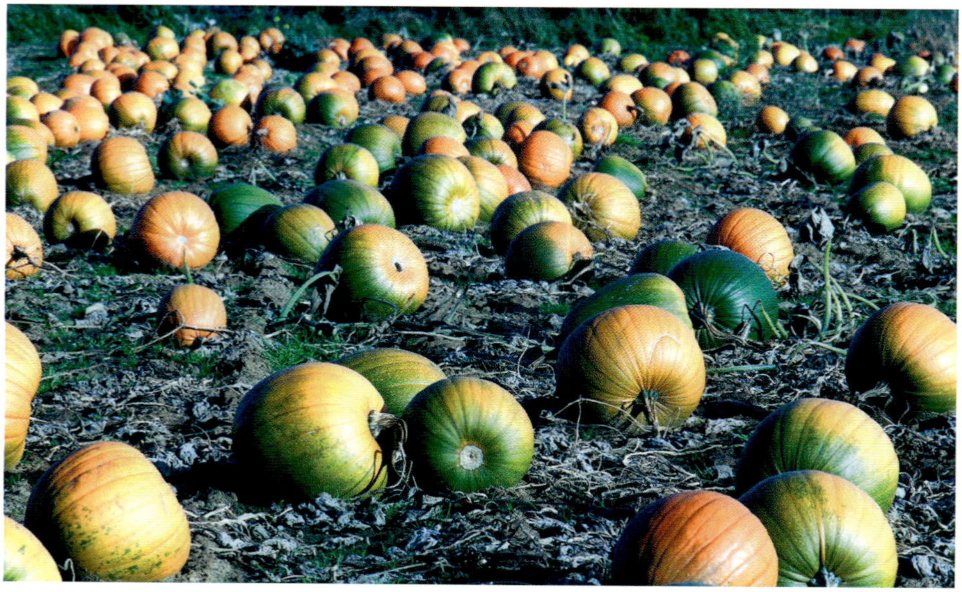

Gourds....some of the many pumpkins grown by Braithwell farmer Peter Dunstan. (YPP2125)

Classic Dales: stone barns near Keld in Swaledale. (YPP2126)

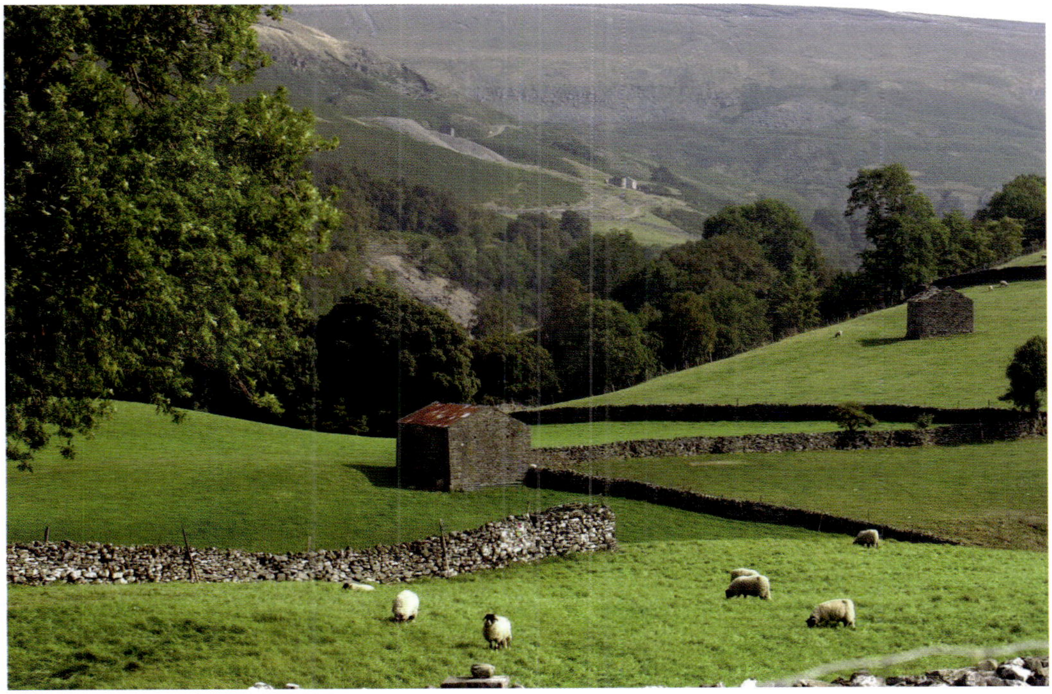

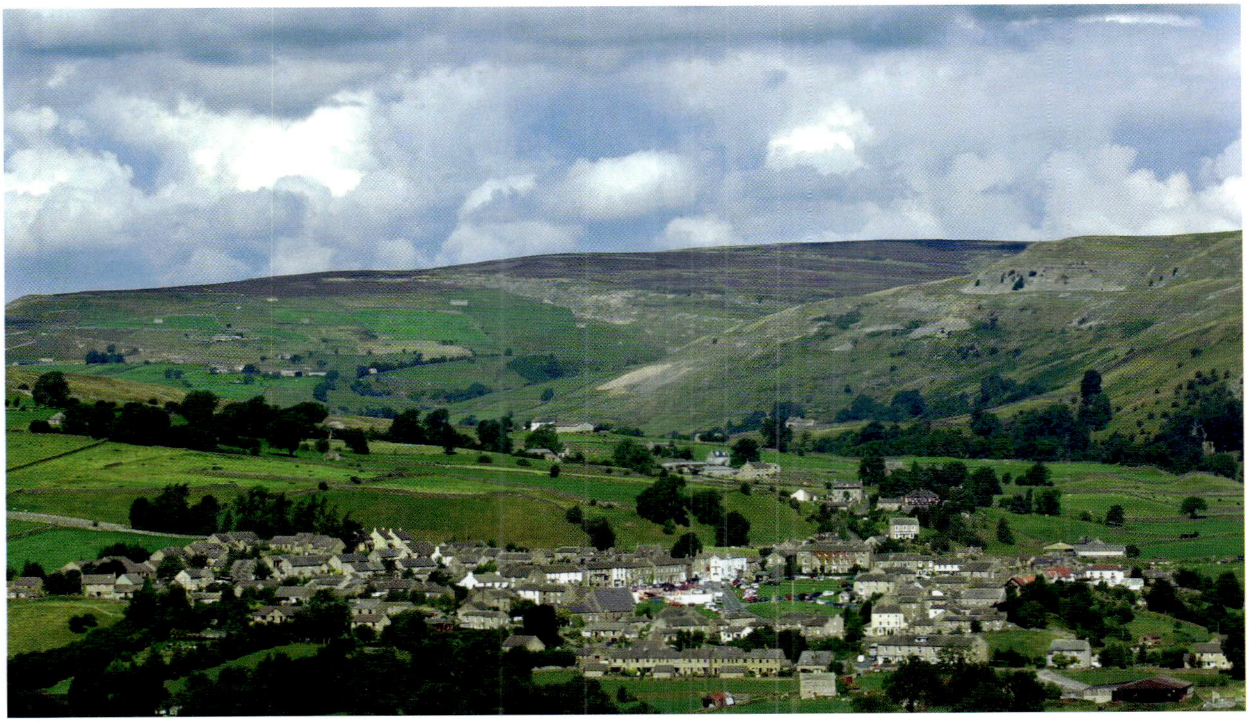

Reeth in Swaledale has long attracted visitors. Years gone by saw miners arriving to work in the surrounding lead mines. Now it's tourists who flock to the dales town. Dominating the skyline, before it breaks away into heather covered moorland is Fremington Edge. (YPP2127)

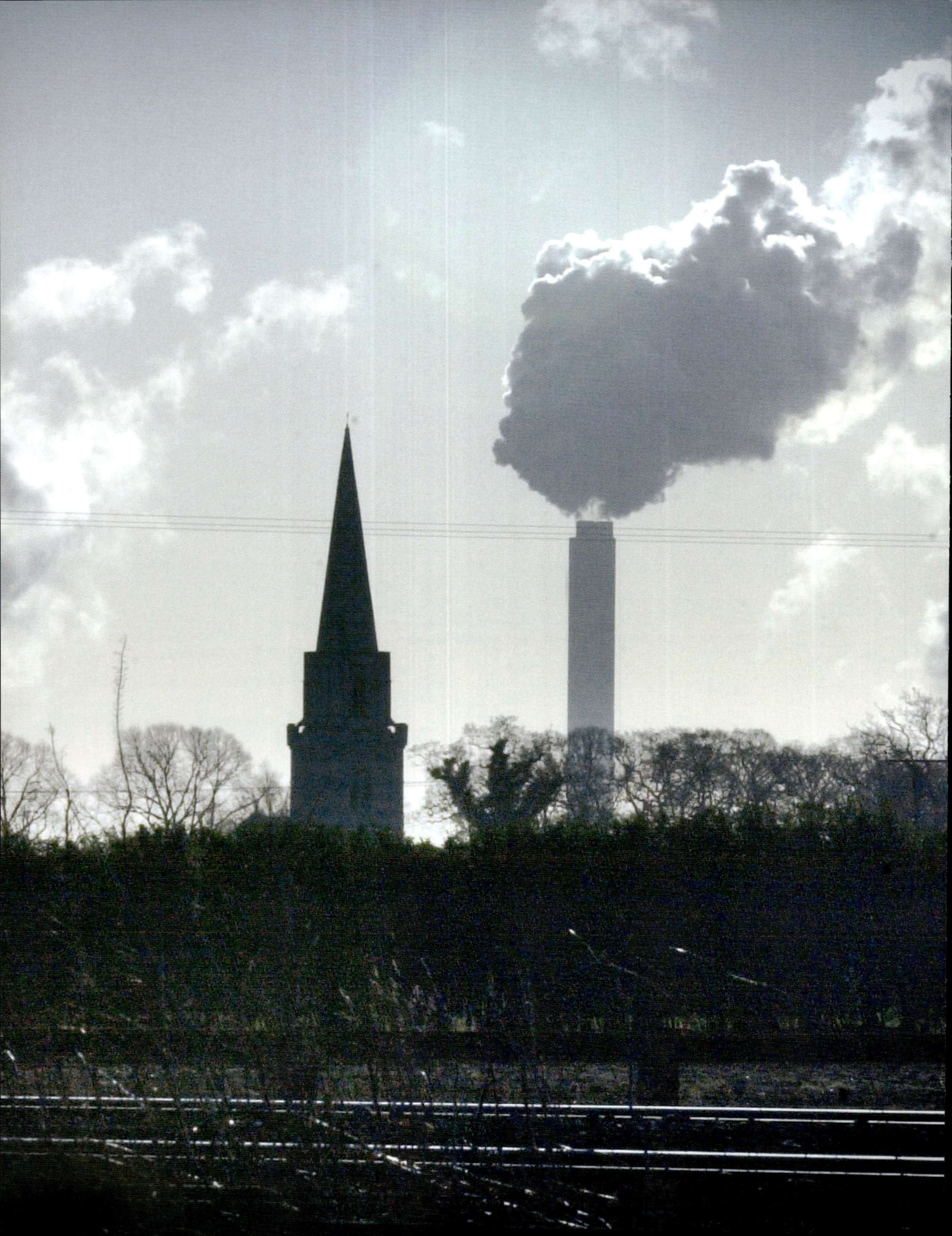

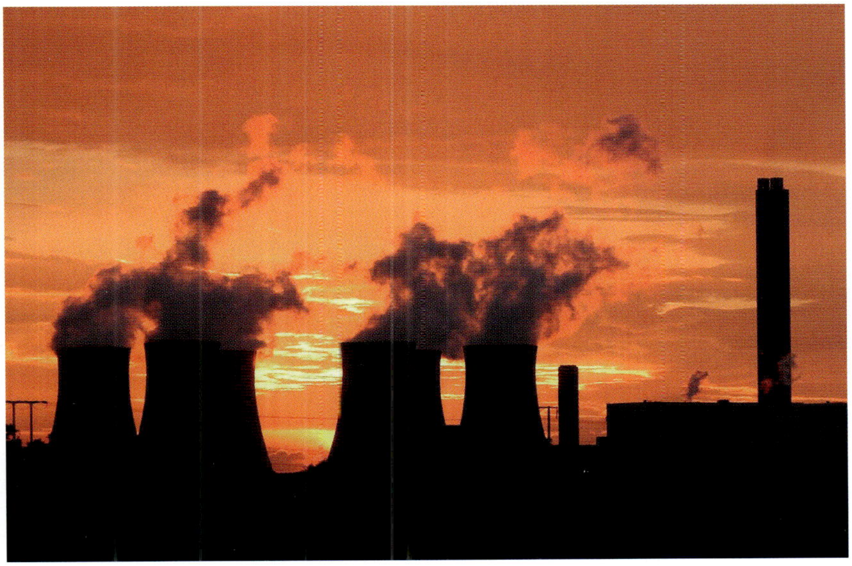

The sun sets behind Drax Power Station.
(YPP2129)

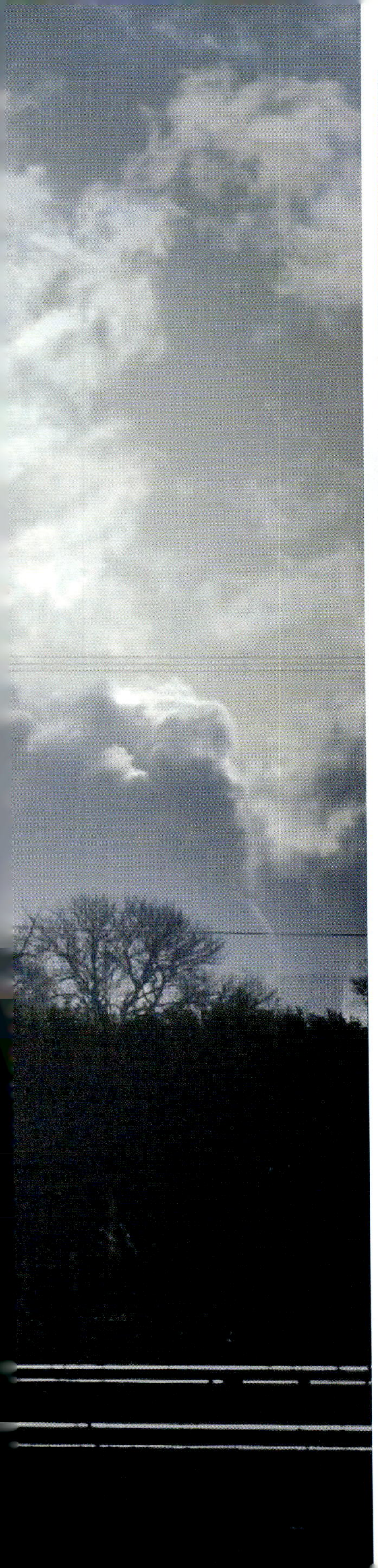

The sharp-pointed steeple of the Parish Church of St Wilfrid, Brayton, near Selby, and in the distance, a stack at Drax power station puffs clouds into the sky.
(YPP2128)

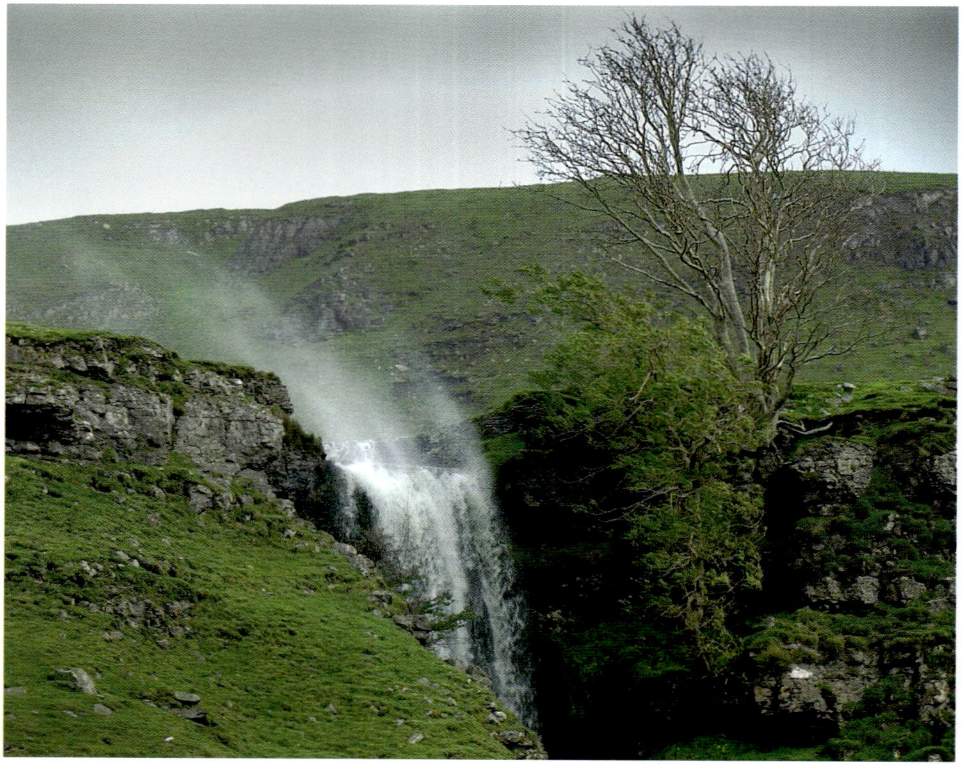

Spray from a cascading stream above Cray near Buckden in the Yorkshire Dales is carried away on a powerful wind. (YPP2130)

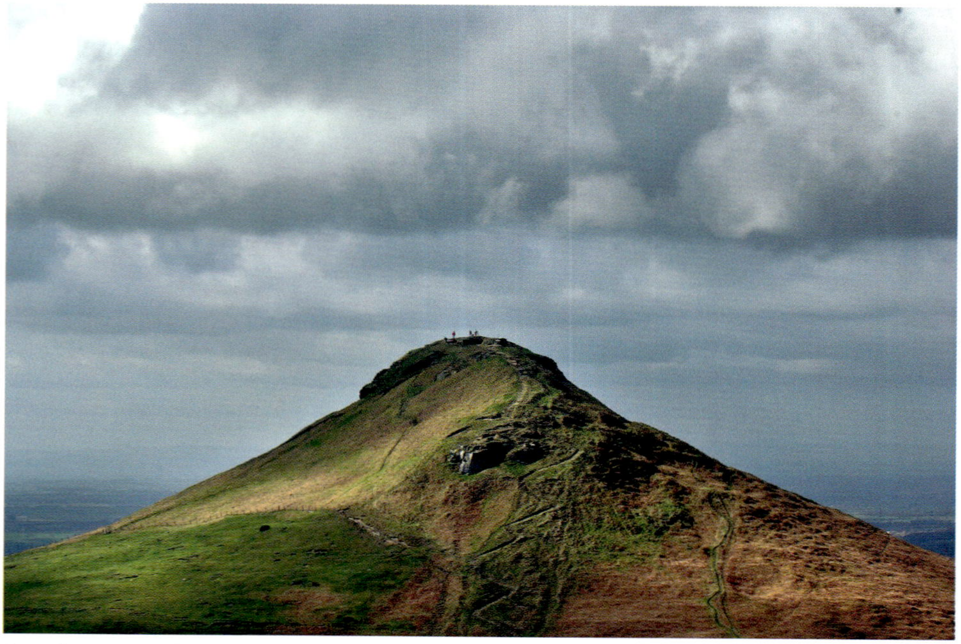

Rosebery Topping, a bit of wilderness near Teesside, is not particularly high, but there's a sense of achievement when getting to the top, especially in the teeth of a howling wind that sweeps over it from across the North Sea. (YPP2131)

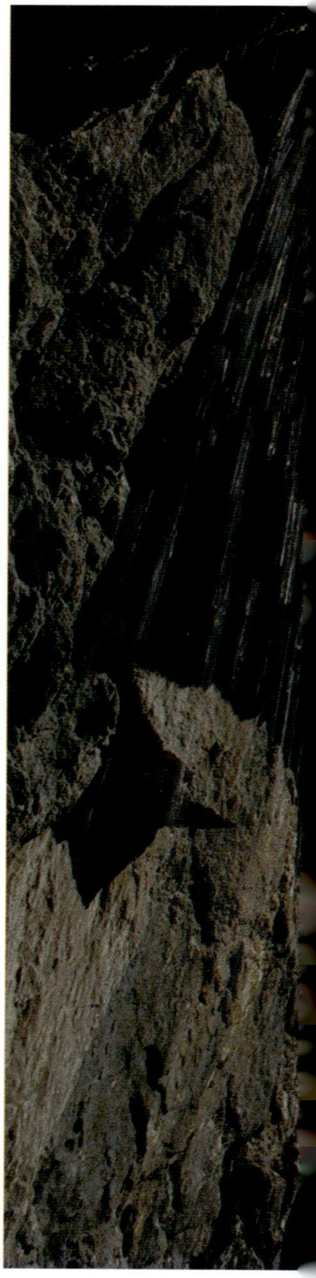

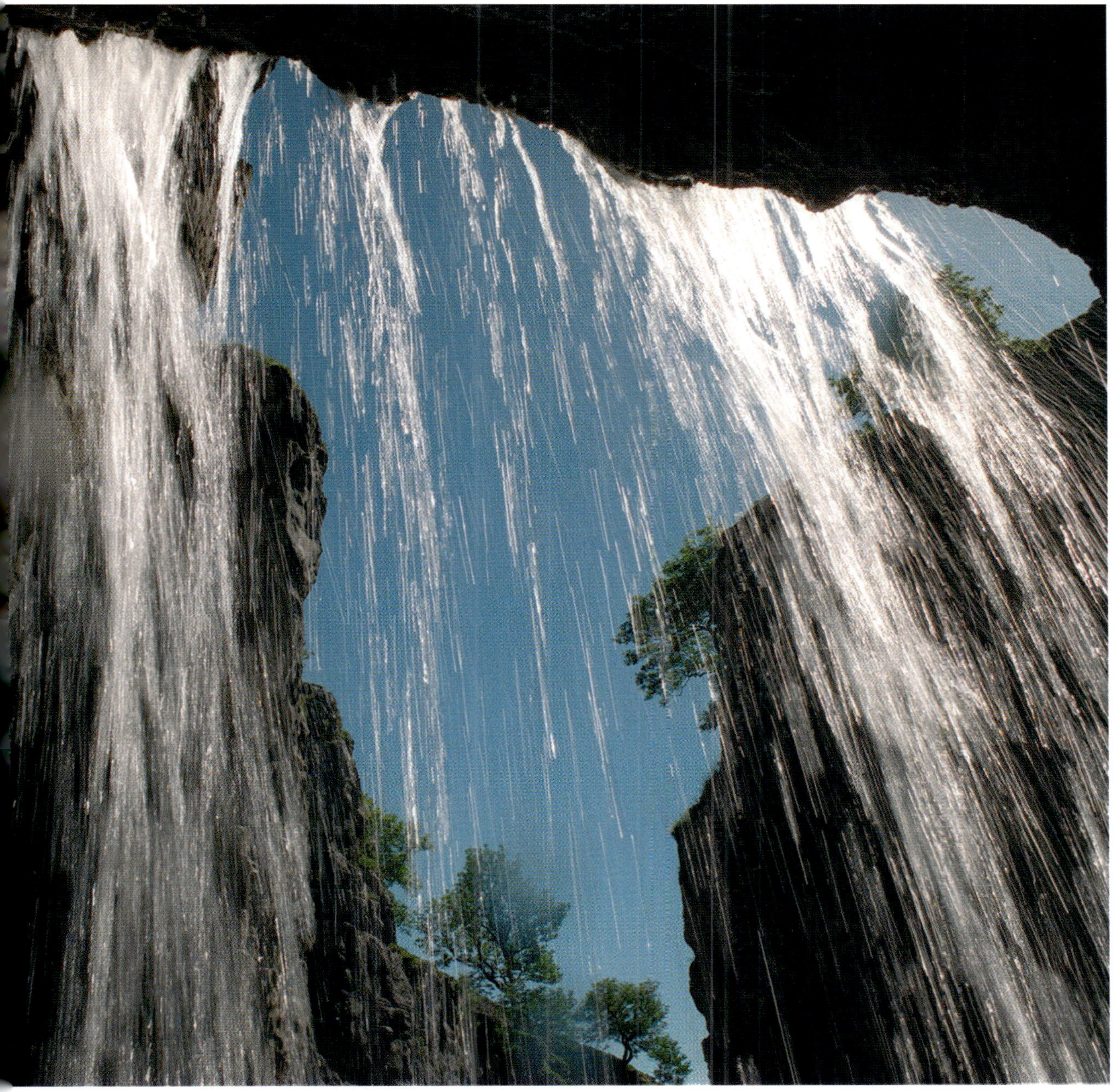

Water like spun glass forms a gleamirg curtain in this picture from behind the upper waterfall in Gordale Scar. (YPP2132)

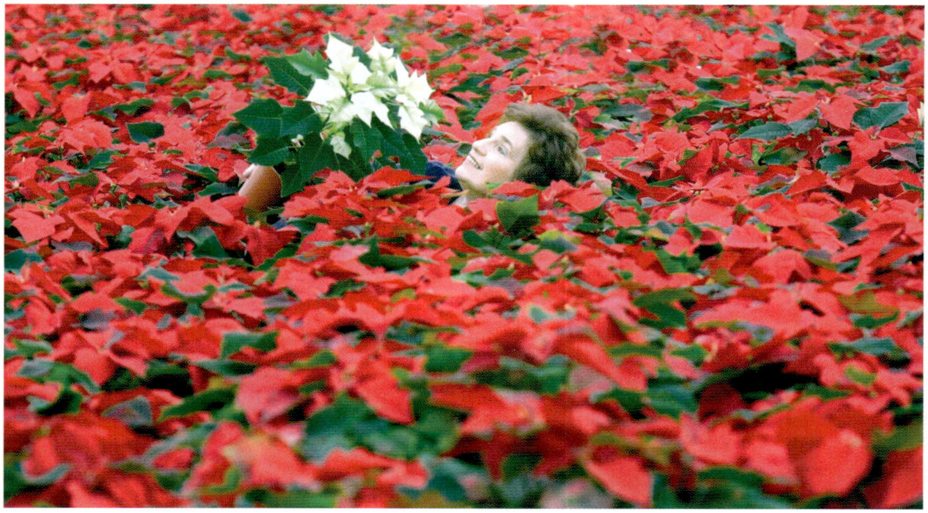

A sea of crimson Poinsettia at Leeds City Council's nursery - over 6,000 are grown for a Christmas display - and in their midst is Judy Goodburn, the Nursery Adminstrator, as though being kept afloat by a cream poinsettia bubble.
(YPP2133)

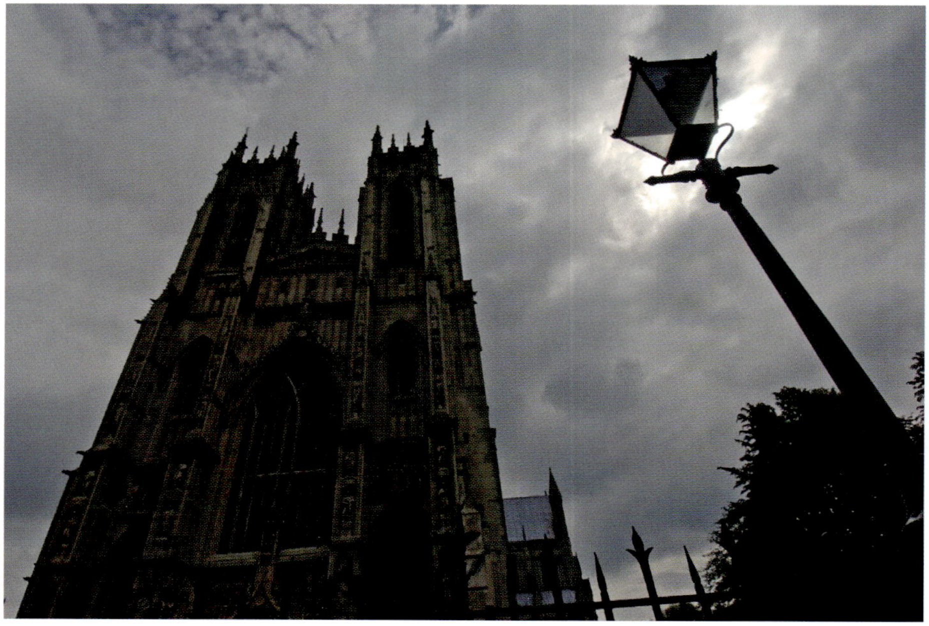

Beverley Minster where masonry experts had started strengthening work on the foundations of the 15th Century Percy Chapel.
(YPP2134)

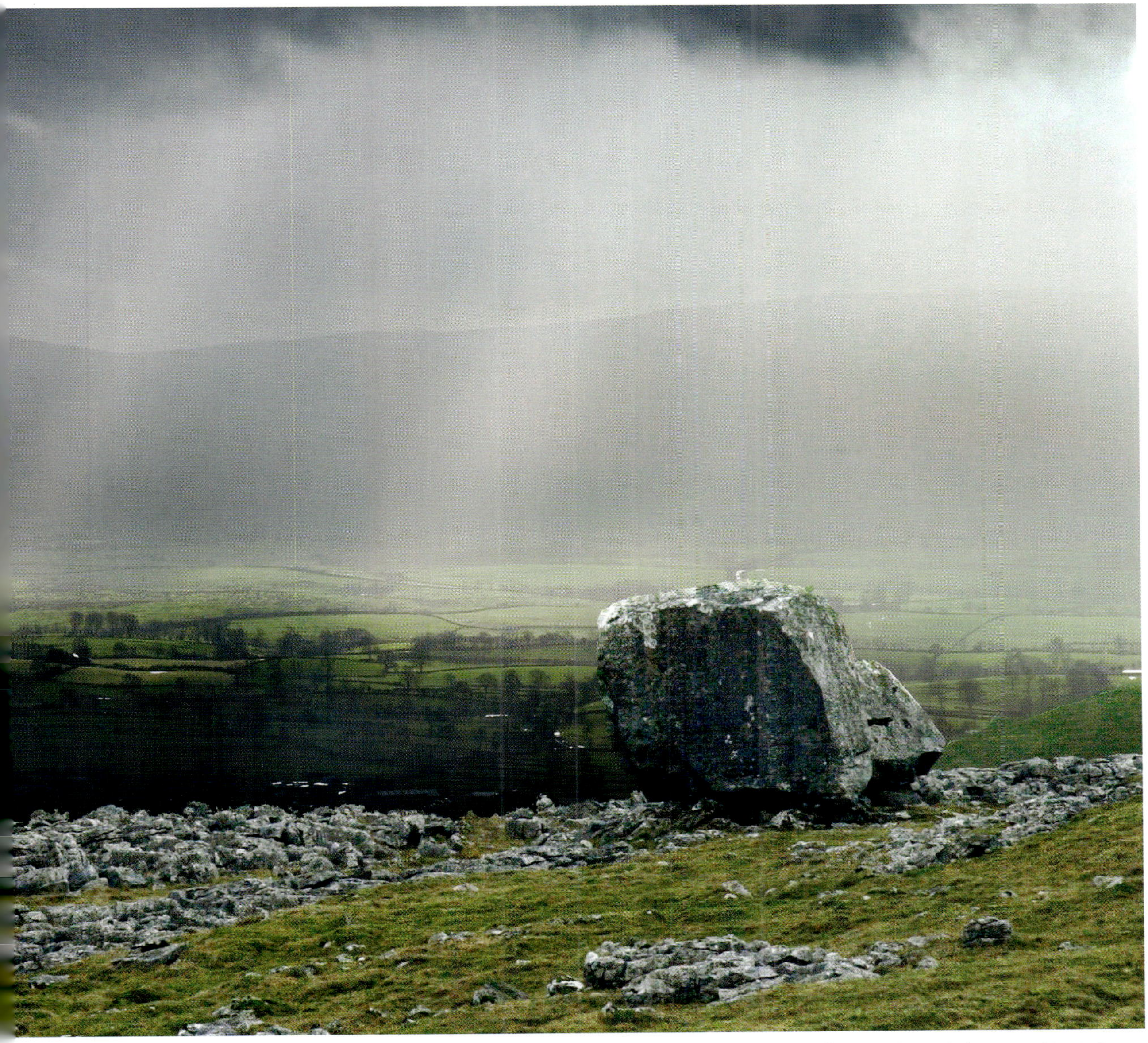

The Cheese Press Stone above Kingsdale near Ingleton.
(YPP2135)

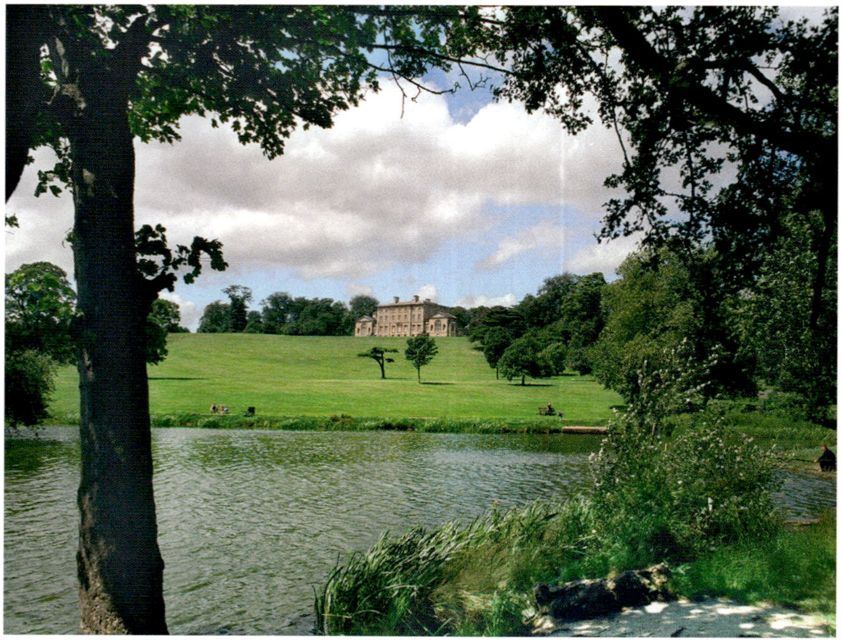

The picturesque lake and grounds at Cusworth Hall, Doncaster. (YPP2136)

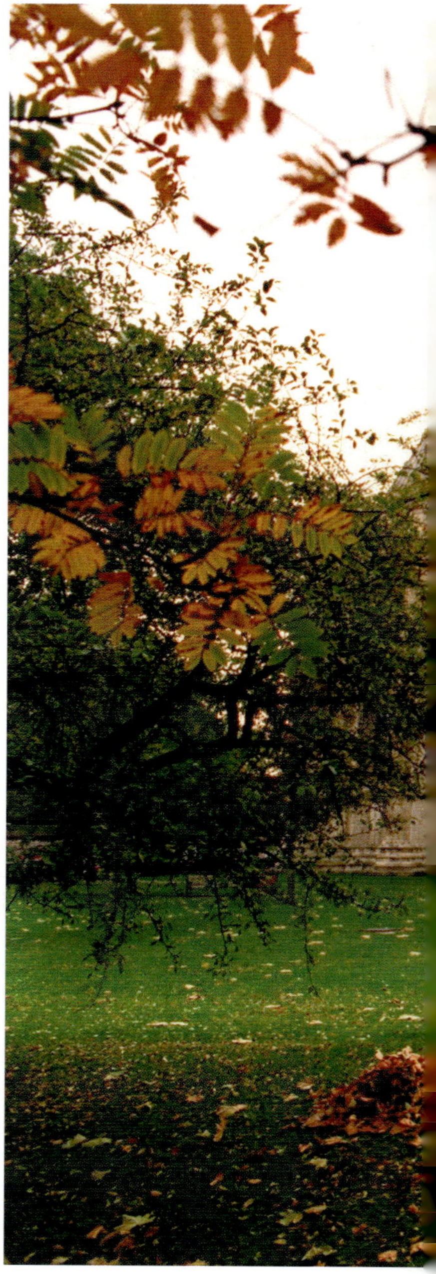

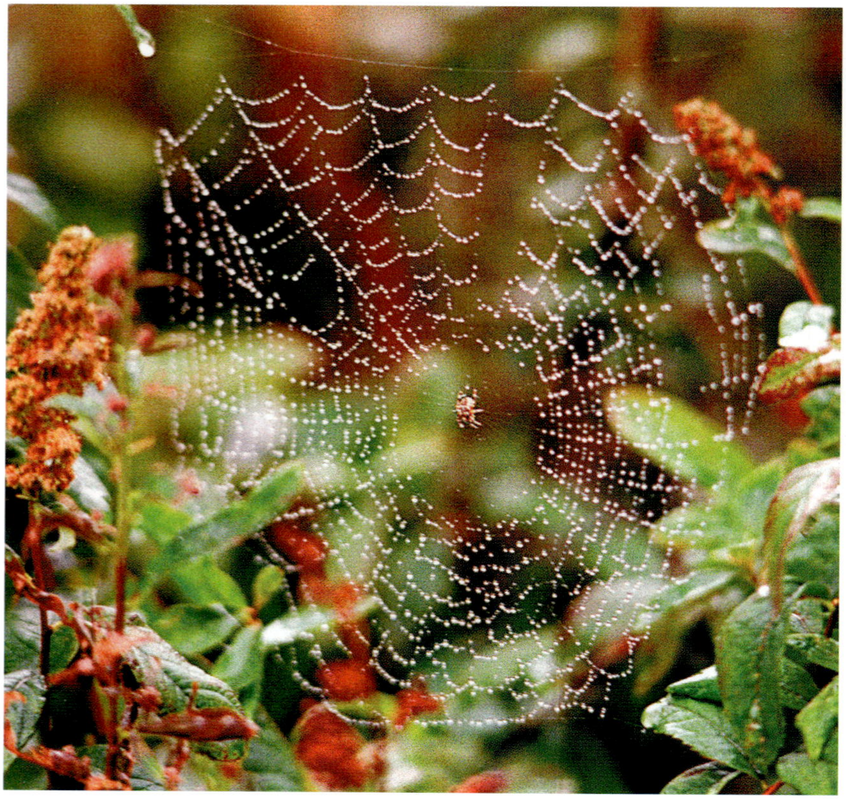

Autumn morning, and a spider fishes for flies with a bejewelled net in a Leeds garden. (YPP2137)

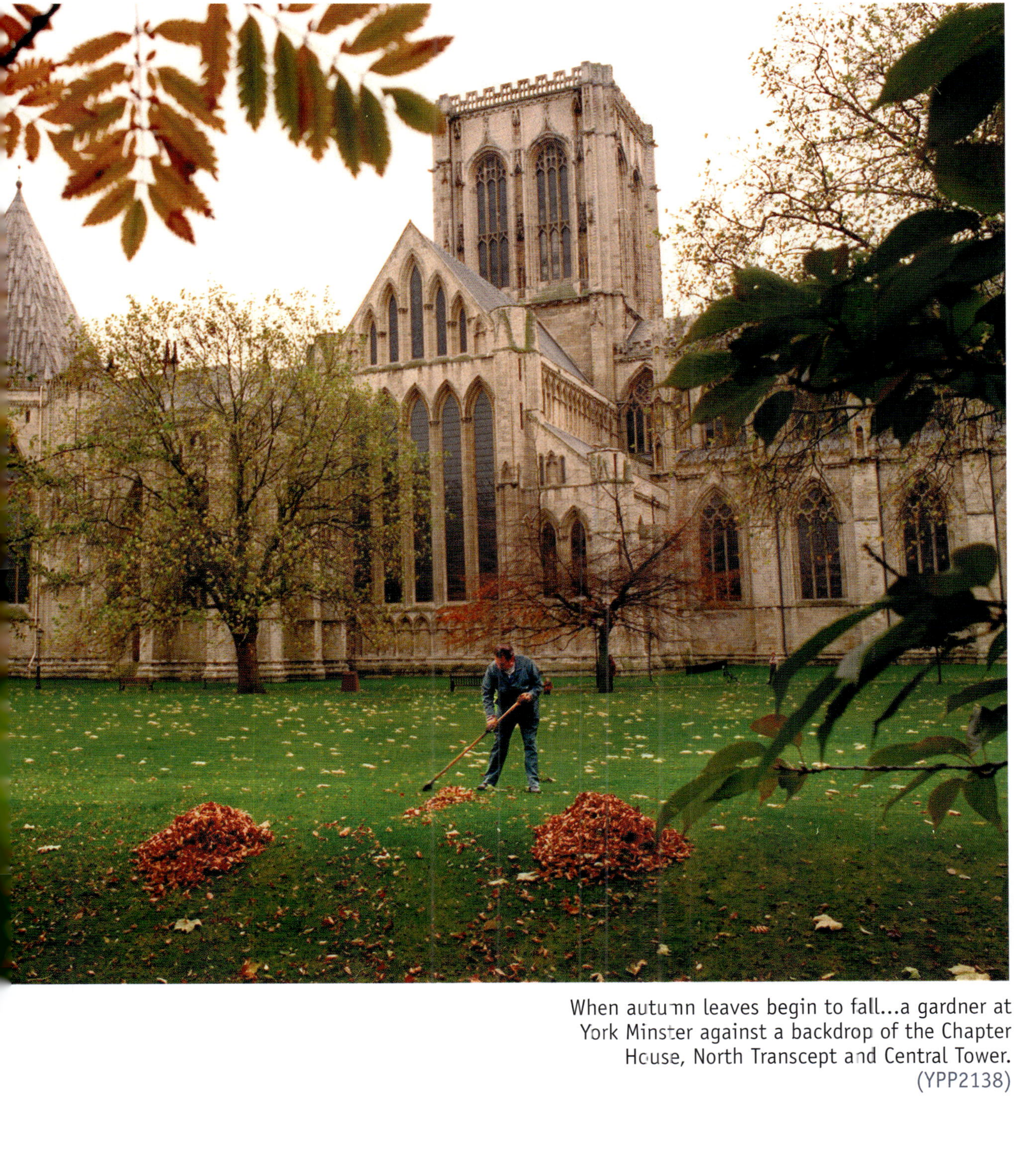

When autumn leaves begin to fall...a gardner at York Minster against a backdrop of the Chapter House, North Transcept and Central Tower. (YPP2138)

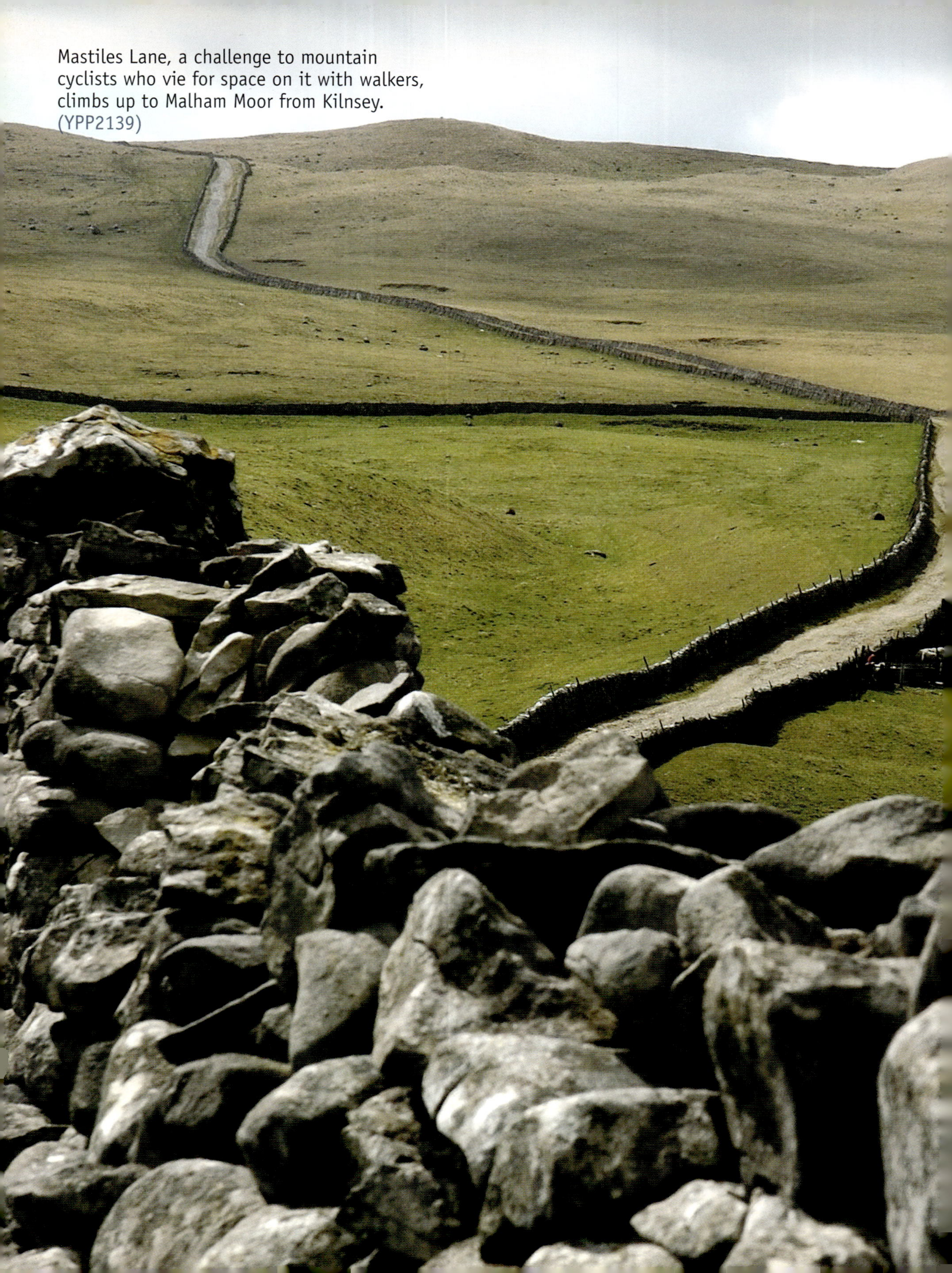

Mastiles Lane, a challenge to mountain cyclists who vie for space on it with walkers, climbs up to Malham Moor from Kilnsey. (YPP2139)

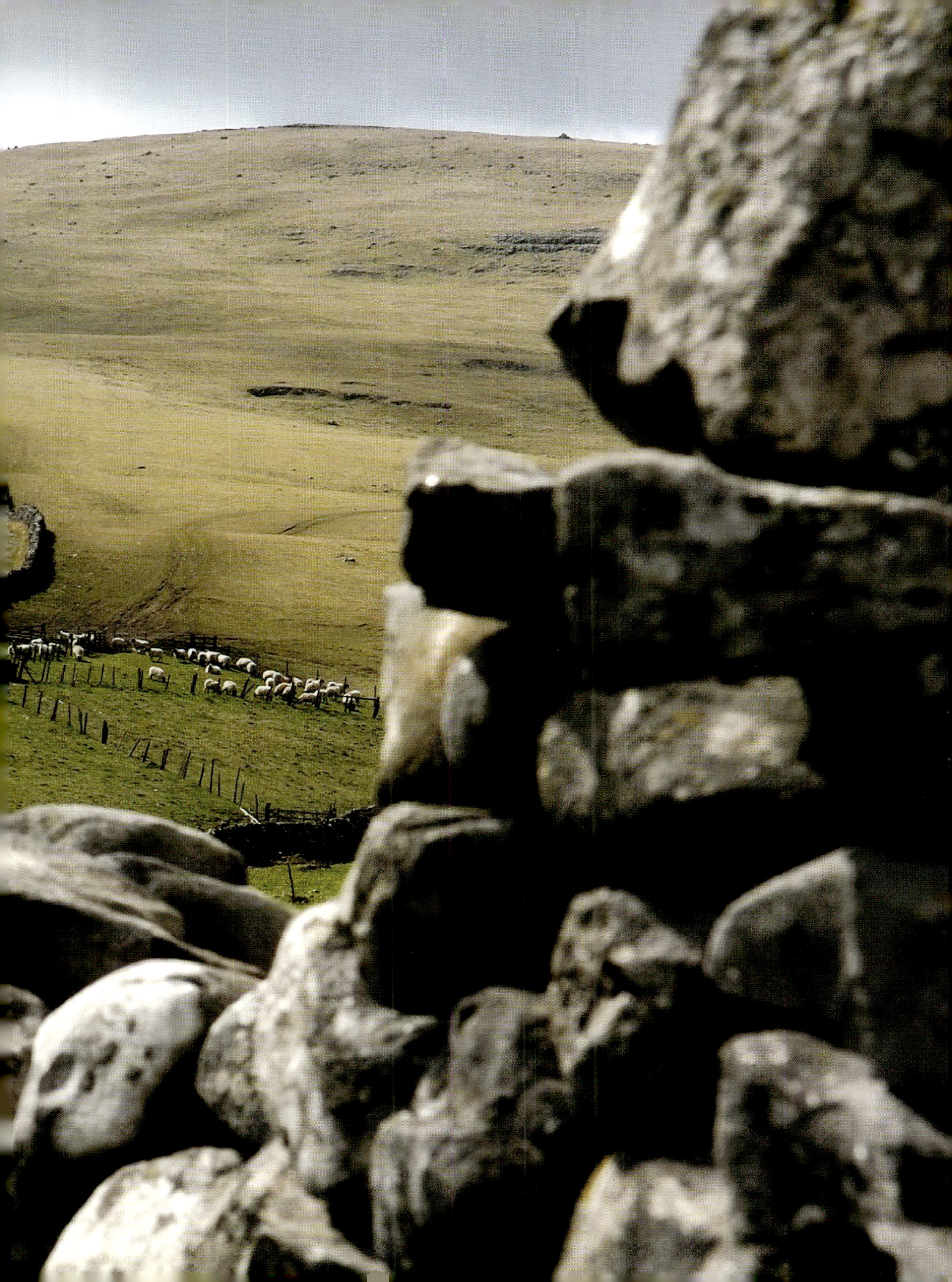

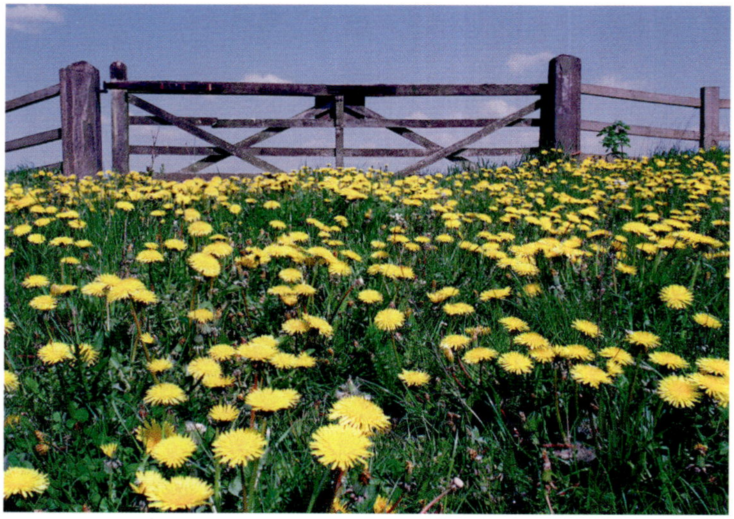

A host of golden dandelions in Bramham Park mark the gateway to summer as day by day the sun climbs higher and lingers longer in the sky. (YPP2140)

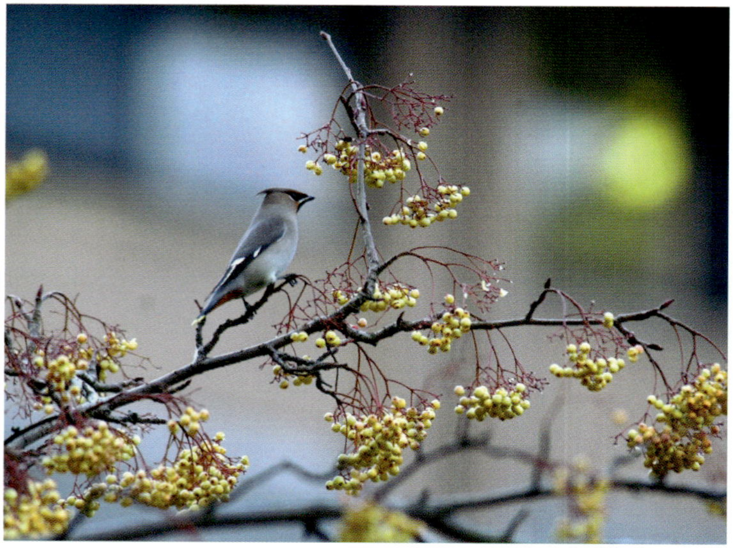

Wax Wings from Scandinavia feast on berries outside Leeds General Infirmary. (YPP2141)

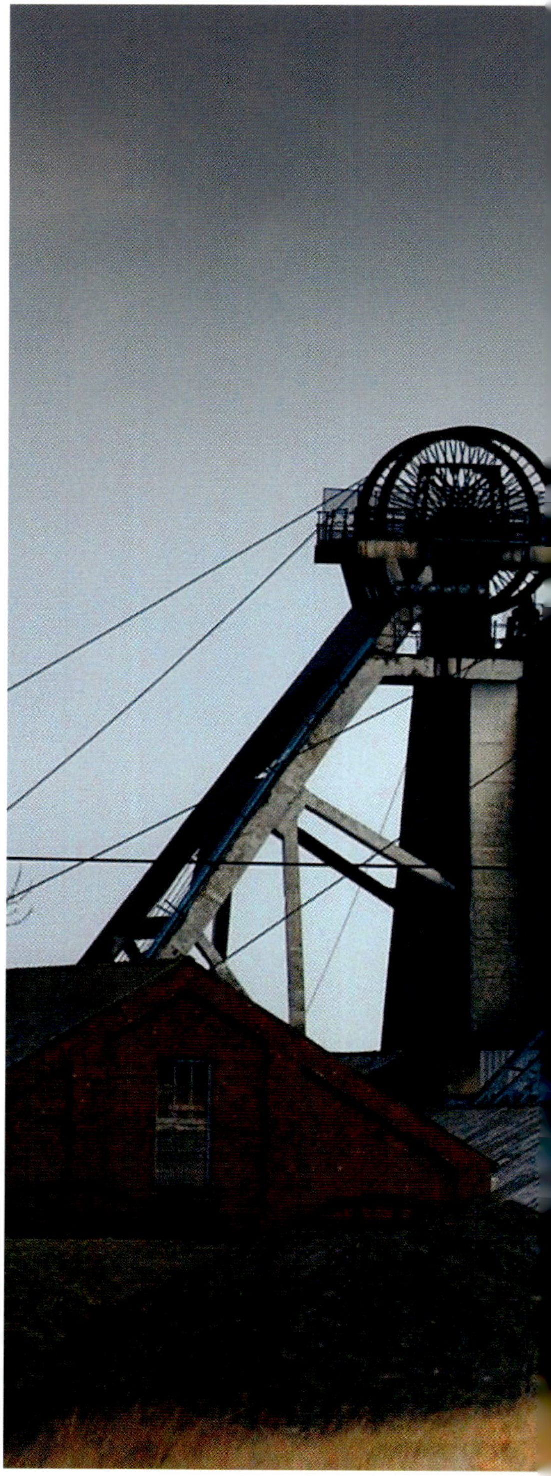

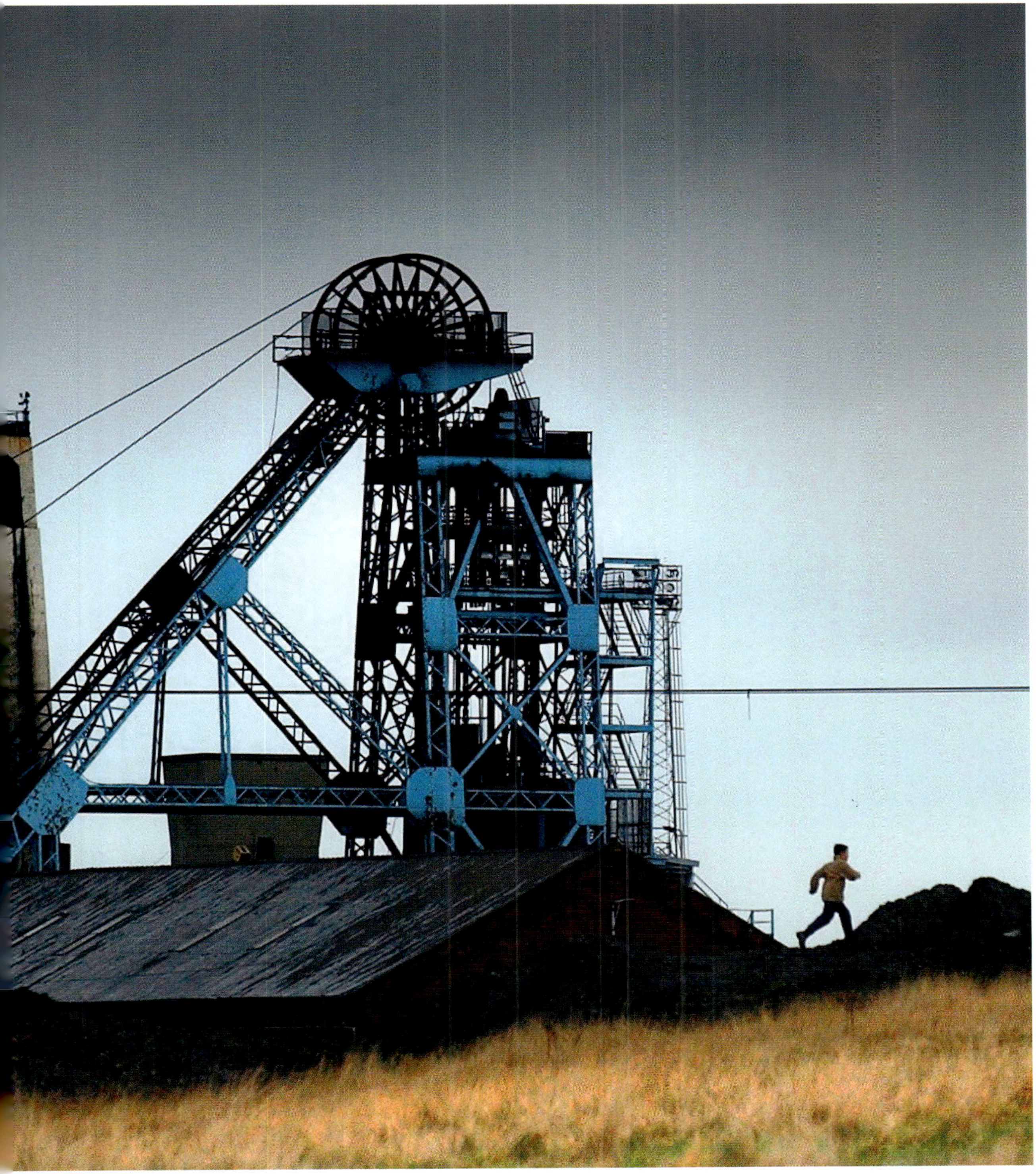

The disused but immaculately-preserved pit-head winding gear at Hatfield Main Colliery, Stainforth, near Doncaster, provides an industrialised backdrop to the boy running across old spoil heaps. (YPP2142)

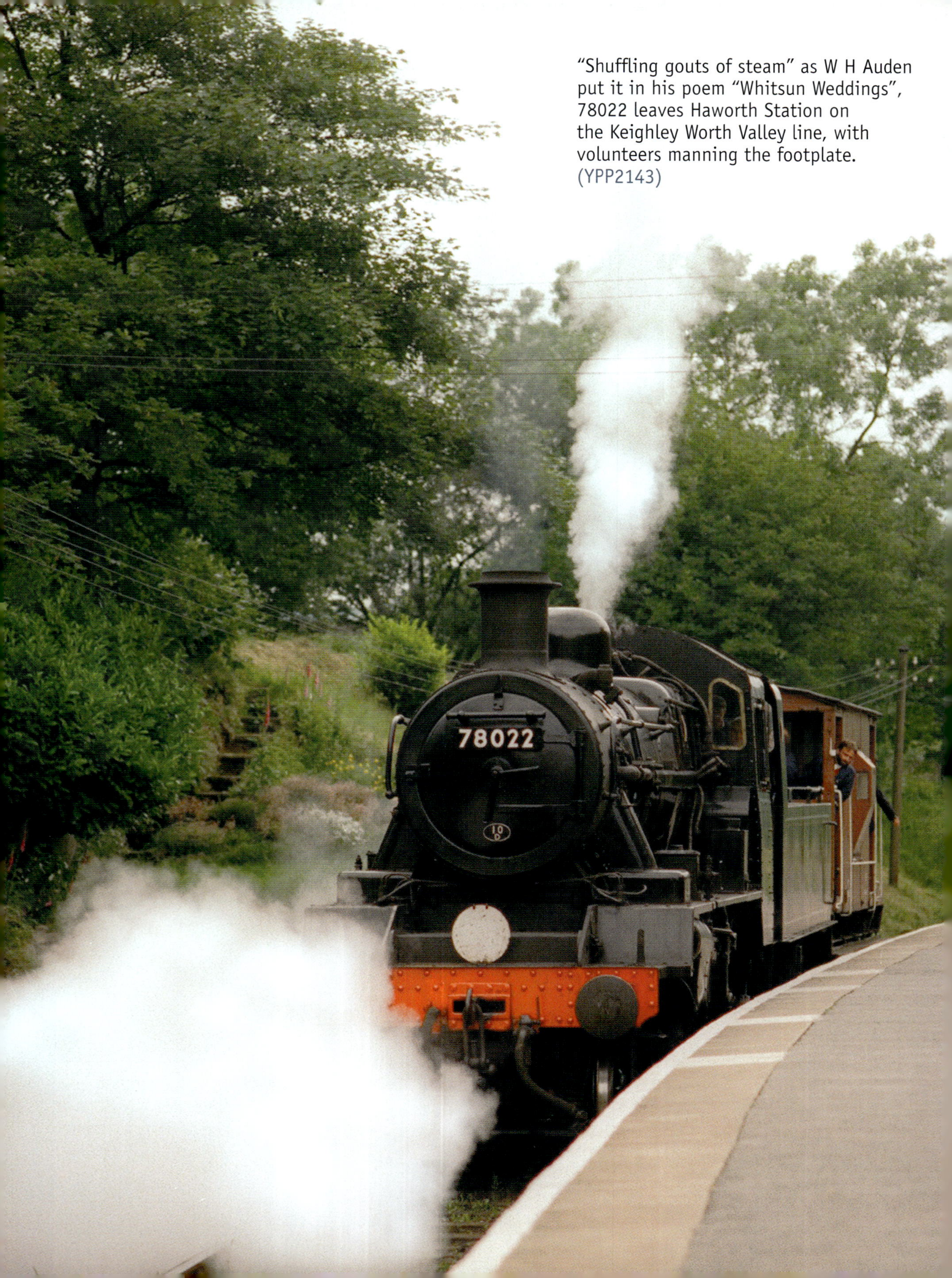

"Shuffling gouts of steam" as W H Auden put it in his poem "Whitsun Weddings", 78022 leaves Haworth Station on the Keighley Worth Valley line, with volunteers manning the footplate. (YPP2143)

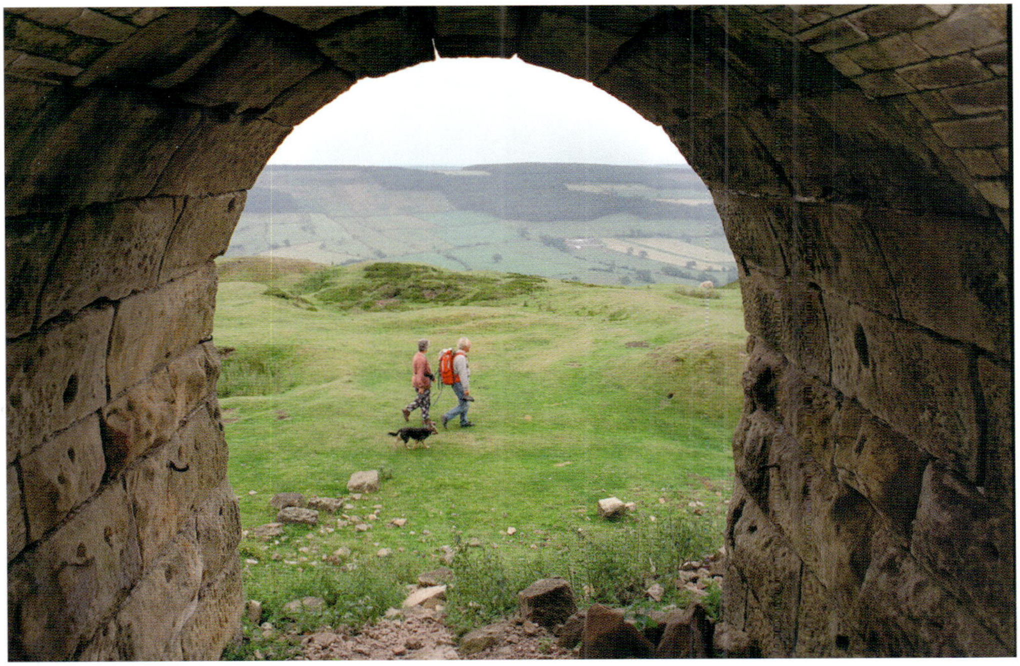

Looking out of one of the old lime kilns at the top of Rosedale Chimney. (YPP2144)

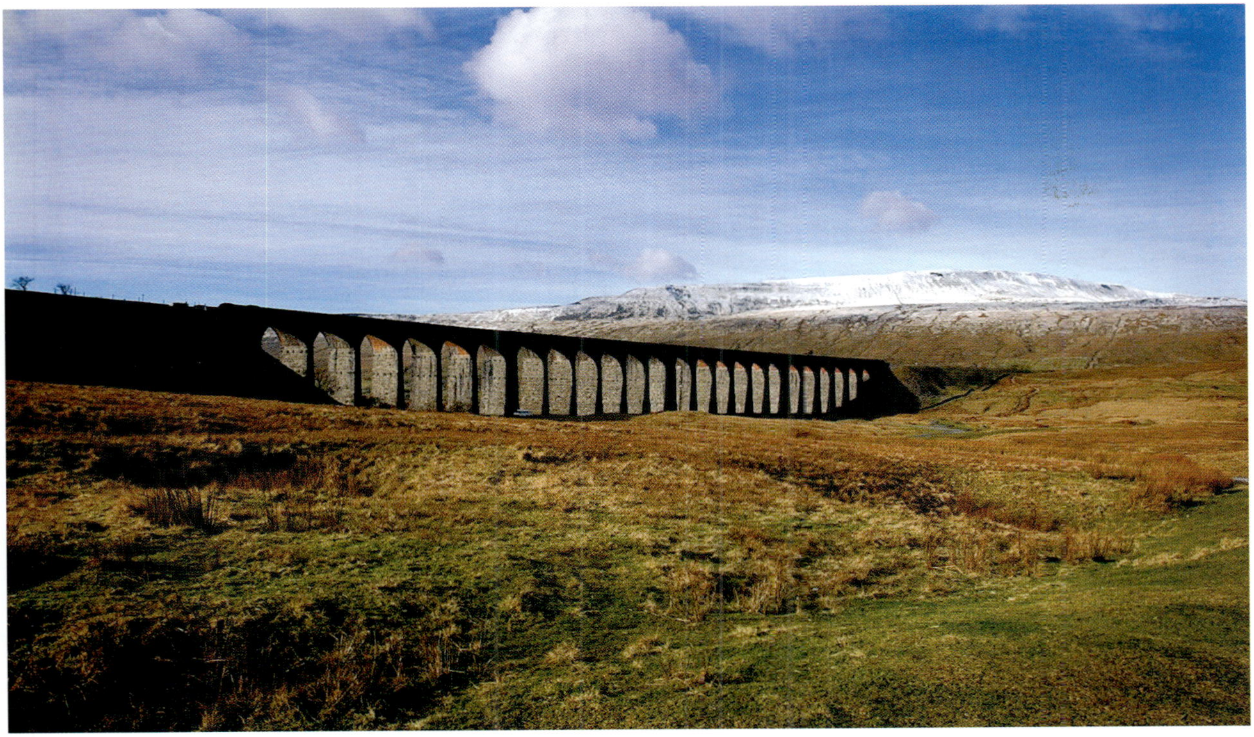

Ribblehead Viaduct spans upper Wensleydale with its 24 arches, and beyond lies Whernside recumbent under a dusting of snow. (YPP2145)

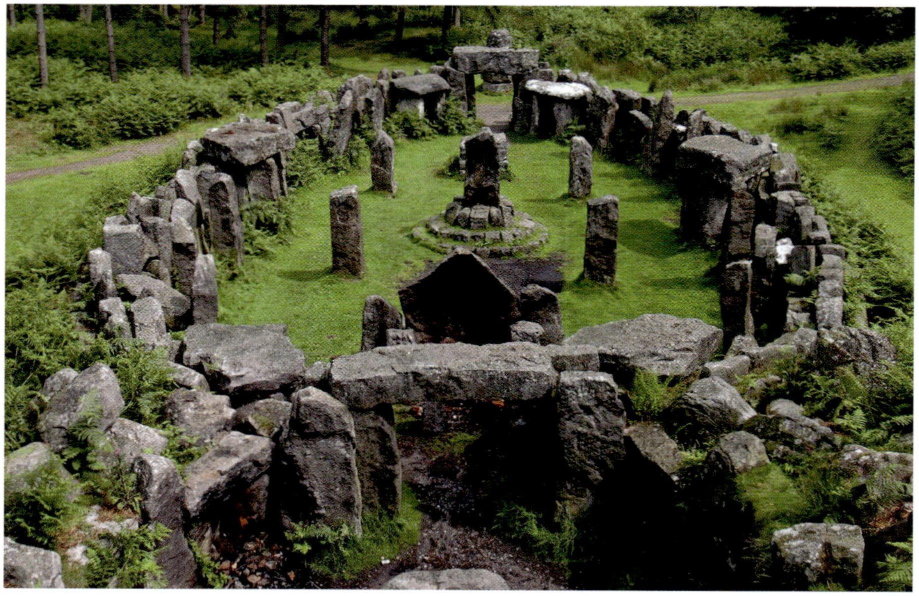

'The Druids Temple', a Folly built by William Danby in the late 1700s on the Swinton Estate near Masham, North Yorkshire. (YPP2146)

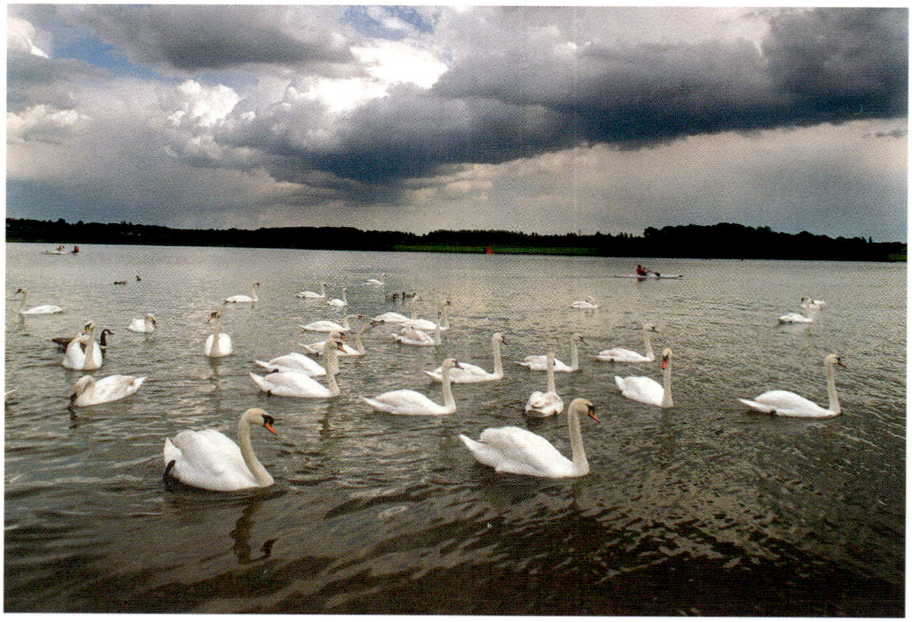

Pugneys Country Park, Wakefield, once an open-cast mine, is now loved by waterfowl, birdwatchers, walkers and water sports enthusiasts. (YPP2147)

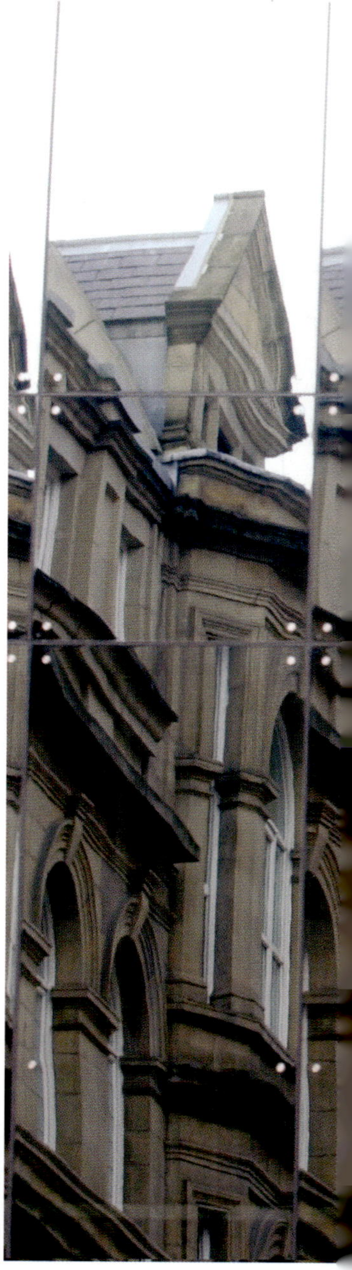

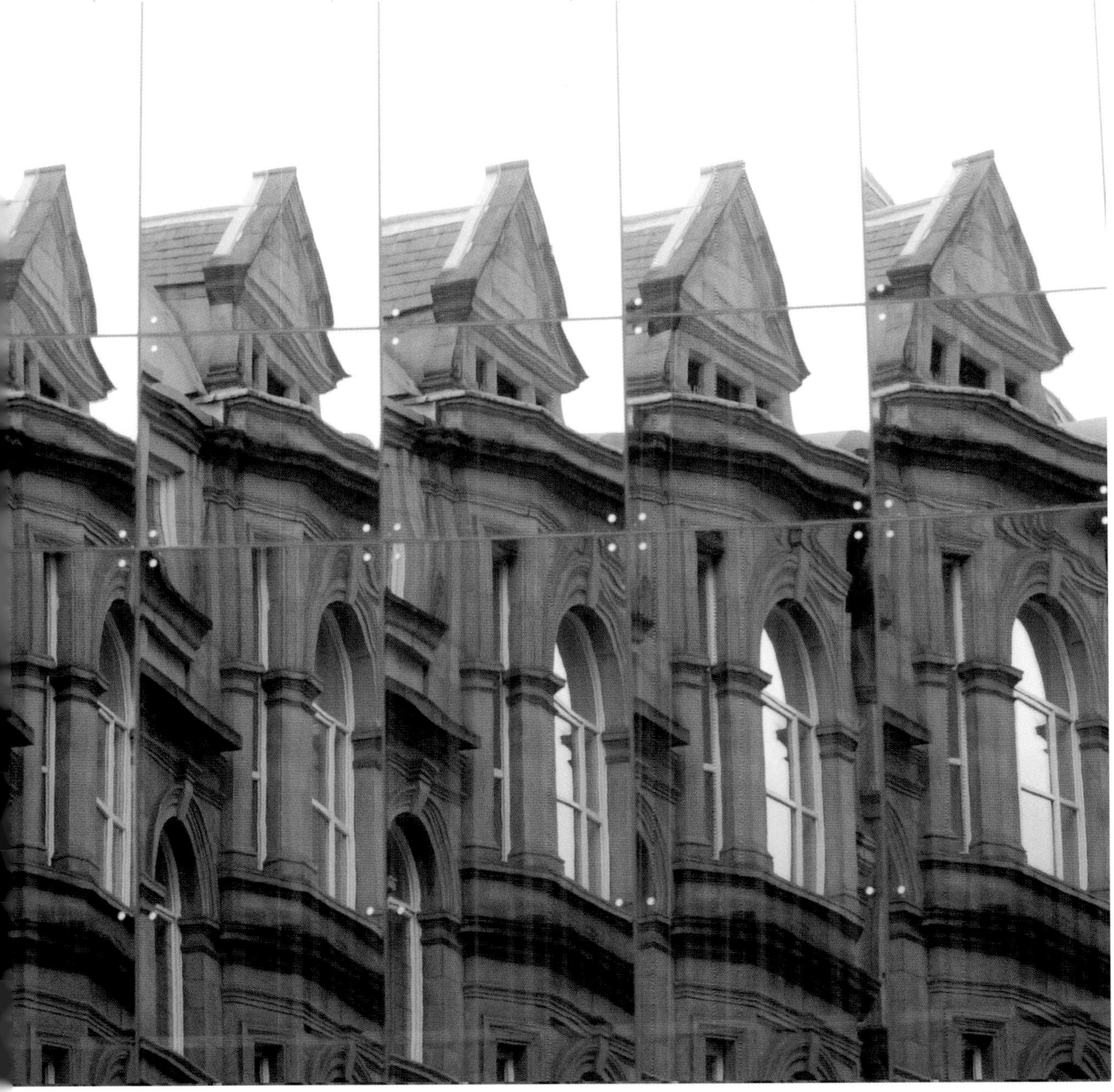

Reflections in the windows of Sterling House off Boer Lane.
(YPP2148)

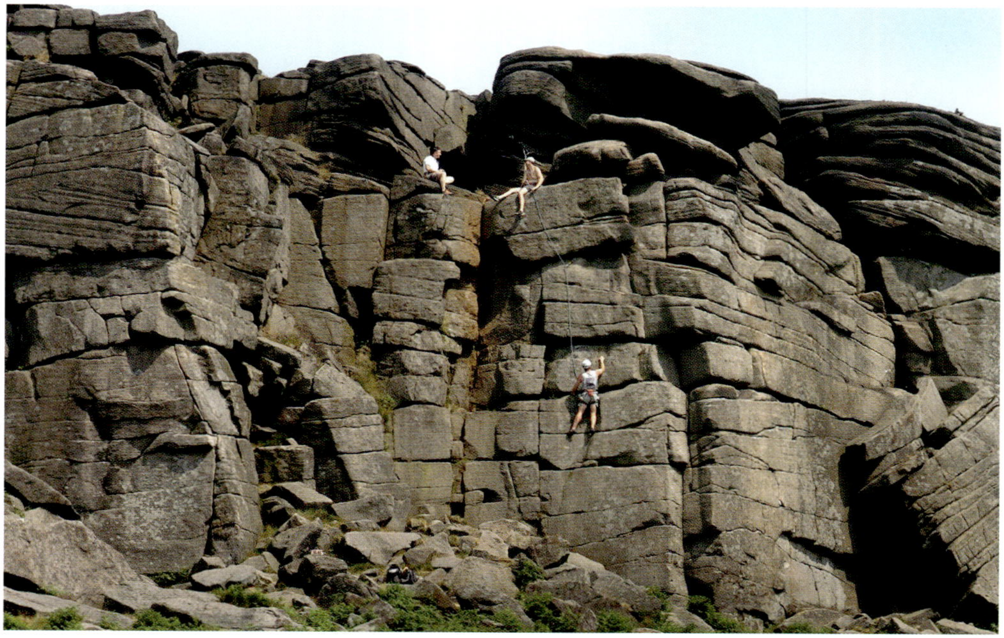

Climbers test their nerves and their skill on the rocky outcrop at Stanage Edge near Hathersage in the Peak District. (YPP2149)

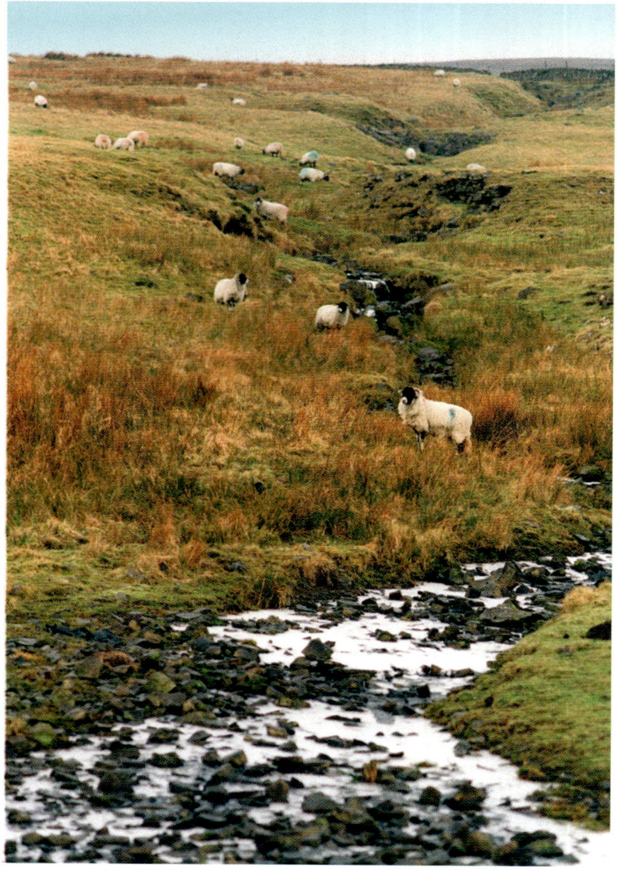

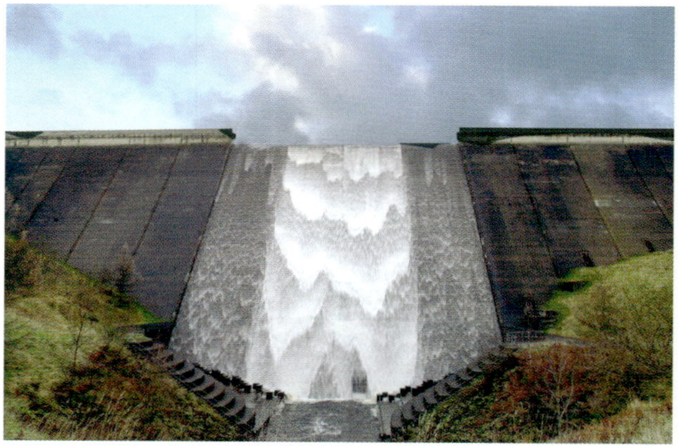

Booth Wood Dam near Ripponden in the Ryburn Valley, the dam wall is 1,160 feet long and 148 feet thick holding back 800 million gallons of water. (YPP2150)

Tough customers are these sheep, and canny too. They need to be if they are to survive up here above Halton Gill in the high Dales. (YPP2151)

"The Reindeer Cavern" at Stump Cross Caves, newly lit to illuminate the amazing formations created by steadily dripping water over a great expanse of time. (YPP2152)

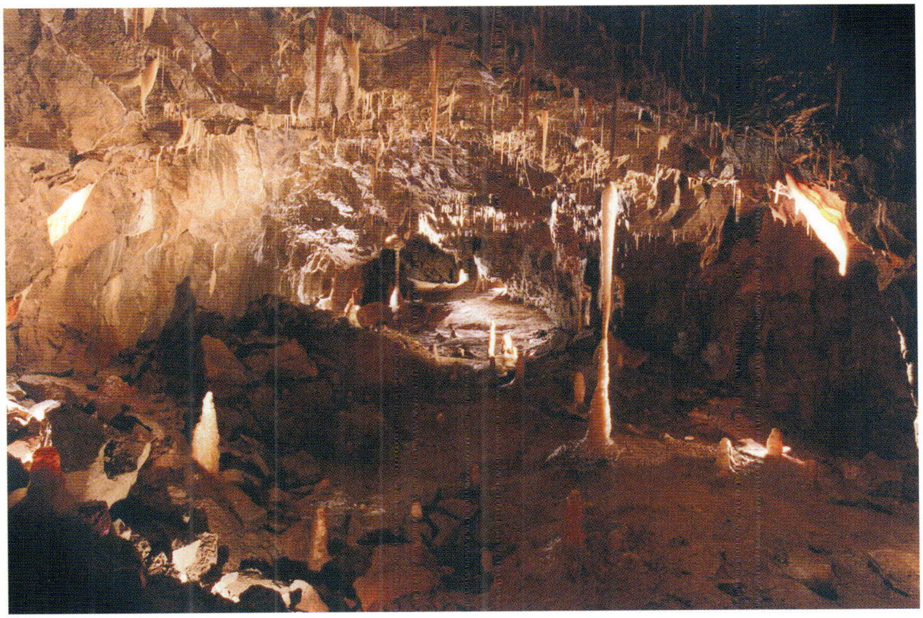

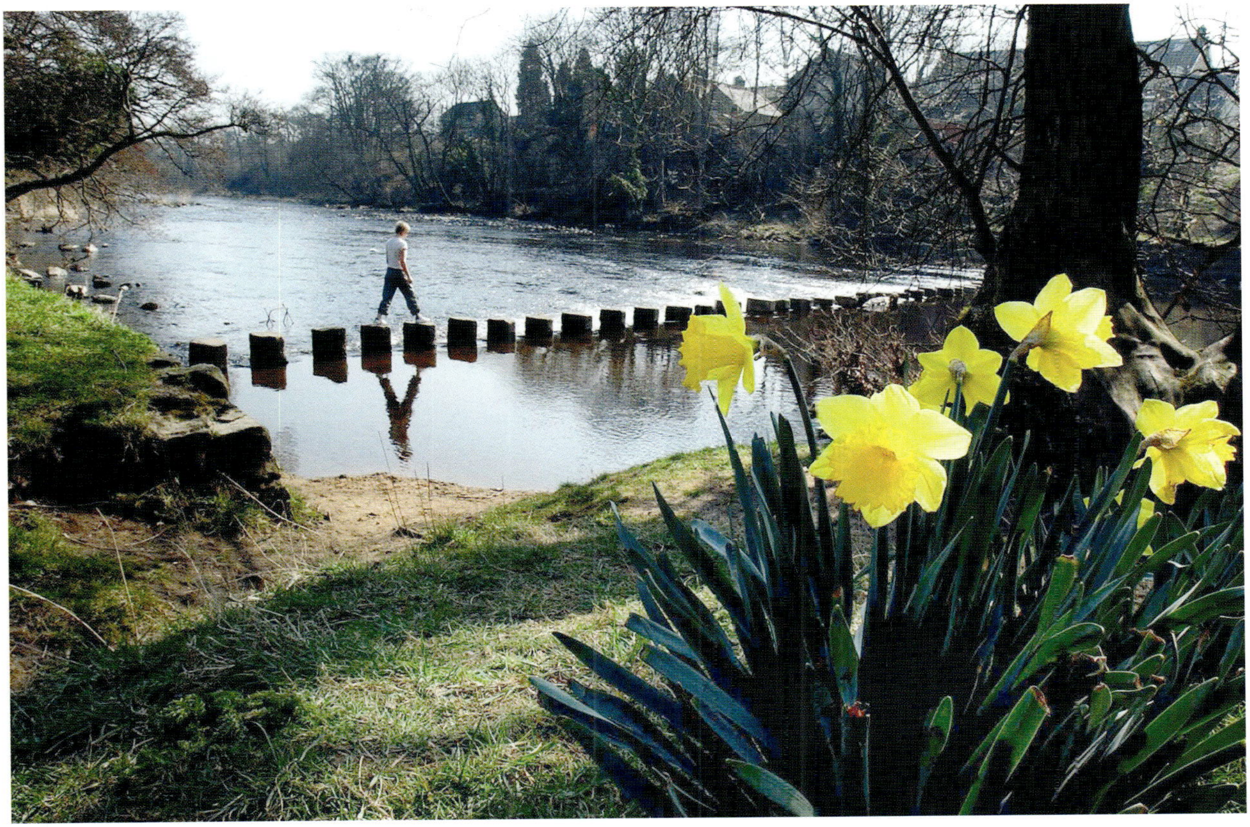

Warm weather and daffodils show spring has arrived at the stepping stones that cross the River Wharfe at Denton. (YPP2153)

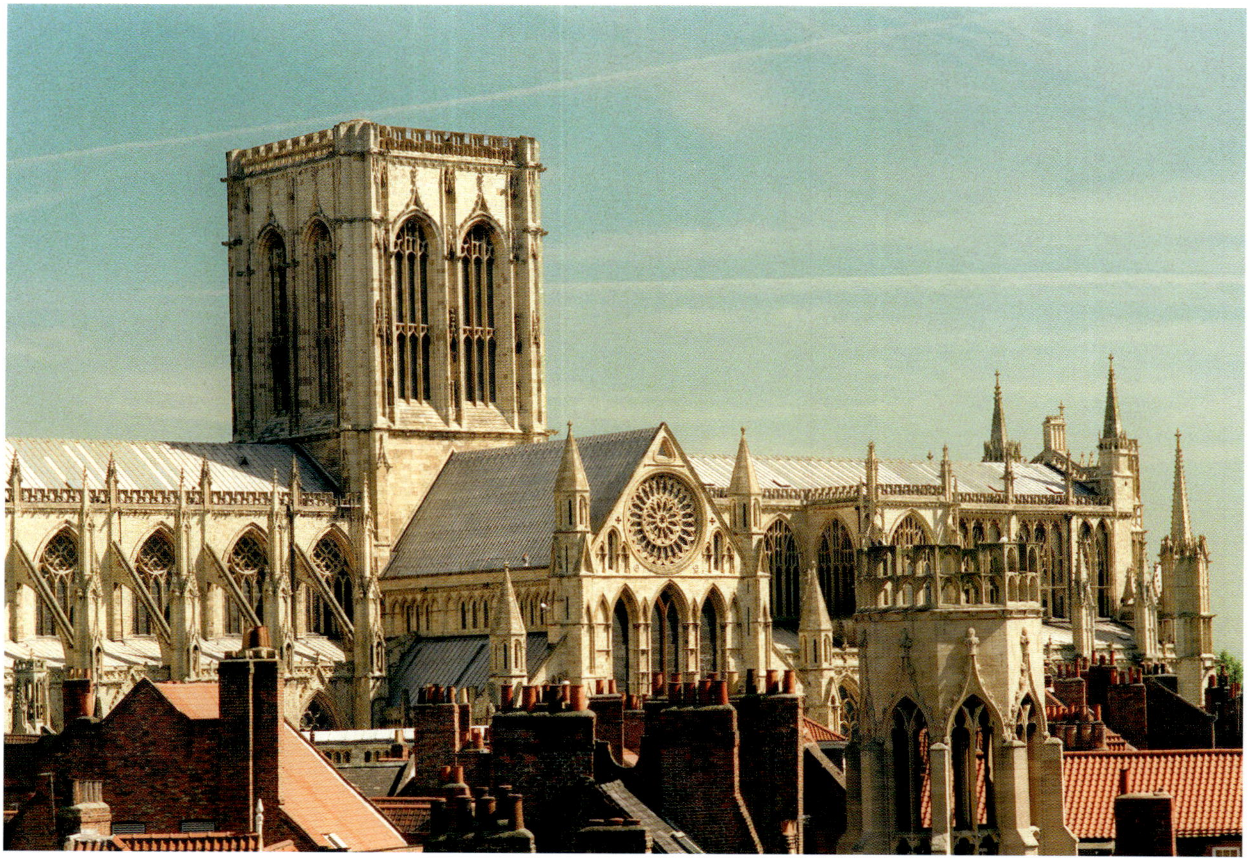

Viewed from the top of Mansion House, York Minster rises imperiously above a crowd of chimneys on a sea of roofs. (YPP2154)

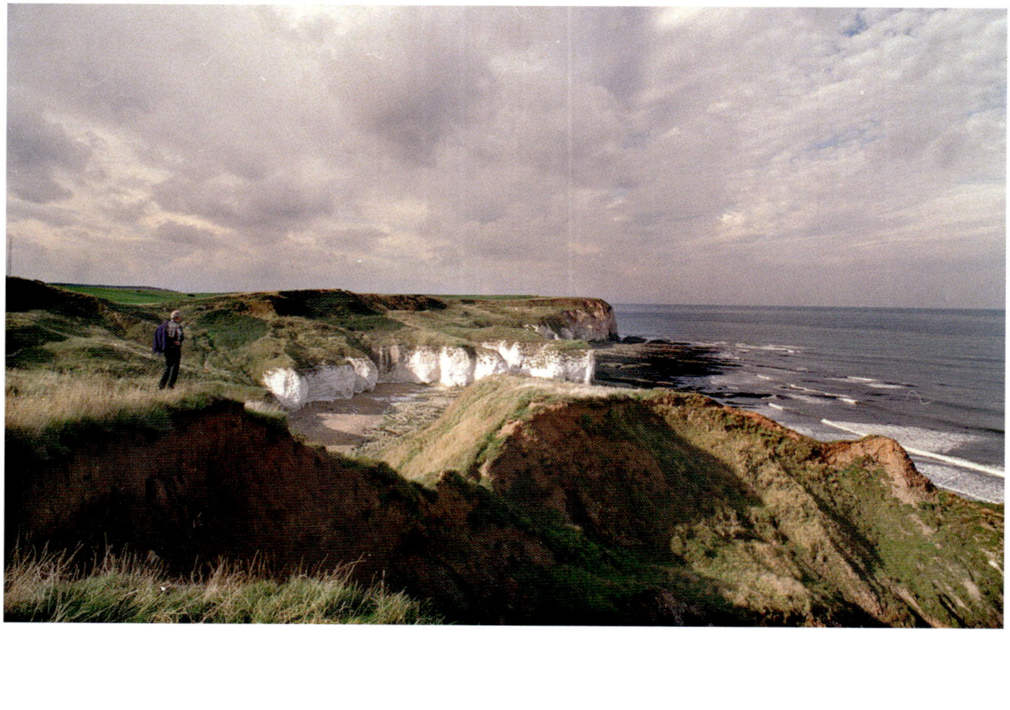

The white cliffs of Flamborough, Bridlington. (YPP2155)

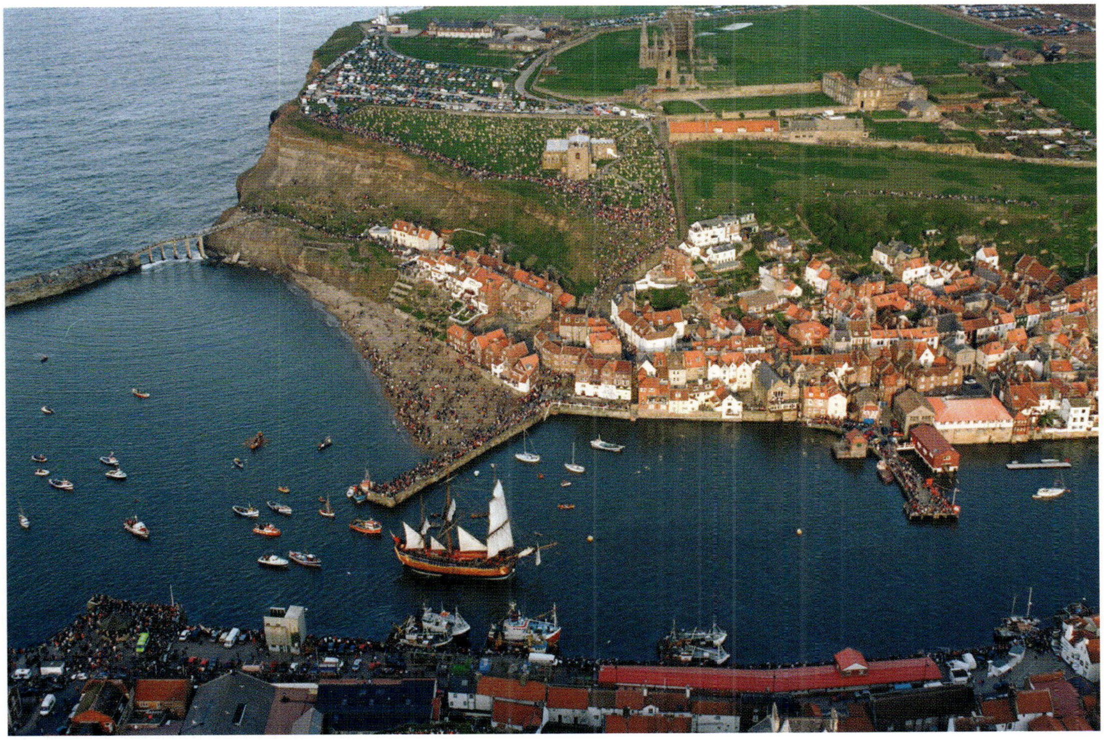

The new Endeavour, built in Australia, arrives in Whitby Harbour - and no-one who saw it will forget it. (YPP2156)

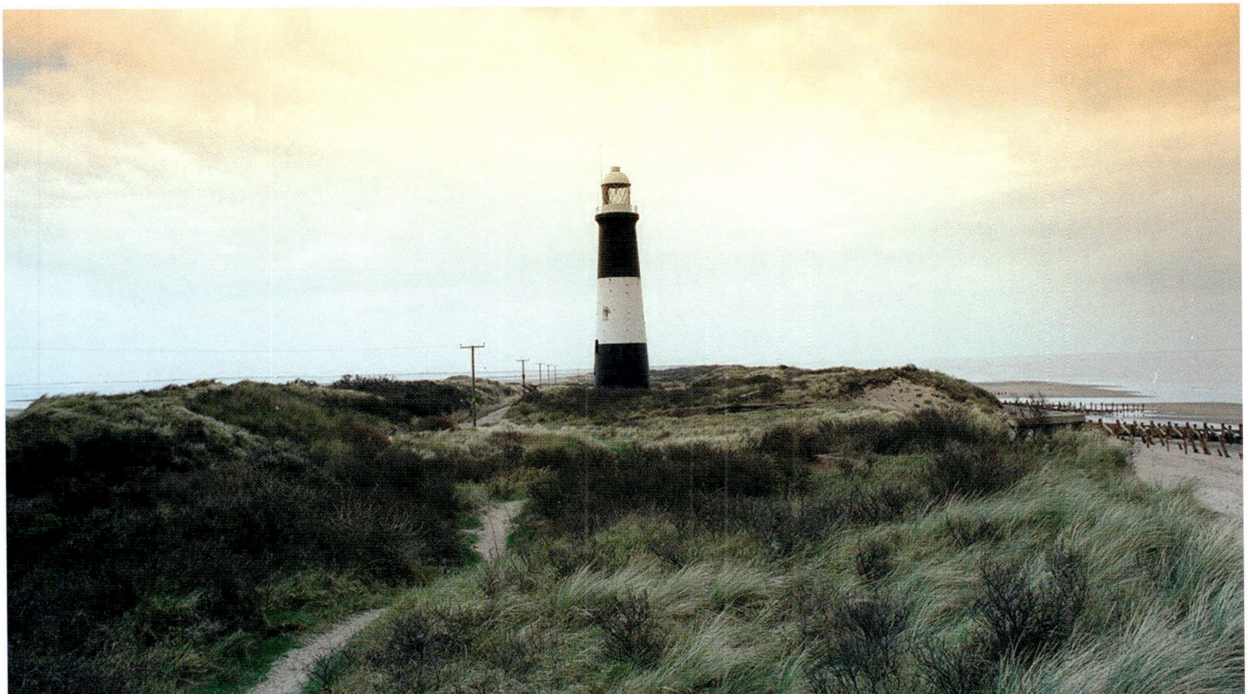

The former lighthouse at Spurn Head. (YPP2157)

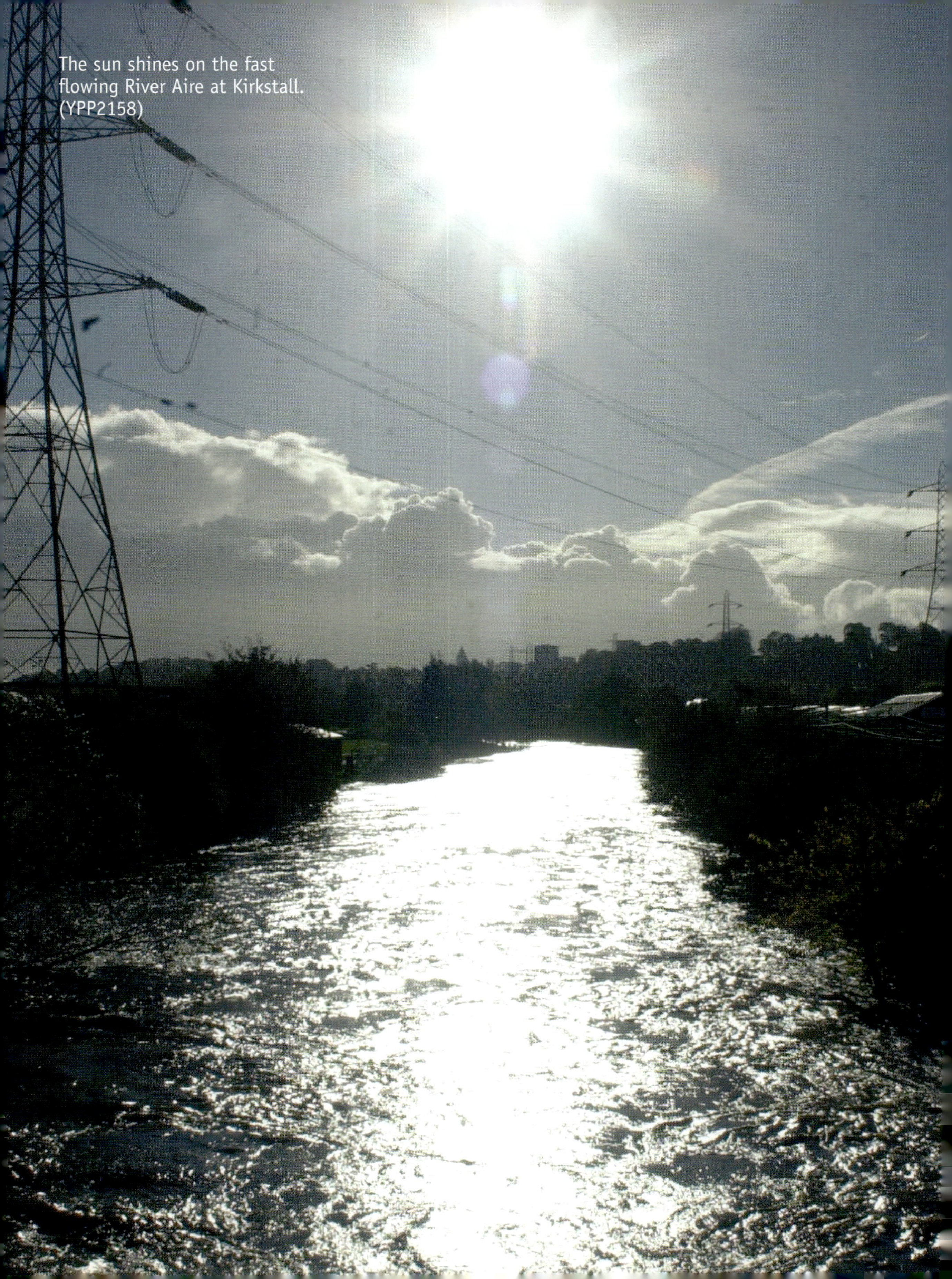

The sun shines on the fast flowing River Aire at Kirkstall. (YPP2158)

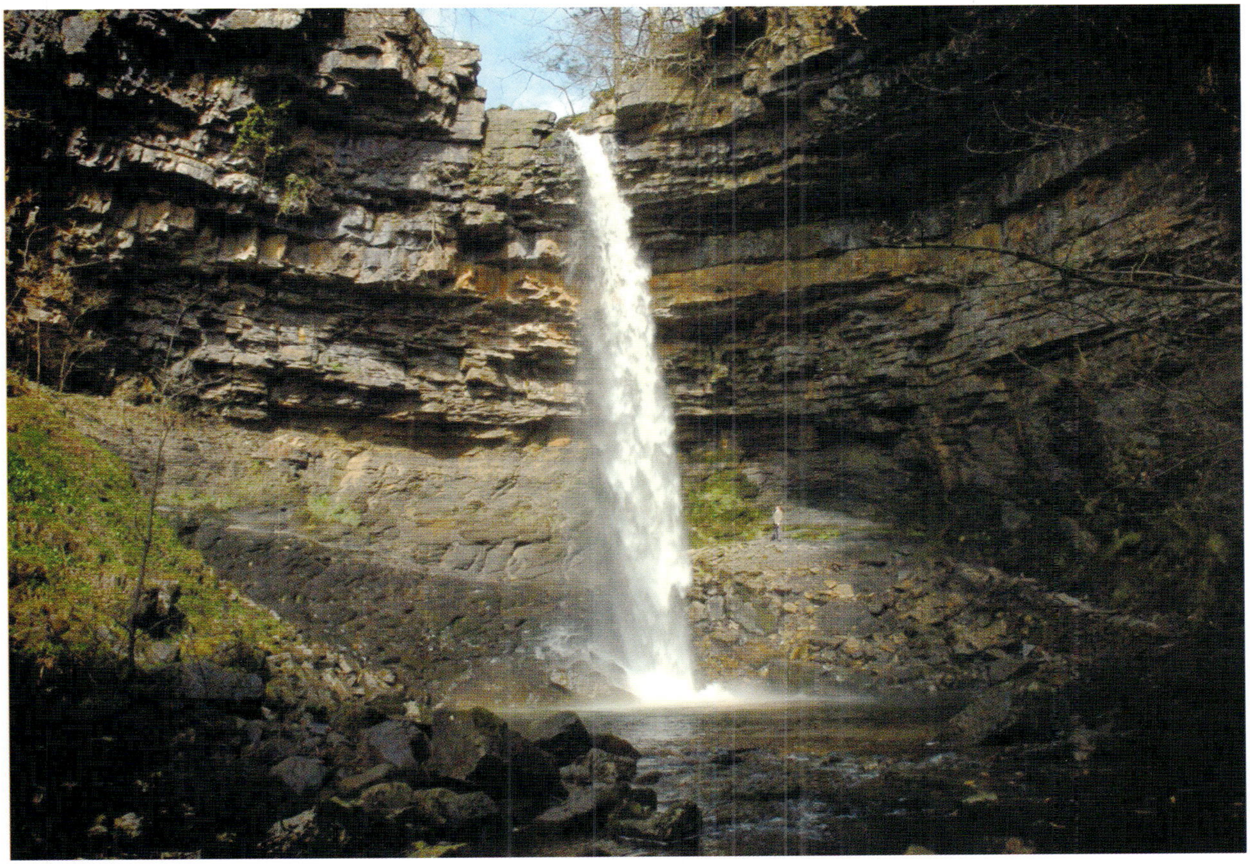

Dwarfed by his surroundings, a visitor takes a closer look at Hardraw Force, at 100 feet, the highest unbroken waterfall in England. (YPP2159)

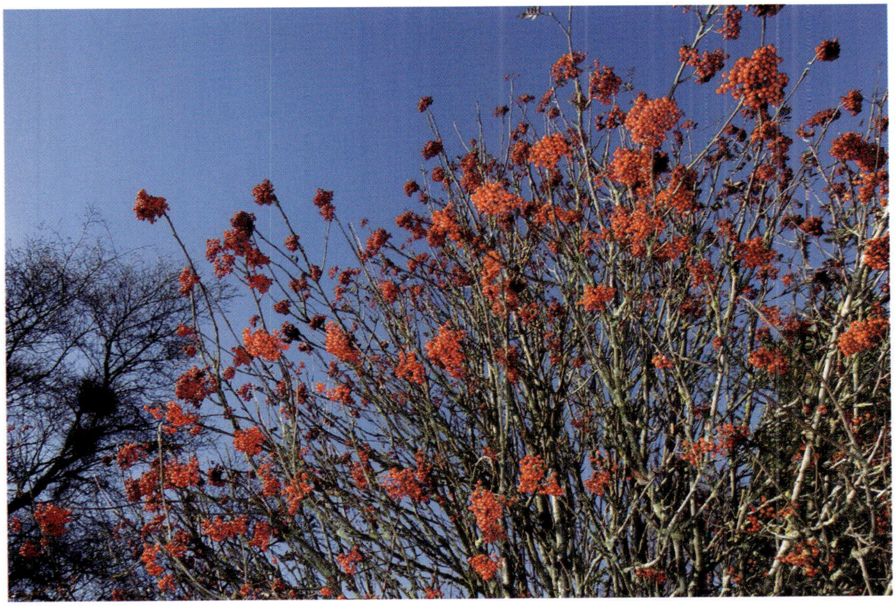

A splash of autumnal colour ... These berries are hanging on at Brimham Rocks near Pateley Bridge. (YPP2160)

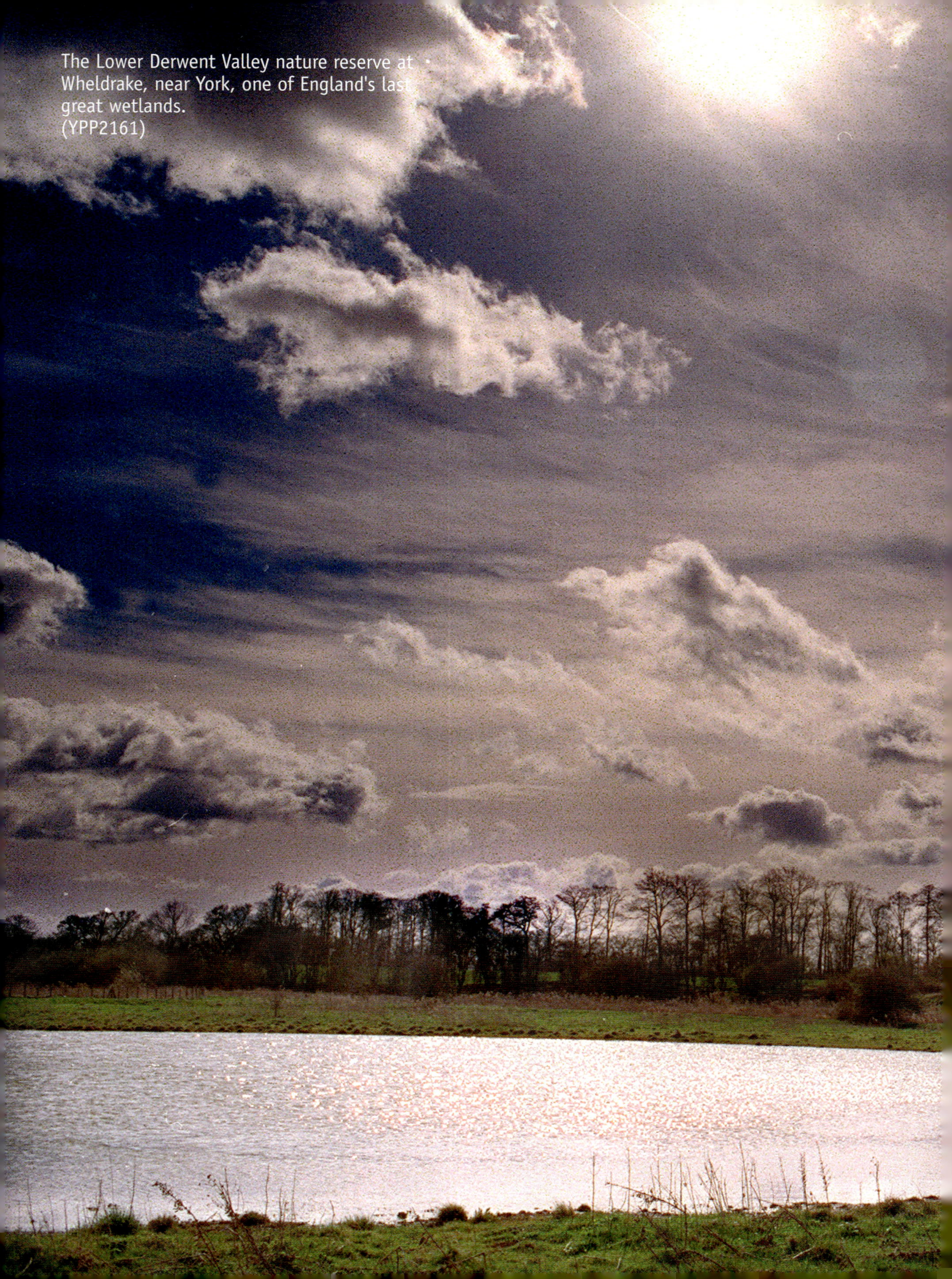

The Lower Derwent Valley nature reserve at Wheldrake, near York, one of England's last great wetlands.
(YPP2161)

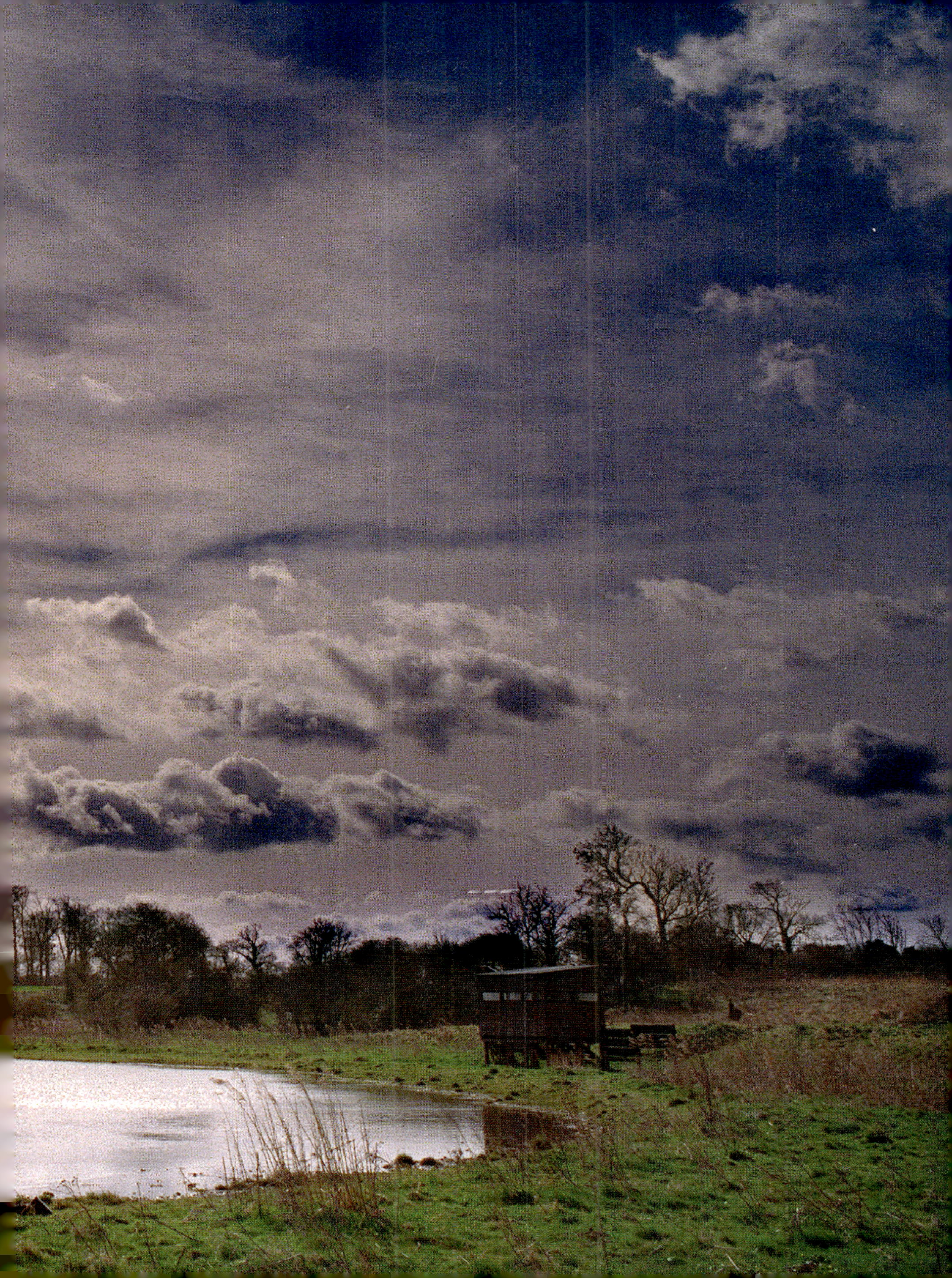

Brian Thornborrow tends to his sheep at the head of Swaledale.
(YPP2162)

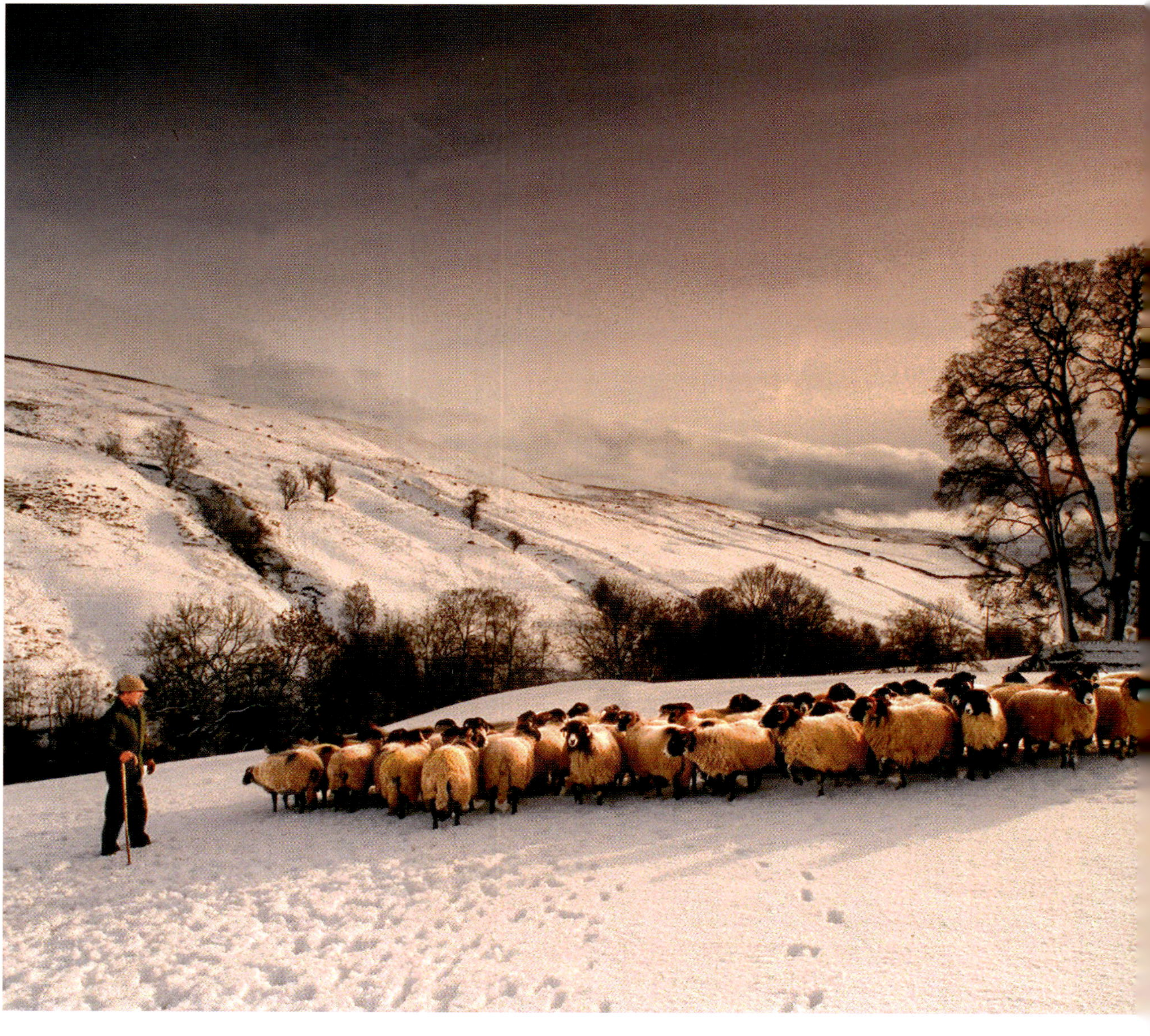

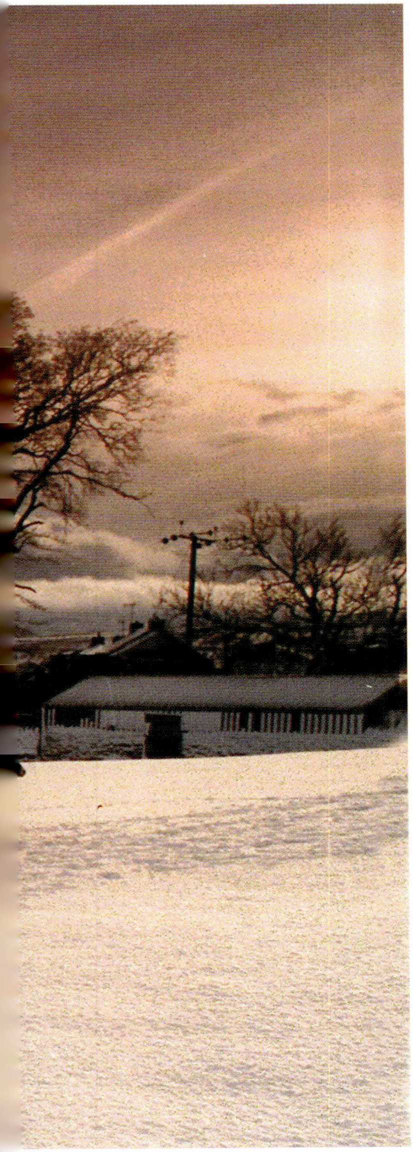

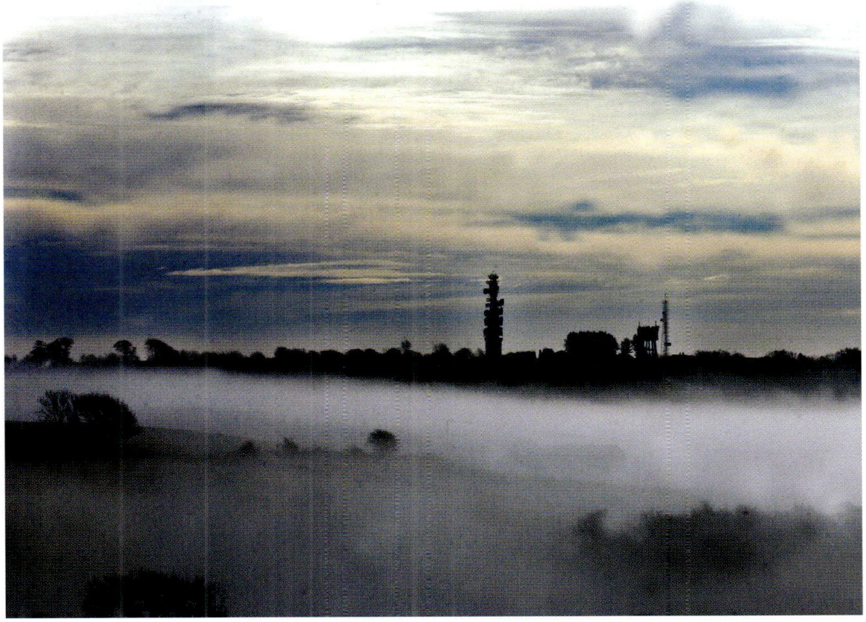

Mist blankets the lower-lying land around Cookridge and its tower on the edge of Leeds. (YPP2163)

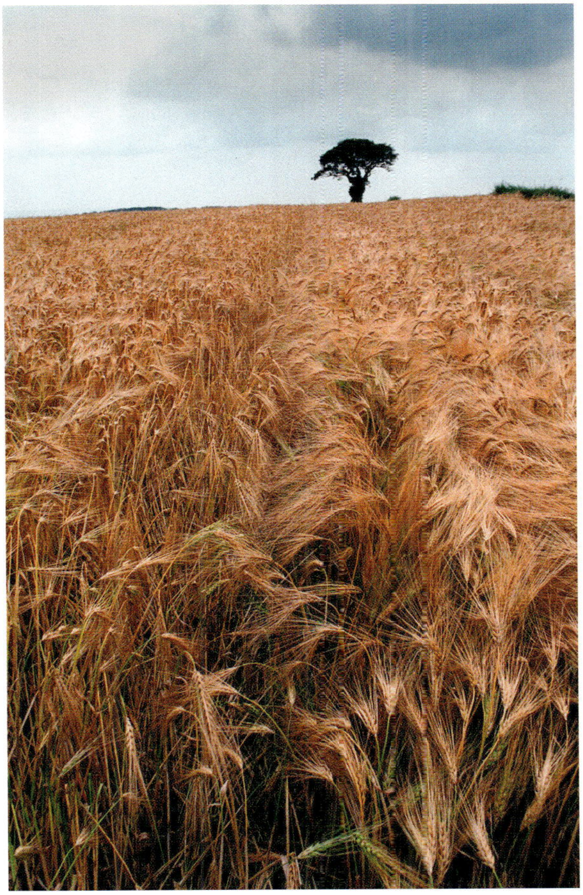

Barley nearly ready for harvesting in a field near Pickering. (YPP2164)

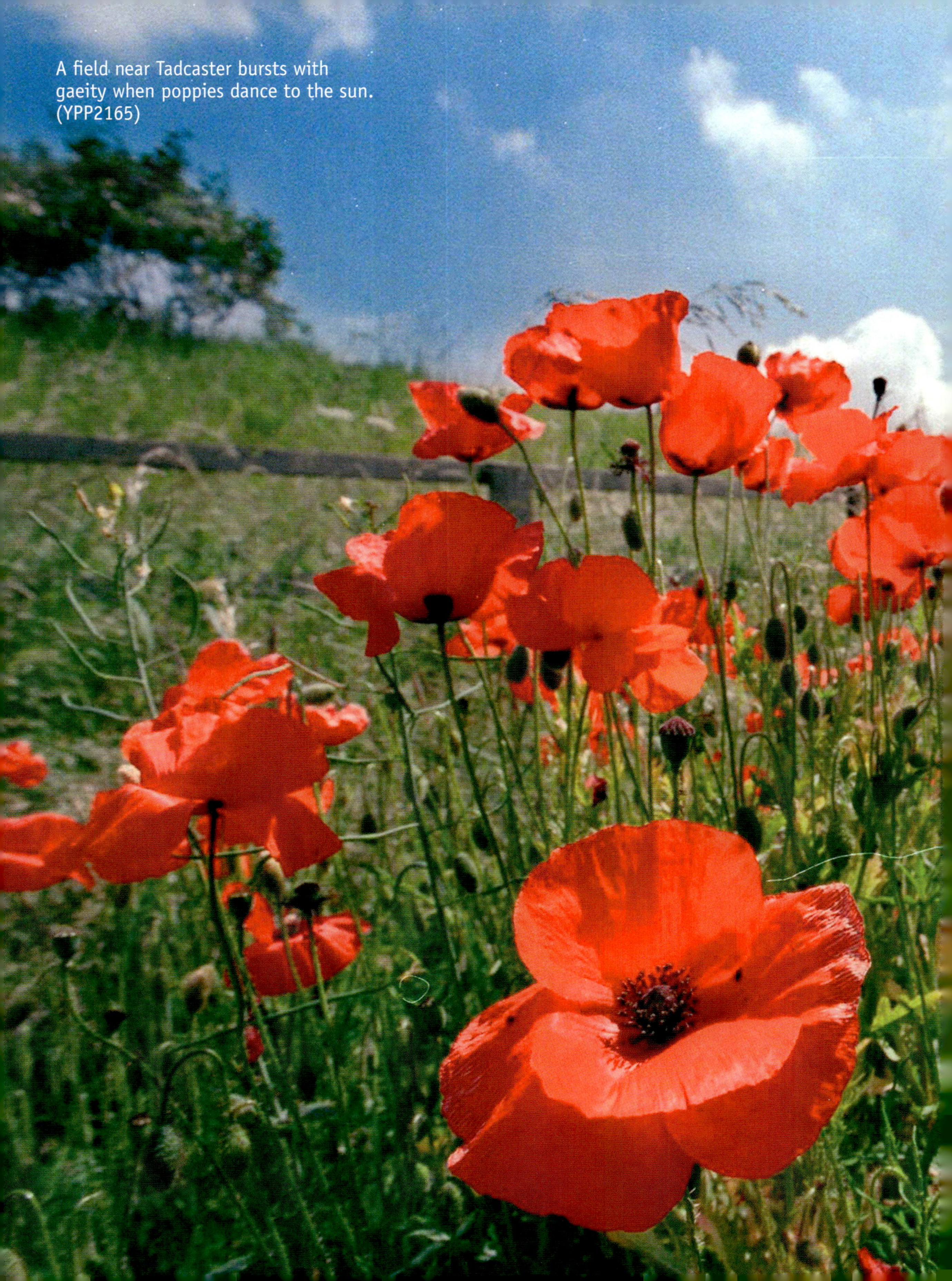

A field near Tadcaster bursts with gaeity when poppies dance to the sun. (YPP2165)

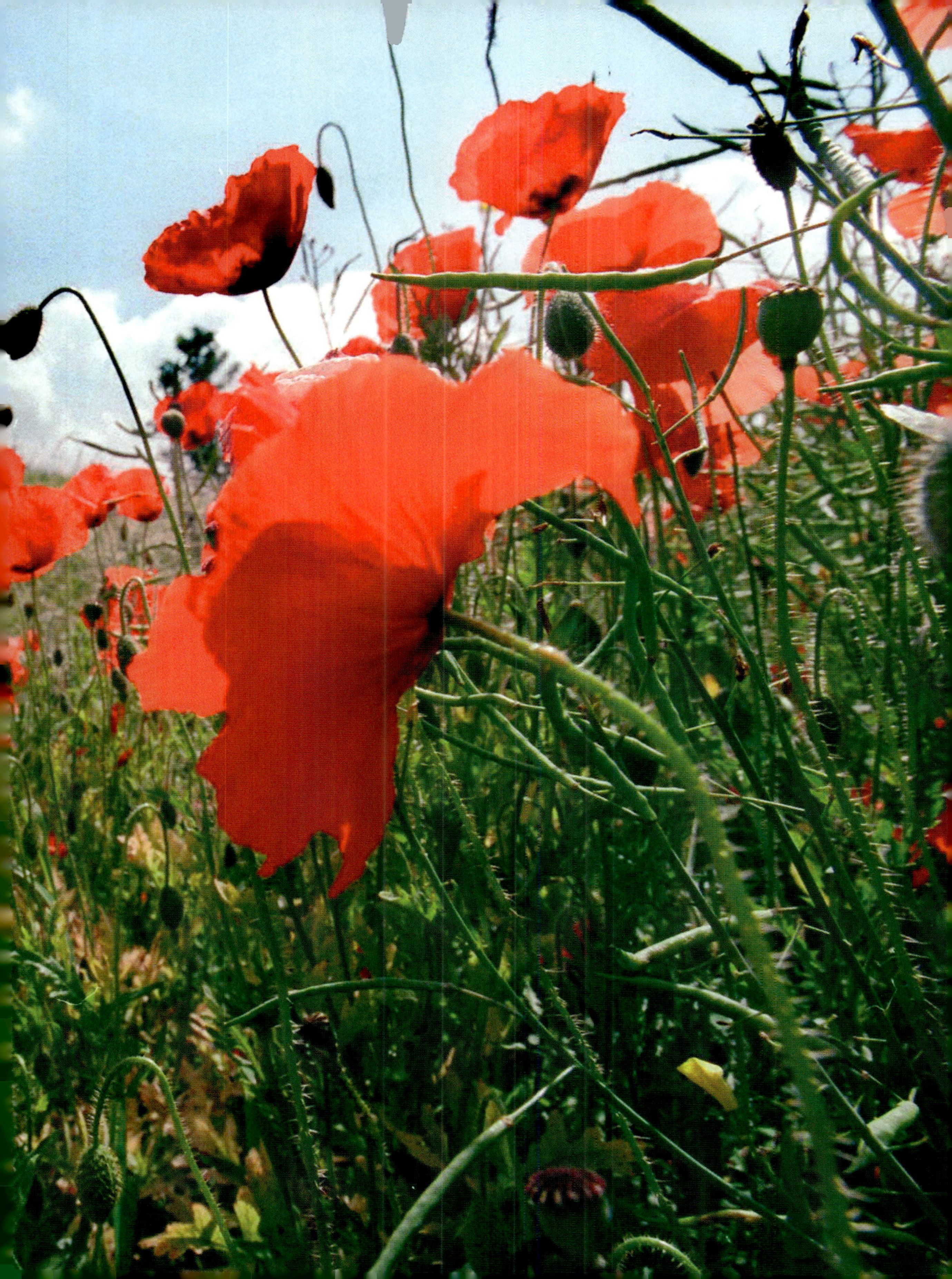

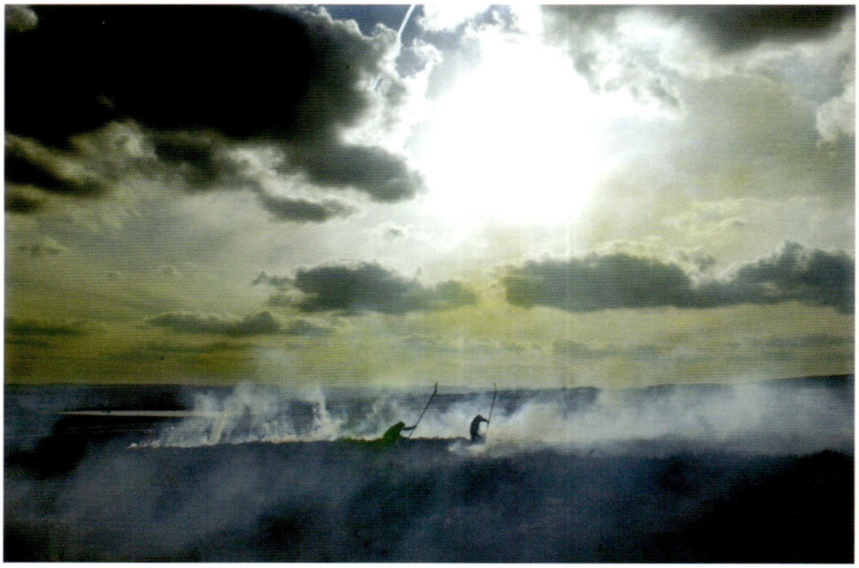

Gamekeepers on Hawksworth Moor control the burning of heather on the moors. (YPP2166)

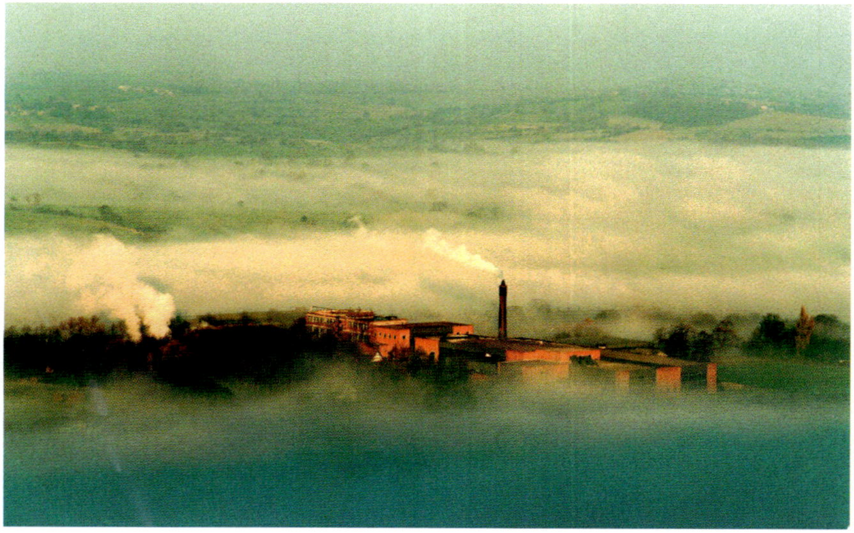

Whiteley Paper Mill at Pool in Wharfedale seems to be floating above the clouds as fog covers lower Wharfedale. (YPP2167)

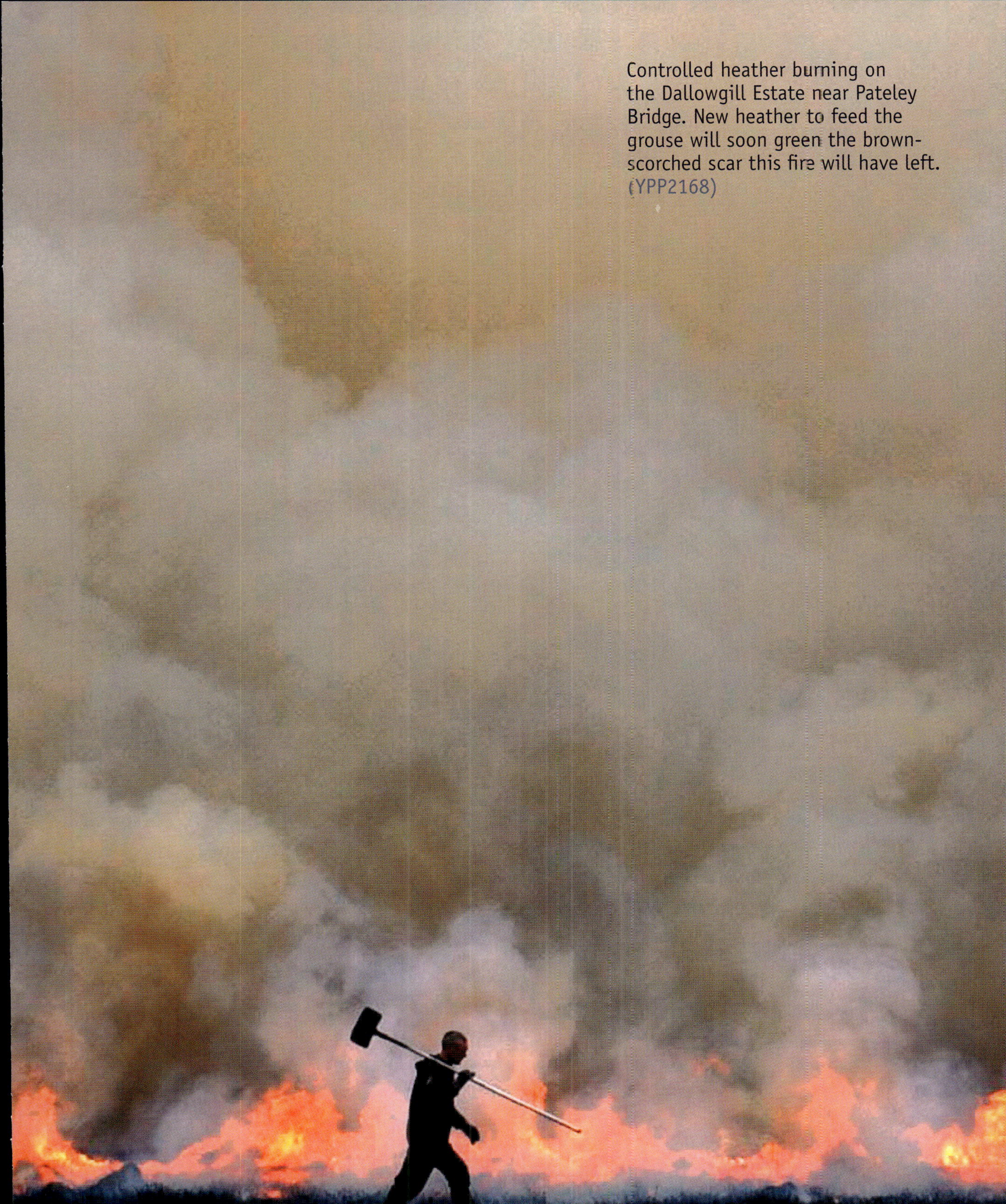

Controlled heather burning on the Dallowgill Estate near Pateley Bridge. New heather to feed the grouse will soon green the brown-scorched scar this fire will have left. (YPP2168)

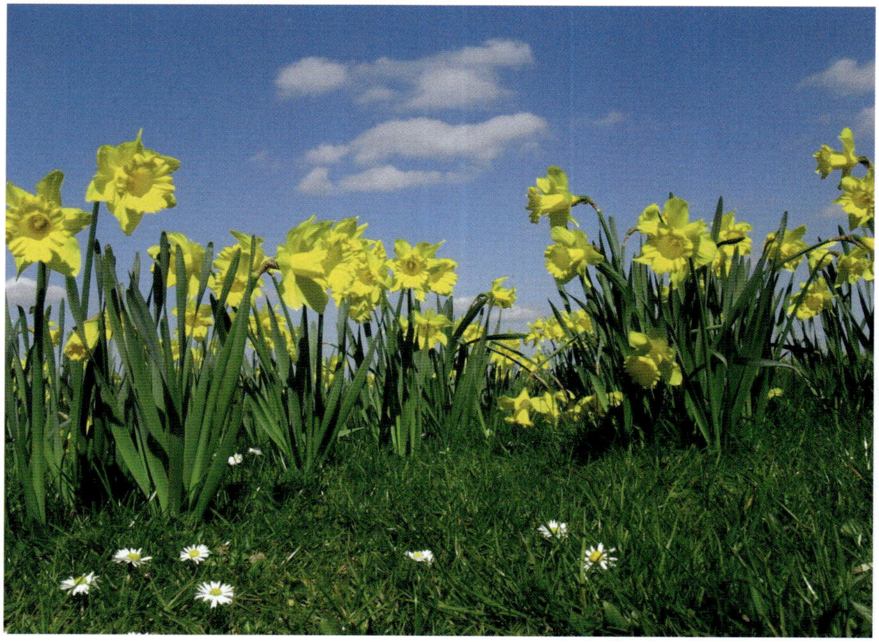

Daffodils and daisies greet the sun in Tickhill near Doncaster. (YPP2169)

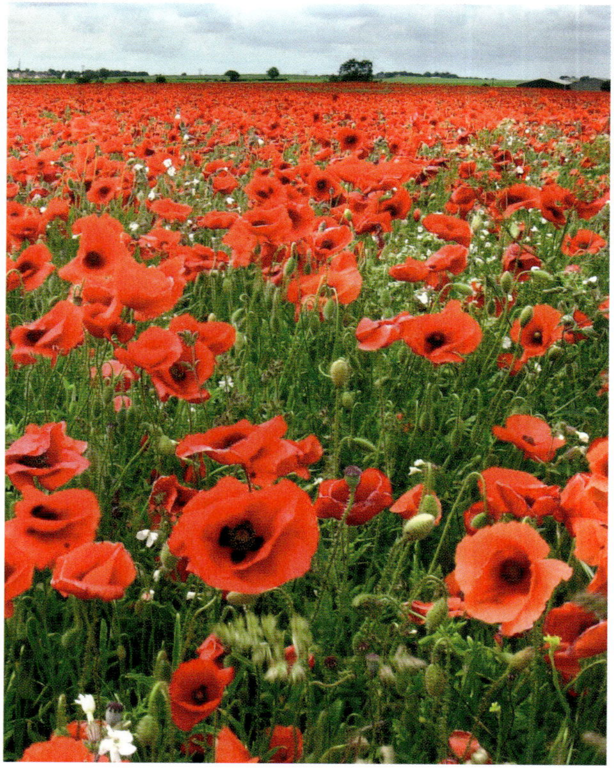

Poppies blowing in the wind in a field at Braithwell, near Rotherham. (YPP2170)

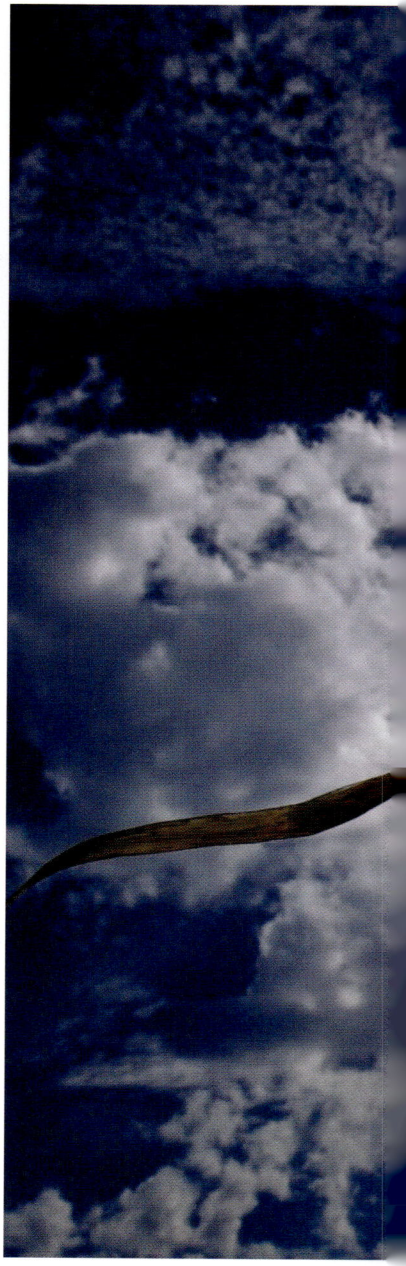

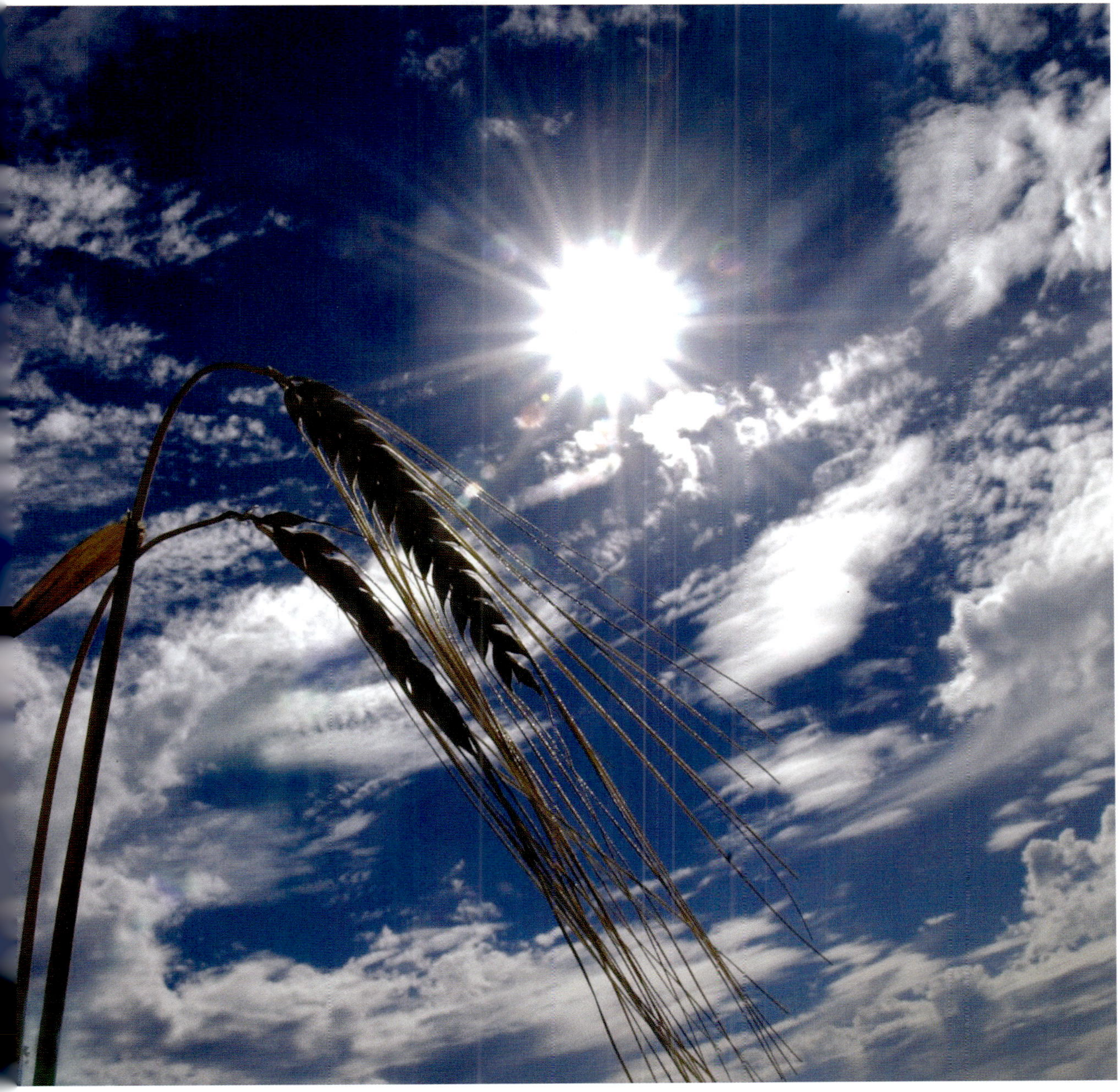

In a field at Robin Hood, near Rothwell, Leeds., two ears of barley perform a pas de deux against a brilliant sky. (YPP2171)

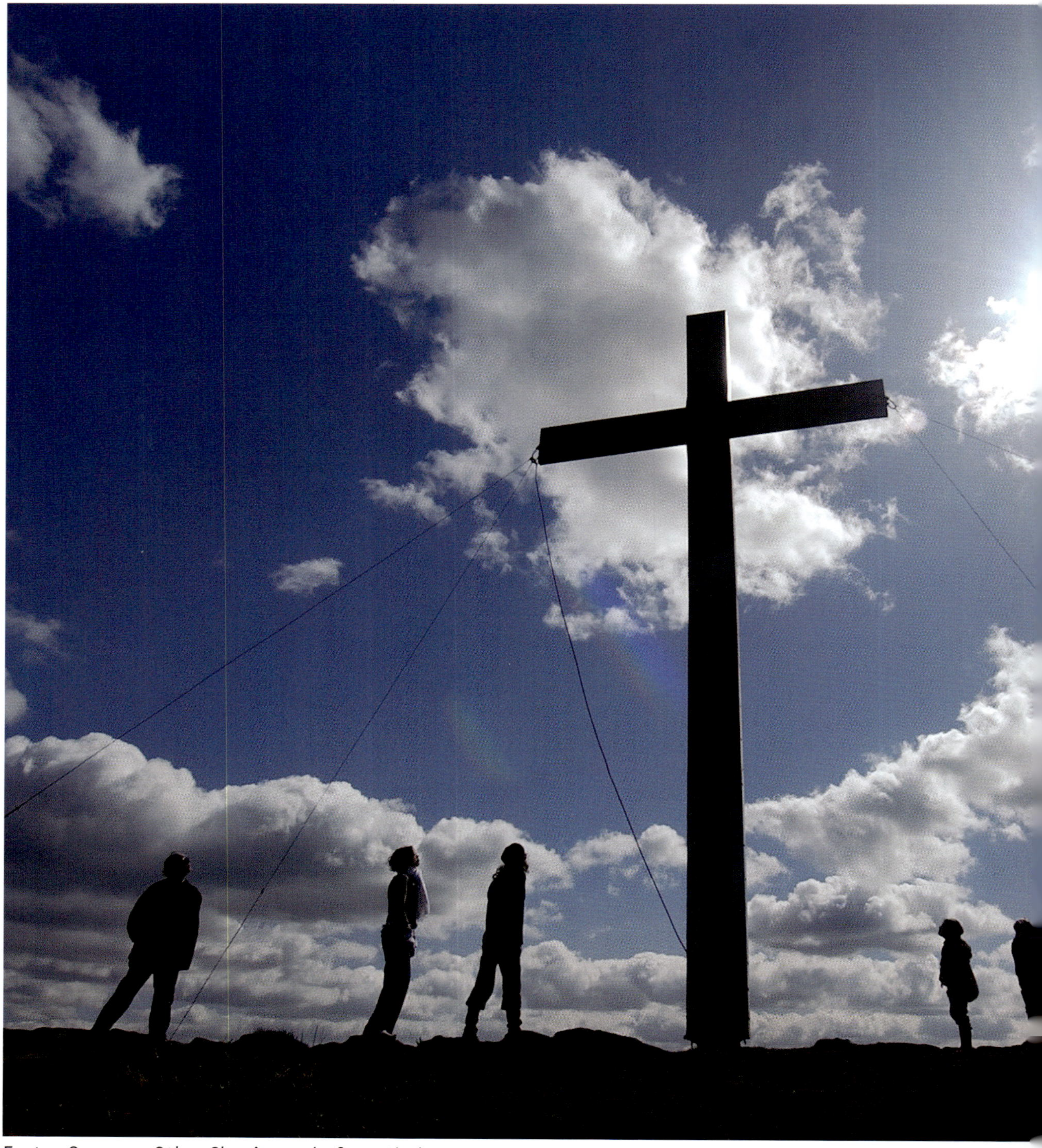

Easter Cross on Otley Chevin made from timber rescued after the IRA bombing of Manchster. It was the 38th year a Cross had been erected on this site. (YPP2172)

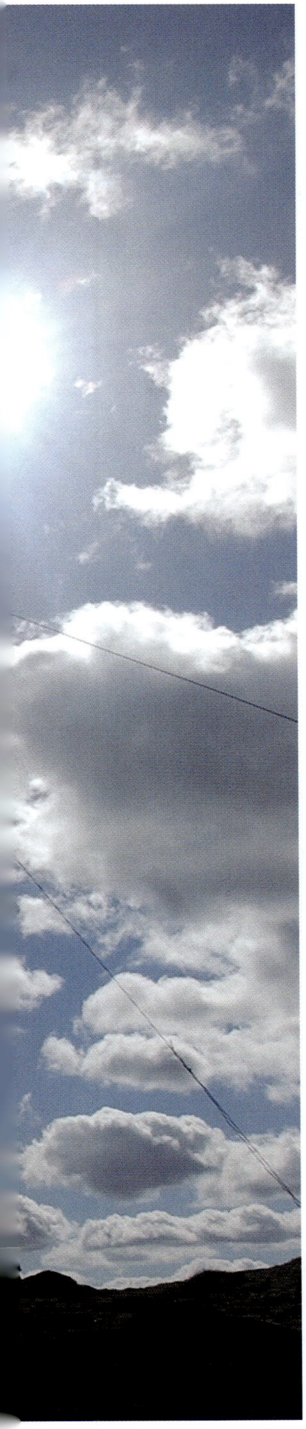

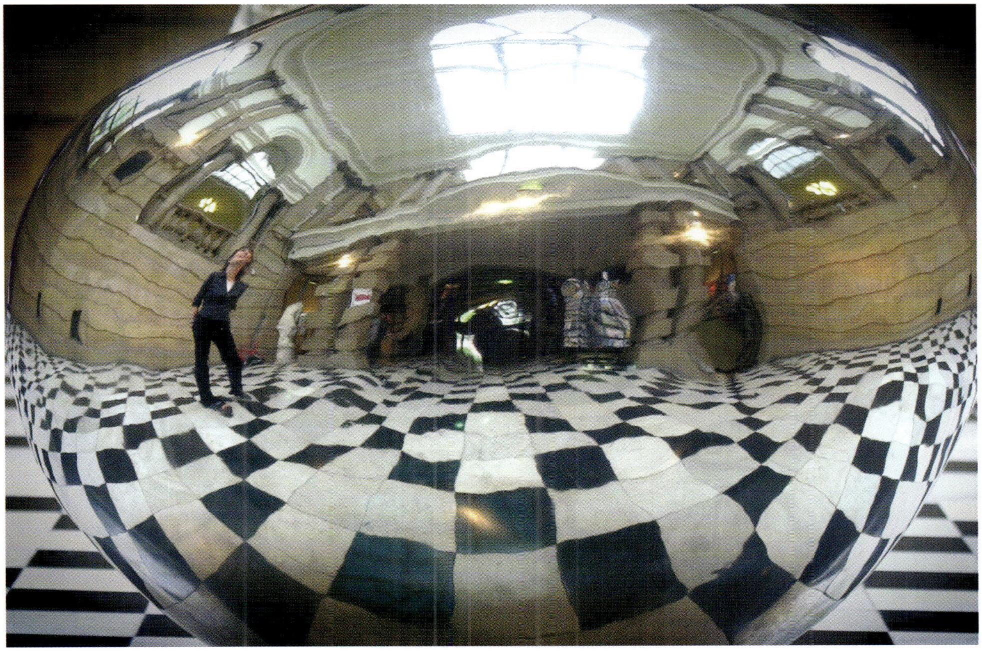

Reflection on the surface of a sculpture "Turning the World Inside Out" by Anish Kapoor at Bradford's Cartwright Hall. (YPP2173)

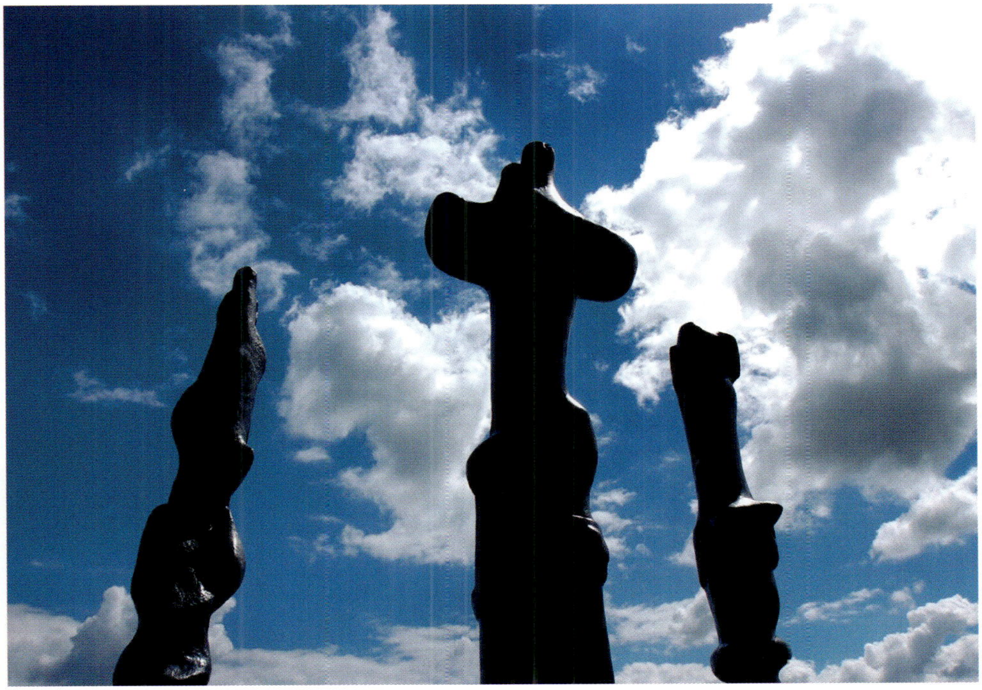

Bronzes by Henry Moor in the Yorkshire Sculpture Park at Bretton Hall with Glenkiln Cross in the centre. Their conception was inspired by prehistoric standing stones known as menhirs. (YPP2174)

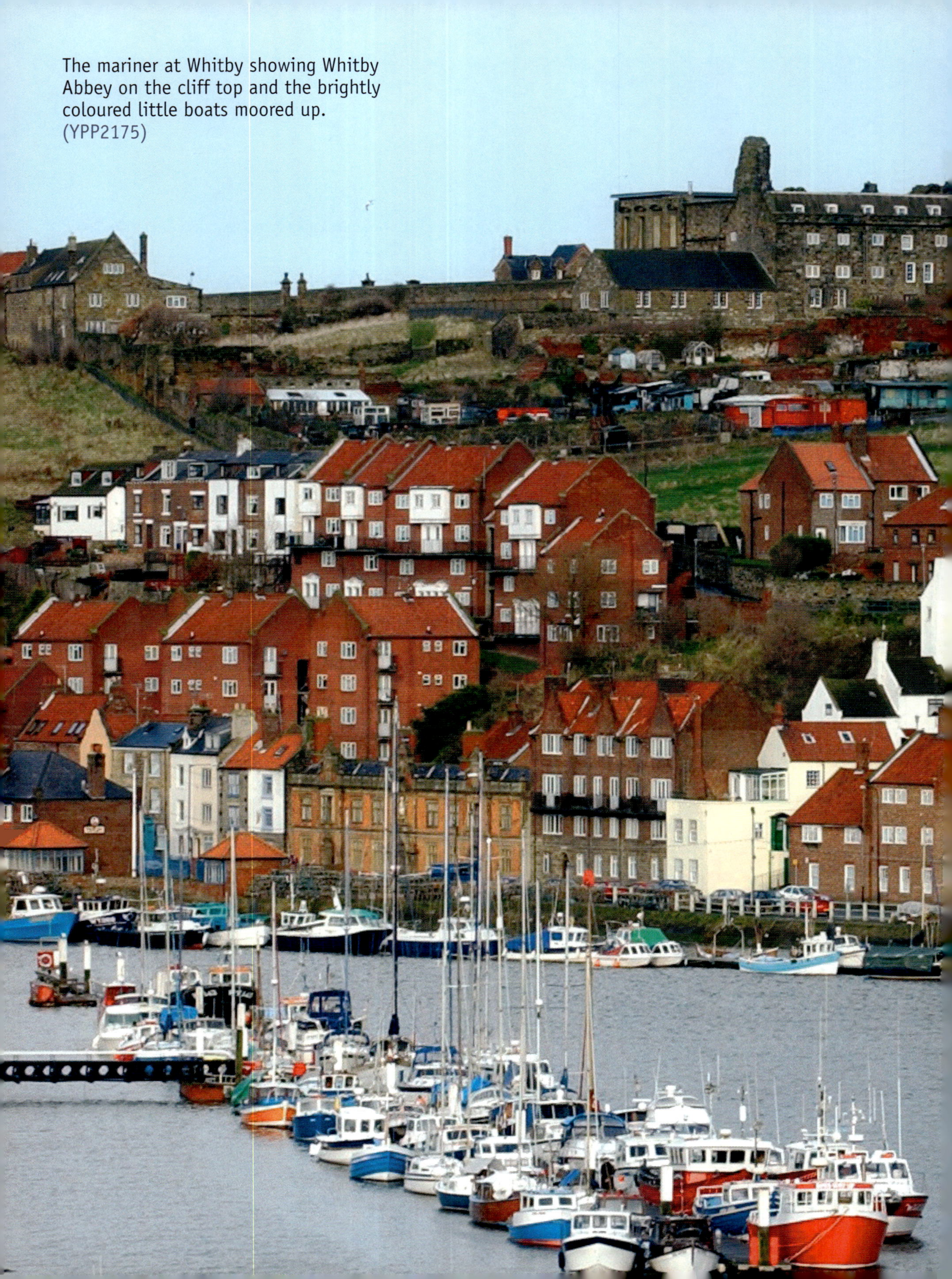

The mariner at Whitby showing Whitby Abbey on the cliff top and the brightly coloured little boats moored up. (YPP2175)

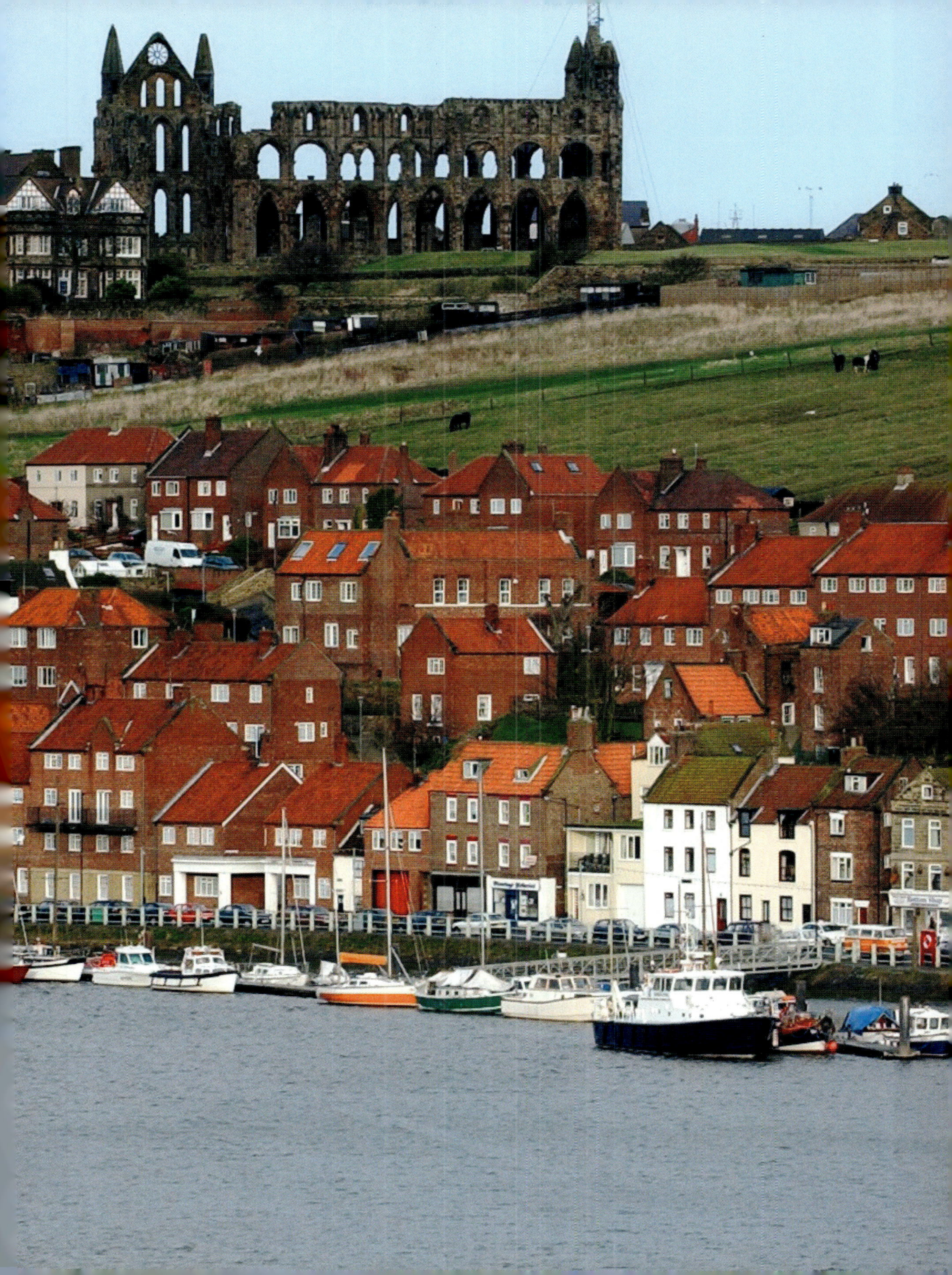

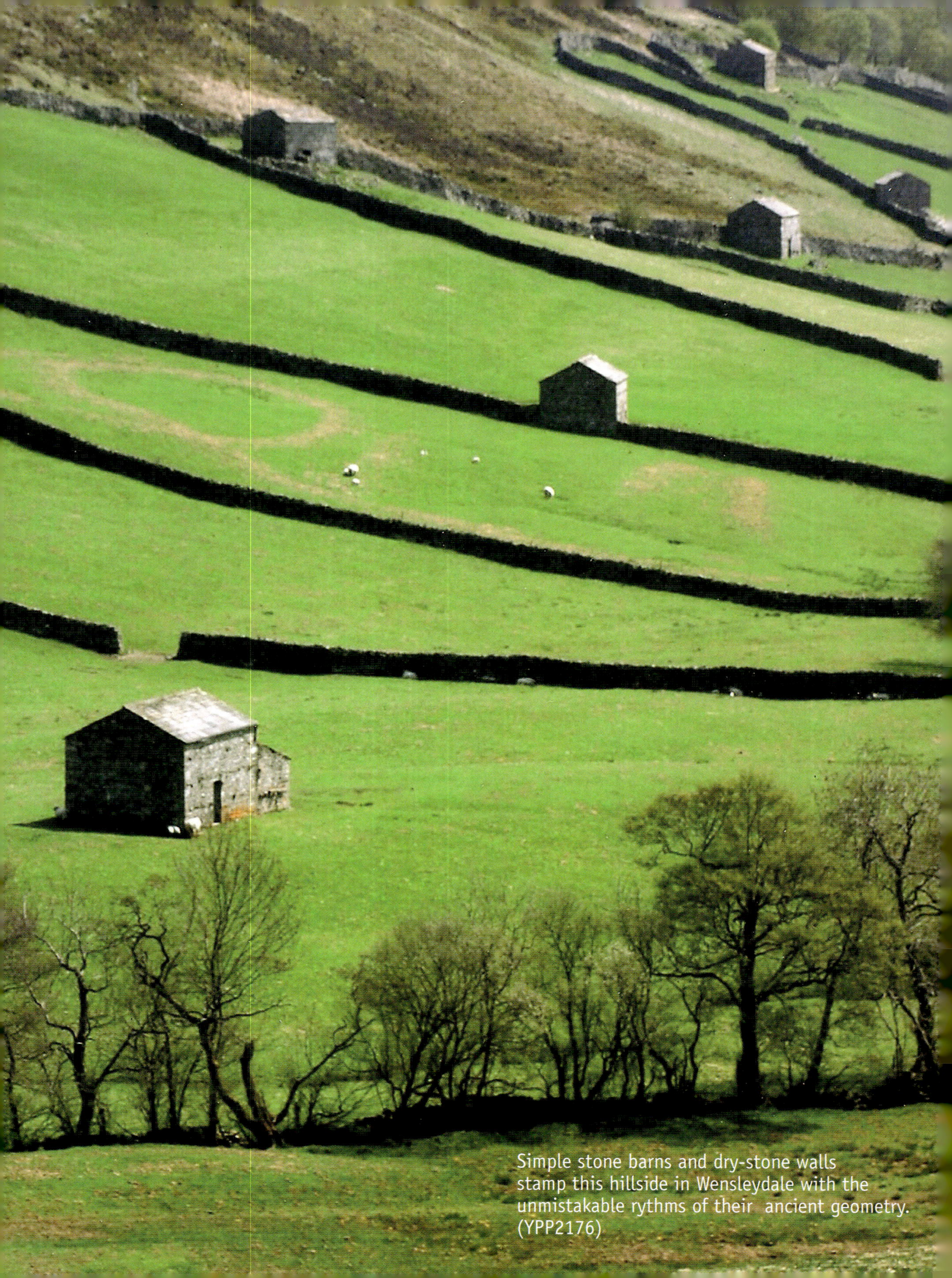

Simple stone barns and dry-stone walls stamp this hillside in Wensleydale with the unmistakable rythms of their ancient geometry. (YPP2176)